Return and Renewal

MISHNAT HARA"L

מגיד
MAGGID

Yeshivat Har Etzion ישיבת הר עציון

Rabbi Aharon Lichtenstein

Return and Renewal

Reflections on Teshuva and Spiritual Growth

ADAPTED AND EDITED BY
Michael S. Berger and Reuven Ziegler

Mishnat HaRAL
Yeshivat Har Etzion
Maggid Books

Return and Renewal
Reflections on Teshuva and Spiritual Growth

First Edition, 2018

Maggid Books
An imprint of Koren Publishers Jerusalem Ltd.

POB 8531, New Milford, CT 06776-8531, USA
& POB 4044, Jerusalem 9104001, Israel
www.korenpub.com

ISBN 978-1-59264-507-7, *hardcover*

A CIP catalogue record for this title is available from the British Library

Printed and bound in the United States

בני בנים הרי הם כבנים

In loving memory of our grandparents

Gertrude and Leslie Zack
גיטל בת שמואל ואליעזר בן איסר

whose legacy of kindness and *chesed,*
devotion to family and to the Jewish people,
continues to light the way for our family

והיו על לב אהרן

We gratefully acknowledge the supporters of Mishnat HaRAL

Steve & Renee Adelsberg
Ben & Aviva Adler
Lior & Drora Arussy
Howard & Chaya Balter
Jack & Giti Bendheim
Etan & Sarah Bendheim
Julius & Dottie Berman
Andrew Borodach & Rachel Wolf
Eli & Judy Clark
Arye & Bashi Colton
Ezra & Adena Dyckman
Michael & Yaffa Eisenberg
Steve & Adina Fredman
Allen & Rachel Friedman
Shai & Tovah Gerson
Joseph & Leelah Gitler
Murray & Batsheva Goldberg
Eric & Tamar Goldstein
Jerry & Anne Gontownik
Ari & Shira Gontownik
Robert & Virginia Bayer Hirt
Yisroel & Shira Hochberg
Simcha & Barbara Hochman
Ben Zion & Naomi Hochstein
Jay & Rachel Jubas
Marcos *z"l* & Adina Katz
Zvi & Tzippy Katz
Kolatch Family Foundation
Rachmiel & Gita Koppel
David & Sarena Koschitzky
Hartley & Faye Koschitzky
Henry & Julia Koschitzky
Joel, Yedidia, Yekutiel & Amitai Koschitzky
Jono & Tamar Koschitzky
Saul & Mira Koschitzky
Emanuel & Ellen Kronitz
Avrom, Zev & Rael Krengel
Gershom & Janine Kutliroff
David & Faye Landes
Eliot & Marilyn Lauer
Josh & Beth Mermelstein
Leon & Marilyn Moed
Sam & Debbie Moed
Terry & Gail Novetsky
David & Andrea Polster
Donny & Arielle Rosenberg
Gidon Rothstein & Elizabeth Holland
Len & Dorothy Sank
Allen & Miriam Schick
Jacob & Vered Schimmel
Menachem & Rena Schnaidman
Kalman & Jordana Schoor
Jacob & Julianne Schorr
Elli & Efrat Schorr
Raphi & Yonit Schorr
Arye & Renana Schreiber
David & Ruth Schreiber
Avi & Sarah Schwartz
Daniel & Debbie Schwartz
Heshe & Harriet Seif
Hillel & Saritte Silvera
Herb *z"l* & Marilyn Smilowitz
Michael & Liora Stein
Richard Stone
Paul *z"l* & Kathryn Wallach
Howard & Tova Weiser
Gary & Hildee Weiss
Mark & Susan Wiesen

Contents

Preface

In 2014, *Tradition* dedicated an issue to an analysis and appreciation of R. Aharon Lichtenstein's religious thought – a volume that came out just a few months before his passing. Scholars joined longtime students in limning the contours of R. Lichtenstein's approach to contemporary religious life and thought, highlighting its uniqueness and assessing its impact.

The majority of these articles, understandably, focused on R. Lichtenstein's published works,[1] or were based on the authors' personal experiences as his students. But R. Lichtenstein had a more public persona as well, which exposed much wider audiences, both in Israel and the United States, to his distinctive brand of religious humanism. One such forum was his *teshuva derasha*, offered annually beginning in 1985, with the first Hausman/Stern *Kinnus Teshuva* lecture at Yeshiva University's Gruss Kollel in Jerusalem, and continuing for the next twenty-five

1. The bibliography of R. Lichtenstein's published works is available at http://etzion.org.il/en/RAL-bibliography. There are more than one thousand entries, which are organized topically.

years in a variety of venues in Israel or in the New York area. This volume assembles twelve of these *derashot,* the earliest from 1989, adding to the *derashot* from 1987 and 2002 already published in *By His Light.*[2]

As in every other area of his intellectual probing, R. Lichtenstein brought to bear on his subject his signature talents: sharp analytic powers and organized thinking, coupled with an almost-encyclopedic knowledge of both traditional Jewish sources and a good deal of the Western canon of literature and religious thought – and all these within a framework of spiritual yearning, ethical sensitivity, and commitment to duty. Readers of the two volumes of *Leaves of Faith* will find familiar structures and comparable breadth in this volume, along with penetrating insight and constructive analysis. Accustomed to seeing sin as a catalog of broken things that the spiritual handyman must fix, we are helped by R. Lichtenstein to see in fact the varieties and gradations of sin ("*Kallot Va-chamurot*"), and commensurately, the many facets and types of *teshuva* of which the tradition was deeply aware – whether over the course of one's life ("*La-kol Zeman*") or in the context of various human conditions ("*Teshuva* of Norm and of Crisis" and "Renunciation, Divorce, and Rehabilitation") – and to which we can commit, if only we are willing to be honest with ourselves.

Given their focus on *teshuva,* the essays in this volume understandably have the added emphasis of the aspirational demands of a life of serious *avodat Hashem* and intensive *talmud Torah* ("Purify Our Hearts to Serve You with Truth," "The Integrity of *Teshuva,*" and "*Teshuva*: Obligation and Opportunity"), themes resonant of the essays in *By His Light* and *Varieties of Religious Experience.* Yet the subject matter of this volume also evokes R. Lichtenstein's candid awareness of, and sensitivity to, the inner life of the human being and of the average Jew. Not surprisingly, in these essays he frequently quotes Socrates' call, cited in Plato's *Apology,* that "the unexamined life is not worth living," an invitation, if you will, particularly poignant during Elul and *Aseret Yemei Teshuva.*

2. If readers can help us locate recordings of the *derashot* not available to us when preparing this volume, we would be happy to consider including them in future editions. The missing *derashot* are those of 1985, 1986, 1988, 1990, 1991, 1994–96, 1999, and 2000. Please contact office@etzion.org.il.

But it is not only our behaviors *per se,* whether major or minor, that need to come under examination. In virtually every essay, R. Lichtenstein forces us to confront and scrutinize the personal religious soil in which these practices were planted and nurtured. The reason our annual resolve to change so frequently fizzles out is that we fail to address the underlying religious beliefs and personality traits that provided such fertile ground for the practices we wish to change.

In this context, citations of Christian thinkers and British poets – at times by way of comparison, at other times by way of contrast – stud these essays next to *Tanakh, Chazal,* and *Rishonim,* highlighting the universal character of many of our religious and aesthetic sensibilities and spiritual challenges. As a religious humanist, Rav Lichtenstein sought out those authors and thinkers who help deepen our human sensitivity and understanding, which can then serve as the basis for more profound spiritual growth and piety within our own lives.[3] As we read these *derashot,* we are brought to acknowledge the painful truth that, without probing to that deeper level, our *teshuva* will almost necessarily be shallow and short-lived. To overcome that tendency, in these essays R. Lichtenstein comes to our aid, spade in hand, to help us dig far below the surface of our selves and achieve more lasting change.

For all their power, many of these essays are admittedly not an easy read – and not in the sense of their syntax or structure. We are referring to the way these essays, if taken seriously, will likely make us uncomfortable. As we read them, we may ineluctably nod our heads in anguished agreement, acknowledging the often-painful accuracy of R. Lichtenstein's descriptions, whether of ourselves individually ("Mediocre *Teshuva* and *Teshuva* of the Mediocre") or of our communities writ large. At the same time, we are helped to see previously unnoticed, or even counterintuitive, aspects of the process of *teshuva* ("*Teshuva*: Impetus and Motive," "*Teshuva* and Joy," and "Humility and Pride in *Teshuva*"), enriching our appreciation of this most basic religious urge and demand, and hopefully finding renewed inspiration to once again try to scale the mountain of our inadequacy.

---

3. See Shlomo Fischer, "The Religious Humanism of R. Aharon Lichtenstein," *Tradition* 47:4 (Winter 2014), p. 22.

More than many of his other writings, these essays in both tone and substance give us the palpable sense of sitting at R. Lichtenstein's feet, and of being in his *beit midrash*. The honesty and candor of the *rebbe-talmid* relationship suffuses this volume, as does the concern of the master for his disciples' improvement. As we read these comprehensive yet personal essays, we are really listening to one who knows us well yet does not despair of our potential and of how we might actualize our better selves. Like his Talmud *shiurim*, these essays reflect R. Lichtenstein's *torat chesed*: each one generously builds a conceptual scaffold upon which seeking, repentant Jews can rise up out of their spiritual morass and change for the better. In that sense, these essays can be read at any time, not only between Rosh Ha-shana and Yom Kippur. To those of us willing to make the effort, R. Lichtenstein extends his hand, not to lift us out, but to help us climb up, to give us firmer footing, as we try to re-create ourselves.

The process employed in converting these oral discourses into written essays is similar to that followed in R. Lichtenstein's earlier volume, *By His Light*. First, all the recordings were transcribed word for word by the people noted below. Next, the transcripts were reviewed and proofread by Rabbi Dov Karoll. Subsequently, the transcripts were adapted for print, which entailed editing for language and content, abridgment, occasional reorganization, removal of tangential remarks to footnotes, division into subsections and addition of subsection headings, translation of sources and terms, and so on. Ilana Sobel copy edited the adaptations, after which the co-editors reviewed the essays and Nechama Unterman proofread them.

The date and venue of each essay is noted in its initial footnote. A list of those who adapted and transcribed the essays follows:

- "*Teshuva*: Obligation and Opportunity," adapted by Michael S. Berger and Reuven Ziegler from a transcript by Michael and Rena Siev

- "Purify Our Hearts to Serve You with Truth," adapted by Michael S. Berger from a transcript by Sholem Hurwitz
- "The Integrity of *Teshuva*," adapted by Michael S. Berger from a transcript by Dov Karoll
- "*Teshuva*: Impetus and Motive," adapted by Michael S. Berger from a transcript by Dov Karoll
- "*Kallot Va-chamurot*: Gradation of Sins in Repentance," adapted by Reuven Ziegler from a transcript by Shlomo Brody
- "Mediocre *Teshuva* and the *Teshuva* of the Mediocre," adapted by Daniel Landman and Reuven Ziegler from a transcript by Michael Platt and Ariela Goldsmith
- "*Teshuva* of Norm and of Crisis," adapted by Reuven Ziegler from a transcript by Marc Herman and David Raphael
- "*La-kol Zeman*: *Teshuva* Within Four Time Frames of Our Lives," adapted by Michael S. Berger from a transcript by Dov Karoll
- "*Teshuva*: Ferment and Repose," adapted by Michael S. Berger from a transcript by Rochie Hurwitz
- "Renunciation, Divorce, and Rehabilitation," adapted by Eli D. Clark from a transcript by Ariela Goldsmith
- "Humility and Pride in *Teshuva*," adapted by Michael S. Berger from a transcript by Dov Karoll
- "*Teshuva* and Joy," adapted by Michael S. Berger from a transcript by David Raphael

Many people contributed to the production of this volume. First, our thanks to Dr. Tovah Lichtenstein for her encouragement and her championing of this project, as well as to Mishnat HaRAL's Yoel Weiss, Noam Shalit, and Aaron Lewin for their help. We are also extremely grateful to all those named above who contributed to this volume, and most especially to Rabbi Dov Karoll for his careful review of the transcripts and Ilana Sobel for her careful review of the adaptations. Our gratitude extends to Matthew Miller, Shira Finson, and the staff of Maggid Books for their professionalism and high standards; to Rabbi Dr. Moshe Berger, Prof. Aaron Segal, Rabbi Yair Kahn, and Debra Berkowitz for their helpful comments; and to Yeshivat Har Etzion, the cherished institution which R. Lichtenstein shaped and guided for more than four decades, for its enthusiastic support.

Most importantly, we thank our revered teacher, *moreinu verabbeinu* HaRav Aharon Lichtenstein *zekher tzaddik livrakha,* for conveying to us in his teachings and embodying in his personal example the highest ideals of Judaism – and, indeed, of humanity. Having been blessed by Rav Lichtenstein's presence in our lives, we are gratified to be able to share his wisdom with others. May his memory continue to be a blessing as his teachings pass on to the ages.

Michael S. Berger and Reuven Ziegler

Teshuva: Obligation and Opportunity

How do we categorize and describe *teshuva*: as an opportunity or as an obligation? The two terms are, of course, quite different. When we speak of opportunity, we generally have in mind some fortunate, perhaps undeserved, option to which we are glad to have access, whereas obligation conjures up a sense of pressing demand, a categorical imperative grounded in an existential situation or mandated by an authoritative commander. One doesn't need to think hard to realize that the answer is that *teshuva* is both. I would like to examine in what sense it is both and how these two aspects of *teshuva* are related.

TESHUVA AS OPPORTUNITY: FREE WILL

We can bring to bear two distinct elements upon the concept of opportunity, one general and one specific. Broadly speaking, *teshuva* is grounded in our faith in and experience of free will. It certainly is no accident that the Rambam, probably the greatest champion of free will among the

---

Delivered as the Hausman/Stern *Kinnus Teshuva* lecture at the Gruss Institute in Jerusalem, Tishrei 5759 (1998).

Rishonim, placed the concept of free will at the very heart of *Hilkhot Teshuva.* In the three central chapters (chaps. 5–7), the Rambam presents what is probably his fullest exposition of the concept and its significance.

> Free will is granted to all people. If one desires to turn himself to the path of good and be righteous, the choice is his. Should he desire to turn to the path of evil and the wicked, the choice is his. (*Hilkhot Teshuva* 5:1)

In *halakha* 2, he presents and rejects the opposing view, a theological, astrological determinism, insisting instead that "each person is fit to be righteous like Moshe *Rabbeinu* or wicked like Yorovam." After expounding upon the theme of free will over the course of two chapters, he draws his conclusion at the beginning of chapter seven:

> Since free choice is granted to all people, as explained, a person should always strive to do *teshuva* and to confess verbally for his sins, striving to cleanse his hands from his sins in order that he may die as one who has performed *teshuva* and [thereby] merit the life of the World-to-Come. (7:1)

Thus, the prelude to discussing the need for *teshuva* is the concept of free will generally, the confident faith – so deeply rooted in the world of Halakha – that we have the capacity to manage our lives in accordance with our moral and religious will. This is the first aspect of the opportunity implicit in *teshuva.*

TESHUVA AS OPPORTUNITY: THE GIFT OF *TESHUVA*

But there is an additional aspect: the *gift* of *teshuva,* which is, itself, multiple. At one plane, it is free will writ large. One might have assumed that while freedom is a gift with which we are initially graced, this gift is given to us when we are a kind of *tabula rasa,* a blank slate unencumbered by sin and degradation; but once the albatross of sinful and immoral behavior has been cast around our necks, we no longer are able to move freely, and no longer possess that capacity for free choice. Indeed, the Rambam states that in extreme cases, such as with Pharaoh, that is exactly what occurs (*Hilkhot Teshuva* 6:3). Fortunately, this is not the norm. The freedom that characterizes our lives generally continues to be in force and allows us to move freely even after sin, even after we have distanced ourselves from God and from our true selves.

Apart from that, there are other elements of opportunity within *teshuva* that have nothing to do with our ability to repent, but rather with the results of *teshuva*, and the readiness of God to accept *teshuva*. We are granted the opportunity of remission of sin; God is willing to waive whatever punishments we had justly deserved. And at the relational level, quite apart from canceling our terrible debts, God is willing to receive us again into His presence and reopen channels of communication. The Rambam, in the continuation of the seventh chapter, stresses this element particularly:

> How exalted is the level of *teshuva*! Only yesterday this sinner was divided from God, the Lord of Israel.... He would call out [to God] without being answered.... He would perform *mitzvot*, only to have them thrown back in his face.... Today, [after having repented,] he clings to the Divine Presence.... He calls out [to God] and is answered immediately.... He performs *mitzvot*, and these are accepted with grace and joy...and, furthermore, God longs for our *mitzvot* and good deeds. (7:7)[1]

Thus, the opportunity afforded by *teshuva*, the gift which, by divine grace, we have received, entails three components: (1) the element of free will, which remains operative, notwithstanding the fact that we have defiled ourselves; (2) the readiness on God's part to forgive our sins;

---

1. The concept of *teshuva* as a gift God has given us can also be found in the way Rabbeinu Yona opens his *Sha'arei Teshuva*:

> Concerning the principles of *teshuva*: among the Blessed One's kindnesses to His creations is having prepared for them the way to rise from the pit of their deeds and to escape the trap of their offenses.... In His great goodness and uprightness, He has taught and exhorted them to turn to Him upon having sinned against Him.... Even if they have offended and rebelled exceedingly and been utterly faithless, He has not closed the doors of repentance to them.

This *chesed* is a gift, an opportunity conferred upon us by God.

(3) His willingness to forget about the past, and to enable us to come unto Him once again.[2]

TESHUVA AS OBLIGATION

But, of course, *teshuva*, for us, is not simply an opportunity, an option of which we can avail ourselves to the extent that we wish. It is – wondrously – that, but not only that. *Teshuva* is also an obligation.

Now, it is well known that the *Minchat Chinnukh* questions the imperative nature of *teshuva*. The Rambam, both in the heading before *Hilkhot Teshuva* and in the *halakhot* themselves, speaks of *teshuva*, but when prescribing actions he seems to focus upon *viddui*, verbal confession.[3] The *Minchat Chinnukh* (364:2) asserts that according to the Rambam *teshuva* is not counted as a mitzva; rather, it is *viddui* that is a mitzva. If a person wants to do *teshuva*, then the Rambam prescribes how it is to be done, just as if one chooses to wear a four-cornered garment, one must affix *tzitzit* according to certain specifications. There is no verse mandating, at least at the halakhic plane, that a person perform *teshuva*.

This is, however, an exceedingly strange position to assume. It is absolutely chilling to think that *teshuva*, the key to our present spiritual state and to our ultimate metaphysical destiny, should be merely a matter of preference and predilection. Is it conceivable that a particular action, *viddui*, is thoroughly legislated by the Torah, yet that which concerns the totality of our being, *teshuva*, is a matter of choice? Both the Torah and the prophets constantly hammer away at the theme, "*Shuvu, shuvu, shuvu*, Return, return, return," speaking in the name of God to

---

2. These different aspects of free will can also be detected in the language of the prophets. They speak not only of *teshuva* "from," turning away from sin, as in the verse: "Turn, turn from your evil ways" (*Yechezkel* 33:11), but also *teshuva* "to," exemplified by: "Return, Israel, to the Lord your God" (*Hoshea* 14:2). [For more on this theme, see the chapter "*Teshuva* of Norm and of Crisis."]
3. *Hilkhot Teshuva* 1:1 states:

> If a person transgresses any of the *mitzvot* of the Torah, whether a positive commandment or a prohibition, whether willingly or inadvertently, when he repents, and returns from his sin, he must confess before God, blessed be He, as the verse states (*Bemidbar* 5:6–7), "Any man or woman who commits any wrong toward a fellow man.... They shall confess their wrongdoing." This refers to verbal confession (*viddui*), and this confession is a positive commandment.

the individual, the Jewish people, and even the other nations! These convey a strong sense that one who is sensitive to his relationship to God, one who is concerned about spiritual values and his own spiritual existence, certainly will want to do *teshuva,* and surely must do *teshuva.* Indeed, other *Rishonim* counted *teshuva* as a mitzva, and, to some extent, the Rambam himself can be construed as believing this.[4] In any event, regardless of whether we accept the position of the *Minchat Chinnukh* or we accept that *teshuva* is an independent obligation, the place of *teshuva* as a central value, as a lynchpin within religious life, is certainly secure.[5]

This obligation is, of course, multiple. Inasmuch as sin itself entails various components, likewise, *teshuva,* which is the corrective of sin, has various components. First, there is the evil in the sin itself that needs to be corrected, be the sin *bein adam la-Makom,* in the man-God realm, or *bein adam le-chavero,* interpersonal. Second, at the level of *bein adam la-Makom,* there is obviously the affront to God in every violation of His will. Furthermore, sin defiles spiritually and religiously, and that requires a corrective. Likewise, at the level of *bein adam le-chavero,* sin defiles a society, a community, and one needs to perform *teshuva* for that defilement, too.

Finally, a sinner must repent for the offense to himself, *bein adam le-atzmo*. To sin, and to remain mired in sin is, first and foremost, to endanger ourselves, as sin is damaging to one's personality, regardless of religious or spiritual consequences. A central aspect of our worldview is that one has responsibility not only to others, but also to oneself. The liberal notion that

4. In the heading to *Hilkhot Teshuva,* the Rambam writes, "There is one positive commandment herein, namely, that a sinner should repent from his sin before God and confess." The emphasis does seem to be more on the act of *teshuva* itself than on the detail of confession.

5. No less an authority than the Vilna Gaon insisted that there are values that may be of the highest order, even though they are not counted among the *mitzvot.* See his commentary on *Megillat Esther,* 10:3, s.v. *doresh tov*:

> This refers to good deeds and proper *middot,* for proper *middot* are more crucial than all the [actions], as I have written that the proper *middot* are not written explicitly in the Torah, for they underlie the entire Torah. As the *Gemara* states, one should regard one who gets angry as an idolater (*Shabbat* 105b), and one who gossips is considered like a heretic (*Arakhin* 15b); and the same goes for all the *middot.*

a person is master of himself and therefore can arrange his life and activities as he wishes, so long as he is ready to bear the consequences, stands totally in opposition to the worldview of Judaism, and indeed to any religious perception. A religious perspective views human life and the human self as a gift or a charge given by God. Hence, we have a responsibility not only to the divine image in others, but to the divine image in ourselves. A person who curses himself or maims himself violates the same prohibition as one who curses or maims others. And, surely, just as we are enjoined to save others from impending disaster, so we are enjoined to save ourselves, and this relates not only to our physical lives, but *a fortiori* to our spiritual lives as well. *Teshuva,* therefore, is demanded of us, quite apart from what we need to do for God, or need to do for our surroundings. We need to do it for ourselves, as part of our responsibility to our Creator who has entrusted us with a *nitzotz Eloka mi-ma'al,* a divine spark embedded within us.

These elements of *teshuva* are clearly obligatory, whether *teshuva* is an independent mitzva or, even failing that, is a religious and moral imperative growing out of our sensibility regarding spiritual matters.

LINKING OPPORTUNITY AND OBLIGATION

When speaking of *teshuva* as an obligation, there is an additional element to be borne in mind. The Rambam states:

> Yom Kippur is a time of *teshuva* for all, individuals and community, and it is the occasion of forgiveness and remission for Israel. Accordingly, everyone is obligated to repent and confess on Yom Kippur. (*Hilkhot Teshuva* 2:7)

The Rambam presents a fact and then draws an inference from it. The fact is that Yom Kippur is a day which is favorable for *teshuva.* That being the case, says the Rambam – and there is a causal nexus here – all are obligated to do *teshuva* and recite the *viddui.* In effect, the Rambam has linked the two elements we are addressing: if you have the opportunity, you *must* avail yourself of it. So, apart from the fact that there might be a mitzva of *teshuva,* just as there is a mitzva of *lulav, sukka,* or *shofar,* there is an additional ground for *teshuva* being obligatory: the fact that it is possible renders it mandatory. The opportunity produces an obligation.

The same thought is presented by Rabbeinu Yona in *Sha'arei Teshuva*:

> Realize that the penalty of the sinner who defers *teshuva* greatly intensifies itself each day. [Why?] For he knows that anger has gone forth upon him and that there is a sanctuary to which he can flee, the sanctuary of *teshuva,* and still he persists in his rebellion and continues in his evil. Though it is within his power to emerge from the turmoil, still he does not fear the scorn and the wrath. His evil, therefore, is great. (1:2)

The reason the punishment increases daily is that person knows he has offended God and is justly liable for punishment, and, additionally, knows that there is an escape hatch, and yet he doesn't avail himself of that opportunity. As an example, Rabbeinu Yona cites a famous *midrash* (*Kohelet Rabba* 7:32) about a group of imprisoned criminals who show some initiative and dig a tunnel underneath the jail. One by one, naturally, they leave, yet one of them remains behind. The jailer comes along, sees the tunnel open, and strikes the remaining criminal with his staff, saying, "Fool! The tunnel is open before you; how did you not avail yourself of it and rush to freedom?" The jailer, who, after all, should be reacting against this escape hatch, regards the remaining criminal as a person to whom freedom – which should be a central value – is of little moment. In effect, Rabbeinu Yona and the *midrash* are saying that the moment the opportunity is there, it engenders obligation, at least to a person who is morally and religiously sensitive; failure to avail ourselves of the opportunity becomes a sin all over again.

So, if we ask ourselves whether *teshuva* is an opportunity, a *chesed* granted by God, or an obligation, a demand imposed upon us, the answer is not only that it is both, independently; it is both, *intertwined.* The very existence of the opportunity imposes a fresh obligation. This is the meaning of the Rambam's expression, "Accordingly." It is inconceivable that a person who attaches significance to his own spiritual state should be totally impervious and insensitive to the ability to restore his relationship to God and to cleanse himself. If, indeed, he does not seize the opportunity, this is both a symptom and a cause of spiritual weakness.

OPPORTUNITY AND OBLIGATION WITHIN A GENERAL RELIGIOUS WORLDVIEW

Within the worldview of *Chazal* and of *gedolei Yisrael*, this sense of both the centrality of opportunity and obligation and their interaction can be viewed as a manifestation of a much broader concept. It can be placed within the more general context of our conception of divine service in particular and of human existence in general. Both opportunity and obligation are central concepts within our view of human life as it is and as it ought to be. At one plane, the sense of obligation, of duty, is both critical and central, whether at the moral plane – we think of humans as *by definition* committed, willy-nilly, to a moral and ethical life as part of having been created in the image of God[6] – or at the religious plane. If we were to take a single term that, more than anything else, we could regard as defining human existence and what frames our lives, it would certainly be the concept of mitzva. A Jew lives, first and foremost, as a called being, as a commanded being.

The very first Rashi in *Chumash* presents this idea not only surprisingly, but I would say audaciously. Rashi quotes the celebrated *midrash* in the name of Rabbi Yitzchak that the Torah ought to have started not with *Bereishit* but with the first mitzva – the implication being that what is important in Torah is the *mitzvot*. This perspective holds that Torah is, essentially, a legislative document that speaks to us in normative terms. The sense of being commanded is central to Jewish existence.

Although the Jew is commanded more thoroughly and extensively than others, divine command is also a universal category. The sense of human life as being guided, informed, and saturated by the sense of command is part of our conception of universal existence. In this context, let us examine two very striking verses in *Bereishit*, chapter 2. The first verse says, "The Lord God commanded the man, saying, 'Of every tree of the garden you may eat'" (2:16). Then the Torah continues, "But of the tree of the knowledge of good and evil, you shall not eat of it, for

6. Like Kant's famous sense of wonder – inspired, as he said, by the starry heavens above him and the moral law within him (*Critique of Practical Reason* 5:161) – the force of moral law is certainly part of our tradition and part of our sensibility.

on the day that you eat of it, you shall be worthy of death." The question arises: Whereas the first verse says that God commanded Adam, the actual command, not to eat from the tree of knowledge, is only in the second verse. Why, then, is initial reference made to "Of every tree of the garden you may eat," which is not part of the commandment?

The question, as I have formulated it, is grounded in the essentially secular conception that God has commanded us only with regard to certain areas of life, and that He has left a large neutral area where our own will and preferences find expression; there we act as we want. He has "His four cubits" (*Berakhot* 8a), but the rest of the ballpark is ours. However, a religious conception does not view any aspect of human reality as devoid of God and His commanding presence. While the Halakha does, at times, distinguish between a *devar mitzva* (obligatory matter) and a *devar reshut* (optional matter),[7] fundamentally, the message is that the realm of *devar reshut* is not outside the ambience of God, but under His tutelage. Thus, not only is abstaining from the tree of knowledge a realization of the divine command, but eating every other fruit in the Garden of Eden – and anywhere else – is likewise part of serving God, part of the realization of "the Lord God commanded." As a verse stated to Adam, it is of universal import.[8]

SEIZING OPPORTUNITY IN THE SPIRITUAL REALM

The sense that opportunity engenders obligation in the spiritual realm is not just a universal religious conception but also a central category of a Torah-based worldview. The failure to exploit spiritual potential, the failure to drink spiritual life to the lees, is not just some kind of pallid passivity, but, in the perception of *Chazal*, it is spiritual rot, described as such and condemned as such.

Let me cite several examples drawn from various areas of human life. The *Gemara* in *Yevamot* speaks of the mitzva of procreation. One would think that if a person is enjoined to procreate and he does not do

7. For example, a person can make an oath with regard to a *devar reshut*, but not with regard to a *devar mitzva*. See Rambam, *Hilkhot Nedarim* 3:7–8.
8. The *Gemara* (*Sanhedrin* 56b) uses this verse as a point of departure for the seven Noachide laws incumbent on all humanity.

it, his failure is only that he has not fulfilled a positive mitzva. While it is not ideal to miss a mitzva, he hasn't taken an evil action; he simply has not done something good. But this is not how *Chazal* speak of him:

> It was taught: Rabbi Eliezer states, He who does not engage in procreation is as though he [is one who] sheds blood.... Rabbi Ya'akov said, It is as if, so to speak, a person has diminished the stature of God.... Ben Azzai says, It is as though he sheds blood and diminishes the divine image. (*Yevamot* 63b)

All this where one has simply not availed himself of the opportunity to fulfill a certain mitzva, that of procreating and building a family.

Let us now take something more directly interpersonal. The *Gemara* in *Berakhot* (12b) states: "Rabba bar Chinnana Sava said in the name of Rav: Anyone who is able to beg for mercy for his friend and does not do so is called a sinner." For example, if a friend of his is ill, he could have said *Tehillim* or he could have implored God on his behalf; yet he didn't do it, either because he didn't think of it, or he was busy with other activities. Again, we would say he hasn't done the mitzva, but we might not have said he sinned. After all, it is not an absolute mitzva like procreation, but rather *gemilut chesed*, an act of kindness. Nevertheless, *Chazal* say, "He is called a sinner."

Or, to take another area: regarding Torah study, the *Gemara* in *Sanhedrin* (99a) is literally frightening. The verse at the end of *Shelach* (*Bemidbar* 15:31) refers to a person very severely: "A person has defamed the word of God and has countermanded His command." Who is considered to have "defamed the word of God"? "Rabbi Nehorai says, He who can engage in the study of the Torah but fails to do so." If one wants to understand how seriously *Chazal* regarded this, you need only to look at the other things listed there: one who maintains that the Torah is not from Heaven, or a heretic, etc. And who joins this list? One who has an opportunity for Torah study and didn't avail himself of it! Then there is the *Gemara* in *Chagiga* (5b) that lists three classes of people over whom God, so to speak, weeps daily. Who is the first on the list? "He who can engage in the study of Torah but fails to do so." God, so to speak, weeps over the failure to translate opportunity into obligation, to avail oneself spiritually of that which was within reach.

Chazal saw the significance of opportunity and the need to translate it into obligation not only in abstract terms; they read *Tanakh* and saw central figures in the Bible in its light. For example, *Chazal* say (*Berakhot* 7a) that when Moshe *Rabbeinu* asked God, "I pray, please show me Your glory" (*Shemot* 33:18), God said to him, "When I wanted to reveal Myself [at the time of the burning bush], you ran away. Now that you want, I don't want." Apparently, this *gemara* regards Moshe critically in the same vein we have been developing: he had an opportunity to see the revelation of the Divine Presence, but he didn't have the spiritual resources or inner strength for that encounter. This was a failing, and that opportunity, having been missed, was not to be restored.

Even more strikingly, the *Gemara* in *Chullin* (91b), cited by Rashi,[9] discusses Ya'akov *Avinu* as he was leaving his father's house. Based on an inconsistency in Ya'akov's itinerary – he seems to have arrived in Charan and then gone *back* to Beit-El – Rabbi Yitzchak says that Ya'akov reached Charan and then realized what he had passed. "Is it conceivable that I passed by a place where my forefathers had prayed and I did not pray there?" I suppose most of us could do that quite readily and quite frequently. What *Chazal* are stating here is that Ya'akov, in what was a critical juncture in his life, suddenly realized, retrospectively, that he had had an opportunity and passed it up. It wasn't a mitzva – there is no mitzva to pray specifically where one's ancestors did – but it was an *opportunity*: to find inspiration, to define his mission and his future, and to derive strength from a return to his roots. He could have done all that, but he did not. He passed by the place at which his ancestors prayed as if it were a subway station. The moment that Ya'akov realized that, he was struck with regret and guilt over having neglected a wonderful opportunity. But being Ya'akov *Avinu,* he didn't just let himself be eaten away by remorse; he turned around.

A remarkable passage in the *Yerushalmi* extends this concept far beyond the spiritual area with which we are dealing.

> Rabbi Chizkiya, Rabbi Kohen in the name of Rav stated: A person will stand in judgment [before the Almighty] for every

9. *Bereishit* 28:10, s.v. *ki va*.

> [fruit] that he saw and of which he did not partake. Rabbi Lazar took this to heart and saved money [to purchase many types of fruit]. At least once a year he took pains to partake of each fruit. (*Kiddushin* 4:12)

A person has the opportunity to partake of God's world, to come in live contact, even as a consumer, with that which the Almighty has created, and that, too, is a form of contact with God. Now, why must a person eat all types of fruit? He has his staple fruits that he enjoys, which he eats from year to year. Even if that means having a more circumscribed experience of God's world, so be it. Yet for that one is going to stand in judgment! If the opportunity to eat a guava engenders an obligation to eat it, what are we to say of the opportunity to pray properly, to learn Torah properly, to engage in *chesed* properly, to be suffused with a sense of God's presence, to perform *teshuva* properly? We are expected to lead a life charged with a sense of obligation, on the one hand, and with a sense of the awareness of opportunity, on the other. We need to keep our eyes and ears open to know where opportunity is present, and to live a life suffused with the interaction of the two.

BRINGING OPPORTUNITY AND OBLIGATION BACK TO *TESHUVA*

These two concepts and their interaction have special relevance to *teshuva*. Life is, to a great extent, a field of opportunity; but at the same time, it is also a field of missed opportunities. When an infant is born, the whole world is potential. Gradually, by the exigencies of life and the need for self-definition, the field of one's activity narrows, and all kinds of opportunities that had, in theory, existed at birth dwindle and eventually disappear from sight. Beyond this natural constriction, there is our failure to seize opportunities that were within grasp. We were not sufficiently sensitive and aware; either we did not realize the importance of the value, or did not sufficiently take heed to look around us and see where the opportunity existed. As a result, we missed *so much* valuable, significant spiritual potential. Retrospectively, we realize we could have structured our lives so much better, suffused it with greater value, organized it more efficiently, utilized time and effort more wisely.

We could have set our priorities more correctly. We look back upon life, and, even when we don't see active evil, we see so much waste. And waste is itself evil.

With regard to the prohibition of *bal tashchit*, of wasting property, the *Gemara* in *Shabbat* (129a, 140b) teaches: "*Bal tashchit* as applied to one's own person stands higher"; waste of human resources is more critical than waste of property. How much worse is the waste of spiritual potential, that gap between what we could have been, what we should have been, and what we are. Everyone has this gap; for some it is enormous, and for others it seems smaller, but there is always the gap. That gap is the waste of human potential that was inherent within us, of the divine image God gave us. We, somehow, "diminished the stature of God" within ourselves. We could have procreated spiritually, but we did not do it. Maybe it sounds too severe to translate this into a kind of bloodshed, choking off incipient life, but we can certainly speak of "diminishing the stature of God." To the extent that we are spiritually sensitive, this is both pitiful and tormenting.

Along comes the opportunity of *teshuva*. *Teshuva* is not just an opportunity *per se*; it is the opportunity to amend for all the missed opportunities. *Teshuva* is the chance to redress the balance, to take all of that waste and not only neutralize it but energize it, even transforming it into a positive force. *Chazal* teach:

> Reish Lakish said: Great is *teshuva*, for one's intentional sins are counted as unwitting transgressions.... Is that so? Did not Reish Lakish say: Great is *teshuva*, for one's intentional sins are counted as merits?... This is not difficult; one is out of love, the other out of fear. (*Yoma* 86b)

Where *teshuva* is properly experienced, even "intentional sins are counted as merits." So if one can speak of life, generally, as opportunity translated into obligation, *teshuva* is the opportunity to bring back all that we missed, to confront the torment and amend the failure. Ultimately, it allows us to restructure and rebuild our lives, and perhaps even more, when *teshuva* is performed out of love, to build upon our failure, our waste, and our diminishing of the divine stature.

TESHUVA: A GATE AND A WINDOW OF OPPORTUNITY

When we speak of opportunity, we can refer to two separate concepts. There is, first, a kind of constant opportunity. One has the ability to involve oneself in Torah every day, every hour, within the limits of other obligations and commitments. Second, there are opportunities that are more specific, that arise at a particular time due to a confluence of circumstances, as when opportunity "knocks." We might speak, then, of a "gate" of opportunity, and a "window" of opportunity. A gate is always open, so that you can walk through it whenever you want. In contrast, a window normally is shut, and during the fleeting moment when it is opened one can hope to extend his hand through it.[10]

Teshuva, as the opportunity to amend for the failure to exploit opportunity, can be viewed in both perspectives. In a certain sense, *teshuva* is always possible. Every moment, every day, a person can perform *teshuva*. "The gates of *teshuva* are eternally open" (*Devarim Rabba* 2:12), and the outstretched hand, as it were, of the Almighty is always there. But there are also moments when He knocks on our window, when we experience "*Kol, Dodi dofek*, A sound, my Beloved is knocking" (*Shir Ha-shirim* 5:2). And then the obligation, grounded in opportunity, becomes that much greater. The constant opportunity is certainly challenging and imperative, but if, beyond that, God does not simply remain majestically ready to receive you, but reaches out to you and descends to you, woe to one who misses that, who relives the verse, "*Dodi chamak avar*, My Beloved has slipped away" (*Shir Ha-shirim* 5:6). When the opportunity is sharper and more immediate, the obligation is much greater as well.

It is in this vein that we are to understand the Rambam and Rabbeinu Yona. Yom Kippur is "the occasion of forgiveness and remission for Israel." This is a time when God is not simply present in the recesses of His infinite being, but has descended to us. The verse commands us to "Seek out the Lord when He may be found, call upon Him when He is near" (*Yeshayahu* 55:6), and *Chazal* say, "These are the ten days from Rosh Ha-shana to Yom Kippur" (*Rosh Ha-shana* 18a; *Yevamot* 49b).

10. These relate to two terms in Modern Hebrew: *hizdamnut*, which by definition is of a particular time and occasion, and *efsharut*, which connotes the possible, something that is always there.

This is "when He is near"; this is the opportunity that beckons particularly. And if it beckons it obligates! "Accordingly, everyone is obligated to repent."

SELF-EXAMINATION DURING THE TEN DAYS OF REPENTANCE

What does this *teshuva* demand of us? Of course, we must view our lives honestly and in detail to see where and whom we have wronged. But that kind of introspection is not sufficient, for if *teshuva* is indeed the opportunity to amend for lost opportunity, we need to address ourselves to that loss, to that waste. We need to confront not simply the active sinner in us, but the indolent in us.

The *Gemara* in *Berakhot* (5a) states:

> Rava, and some say Rav Chisda, said: If a person sees that painful sufferings visit him, let him examine his conduct, as the verse states, "Let us search and examine our ways and return to the Lord" (*Eikha* 3:40). If he checked and did not find [sinful behavior], let him attribute it to the neglect of the study of Torah.

The question arises: when he examined his conduct, did he not look into neglect of Torah study? I think the answer is clear. Of course, when a person examines his conduct, among the various areas he investigates is whether he is learning Torah: "The study of Torah is equal to all the others" (*Pe'a* 1:1). But he conducts his self-examination only at the level of whether he sinned by neglecting the mitzva of Torah study. Yet neglect of Torah is not just a question of a sin. While the *Gemara* in *Sanhedrin* castigated one who had the opportunity to study but did not, the *Gemara* in *Chagiga* discussed another dimension of neglect of Torah – one that caused the Almighty, so to speak, to weep! Why is He described as weeping only over neglect of Torah study, but not over desecration of Shabbat or eating non-kosher food? It is because the weeping is not over sins as such; it is over the waste of this wonderful resource of human life that could have been developed and was instead left to rot. When *Chazal* speak of attributing suffering that has no discernible cause to "neglect of Torah study," they refer to the waste, the failure to energize spiritual potential.

That examination of deeds of which Rava speaks has various components. Broadly speaking, we certainly subscribe to the Socratic axiom that the unexamined life is not worth living – but we need to bear in mind what it is that we examine. We need to undergo self-examination at three different levels. There is the examination of which the Rambam speaks at the beginning of *Hilkhot Teshuva*, where a person examines his *actions*: I did this, or I didn't do that. There is, at the other extreme, the examination of one's *self*: who am I, and where do I stand in relation to who I could be? Between these extremes, the *Gemara* quotes the verse in *Eikha*, "Let us search and examine our ways" (3:40), referring to the totality of our behavior. The Rav *z"l* used to speak frequently of "sin," meaning specific actions, and "the ways of sin," the whole context of lifestyle and personality out of which sin develops and by which it is sustained. This direction that life takes, this modality of activity, stands somewhere between the definition of self and the analysis of particular actions.

With regard to the concept of the waste of spiritual resources, of the failure to implement a kind of spiritual *carpe diem*, we need to examine ourselves at all three levels: we check our actions, we examine our ways, and, perhaps most profoundly and painfully, we investigate our very being, our inner self.

All of this is extraordinarily demanding and difficult. It is hard enough to do what we are supposed to do and abstain from that which we are proscribed from doing, clearly and narrowly defined. But, when we not only hold ourselves to a standard of what we do, but gauge ourselves by optimum, by potential, and therefore hold ourselves accountable for every opportunity we could have seized and did not – this is, as I said, painful, even tormenting. Yet here we encounter not only the obligation of *teshuva*, but the *chesed* of *teshuva*.

TESHUVA AS TASHLUMIN

I spoke earlier of a kind of opportunity to make amends for missed opportunity. In the world of Halakha, this is known as *tashlumin*. We have two models for this, and there is a clear difference between them.

First, there is a type of *tashlumin* where, if you missed the first opportunity, you have a second chance. The paradigm is *Pesach sheni*

(*Bemidbar* 9:9–14).[11] If you didn't bring the *Pesach* offering on the fourteenth of Nisan – not only, as in the passage in the Torah, where a person was at a distance or impure (*Bemidbar* 9:10), but even if you violated intentionally – you bring *Pesach sheni*, the compensatory *Pesach* offering on the fourteenth of Iyar. Similarly, if you didn't bring the mandatory festive offerings, the *korbenot ha-regel*, on the first day of a Festival, you can bring them during the entire holiday.[12] Or, if you didn't make *havdala* on Saturday night, according to many *Rishonim*[13] you can make *havdala* until Tuesday, *be-torat tashlumin*, as a compensation. We don't know why the Torah gave *tashlumin* for *korban Pesach* and didn't give *tashlumin* for hearing the *shofar* or sitting in the *sukka*. Whatever the reason, with regard to certain *mitzvot*, there is a second chance.

The second type of *tashlumin* is applicable to prayer. The *Gemara* says that since prayer contains an aspect of *rachamei*, supplication for mercy, the *halakha* of *tashlumin* applies to it. Unlike the earlier cases, here the *Gemara* explains *why* there is a second opportunity for prayer. The reason is that prayer is an expression of our quest, our pleading, and a plea can never be shut off. Therefore, there is a halakhic difference between the *tashlumin* of *korban Pesach* and *korbenot ha-regel*, and the *tashlumin* of prayer. Regarding *Pesach* and *regel*, even if a person violated the mitzva intentionally the first time around, he still has *tashlumin*. It's a *gezerat ha-katuv*, a Torah edict. With regard to prayer, however, there is *tashlumin* only for unintentional neglect of the mitzva, such as if he accidentally forgot, or if circumstances did not enable him to pray, but not if he omitted prayer intentionally. The *Gemara* implies that, fundamentally, prayer should not have *tashlumin* – it should be like most other *mitzvot*. But at the level of *rachamei*, mercy, prayer is essentially a plea, a turning to the Almighty, and those gates can never be closed. That being the case, if one wantonly missed the prayer, if one knew it

11. There is a dispute in the *Gemara* regarding exactly how to define *Pesach sheni* (*Pesachim* 93a–b), but, for our purposes, I will regard it as a *tashlumin*, compensation.
12. Here, again, there are two views in the *Gemara* (*Chagiga* 9a) whether this is regarded as *tashlumin*, compensatory, or not.
13. *Tosafot, Pesachim* 107a, s.v. *Ameimar*; Rosh, *Pesachim* 10:13; Rambam, *Hilkhot Shabbat* 29:4; see *Tur* and *Shulchan Arukh, Orach Chayim* 299:6.

was taking place but did not want to stop what he was doing and pray – such a person is denied the opportunity to make it up later.

Teshuva is a kind of *tashlumin,* an opportunity to amend that which one did not avail himself of initially, and it is an opportunity grounded in *rachamei. Rachamei* here has a dual sense. On God's part, it is an expression of compassion and kindness. It defies all logic to turn back the clock, to restructure the past; this is divine *chesed.* On our part, it means a plea, turning to God out of the depths of our remorse and our desire, not only to amend but to build. And where there is *rachamei* on our part and on His, then, indeed, the great burden of trying to review one's life, with all the concern and all the anxiety accompanying that review, is then channeled into *teshuva.* This introspection into one's actions and into the path of one's life, which in one respect is so difficult and perhaps tormenting, becomes – to the extent that it is our *rachamei* and His *rachamei* – so uplifting, so ennobling. It becomes, indeed, a manifestation and a realization of the opportunity to restore everything we had missed and which now, in the infinite kindness of the Almighty, we are able to sustain and to develop.

We do not want to be like the prisoner in Rabbeinu Yona's *midrash*: not to be prisoners of ourselves, of our past, or of our failure. If we have within us the spiritual resources, the desire to move, to build, and to avail ourselves of that remarkable *chesed* of the Almighty – the *chesed* of *teshuva,* of forgiveness and atonement, of the remission of sin and of punishment, and, above all, the *chesed* of the restoration of our relation to Him – then what might seem almost an unbearably difficult task becomes a source of joy. Then we encounter the Almighty receiving us, opening the gates, "*Petach lanu sha'ar... ki fana yom,* Open the gate for us ... for day is nearly past" (*Ne'ila* prayer).

Purify Our Hearts to Serve You with Truth

The Rambam notes in his opening discussion of prayer (*Hilkhot Tefilla* 1:4) that standardized *tefilla* provides a ready instrument of prayer for all, thus upgrading the fulfillment of the mitzva by those who, left to their own devices, would be hard put to implement it properly. Nevertheless, as critics have often noted, what frequently governs our perception and experience of these texts is the fact that they are imposed ritual obligation; the specific content of the texts influences us less.

Everyone can attest to the extent to which his experience has assumed this character, and everyone, therefore, can define for himself the concomitant need to cope with the natural tendency toward rote recitation, against which moralists and pietists of all persuasions have railed persistently.[1] Nevertheless, each of us can also attest to a special affinity for specific texts, which penetrate the barriers of routine

Delivered at Kehillath Jeshurun in Manhattan, Elul 5752 (1992).

1. *Yeshayahu* (29:13) poignantly refers to this phenomenon when he says, "And their fear toward Me has been *mitzvat anashim melummada,* A commandment of men learned by rote."

performance, speak to one's particular situation, and address themselves to one's innermost being. These texts permeate the spiritual self with richness and intensity, and therefore occupy a special place in one's heart.

For me, one such text is the familiar supplication, "*Ve-taher libbenu le-ovdekha be-emet,* Purify our hearts to serve You with truth." Since it is recited not only on the High Holidays, but on every Shabbat and Festival, it has always struck me as the conspectus of a number of central themes telescoped within it. I would like to share with you some thoughts and feelings about this plea, by analyzing the substantive content and various interwoven strands of its highly compressed conclusion, "*le-ovdekha be-emet,* To serve You with truth."

WHAT DOES *EMET* ADD TO *AVODA*?

To plead, "*Ve-taher libbenu le-ovdekha be-emet,*" is to imply that *avoda,* service, does not include *emet,* truth, by definition; that one could halakhically be regarded as serving the Almighty even when serving without *emet.* What, then, we ask ourselves, is the incremental demand or, at the very least, aspiration, entailed by the additional dimension of *be-emet*?

I believe we ought to speak, rather, of demands and aspirations in the plural. This point is best borne out if we ask ourselves to what *be-emet* is counterposed. Having raised the question, one readily perceives that truth has at least two distinct, primary opposites, each of which is itself multifaceted: error and falsehood. Anyone endowed with even minimal moral sensibility, let alone philosophic insight, recognizes the radical difference between *ta'ut,* error, and *sheker,* deception. The former is concerned with correlation to fact, the latter with its distortion. When we articulate "*Ve-taher libbenu le-ovdekha be-emet,*" we pray for truth in both respects. We pray that our *avoda* will be devoid of both error and falsehood, that we serve in accordance with truth; and we pray that we do so, at a personal level, truthfully, without deceit or self-deceit. But what, more specifically, is the substance of our petition? We can appreciate this more fully by examining the components of truth's antitheses.

EMET AS OPPOSED TO ERROR

When we analyze error, we can distinguish at least three significant elements: errors in Halakha, in *emuna,* and in seeking to understand God.

Halakhic error entails the misinterpretation or misapplication of "the word of God," namely, Halakha.[2] On the basis of the practice of Rabbi Nechunya ben Ha-kaneh,[3] the Rambam (*Hilkhot Berakhot* 10:23) postulates that one who enters the study hall should recite a short supplication. This brief prayer begins with a request not to stumble with regard to a matter of Halakha, and the same request is repeated at the prayer's end in order to prevent his colleagues' rejoicing over his stumbling, and, contrarily, to preclude his own rejoicing over their stumbling.

The repetition seems redundant, but the explanation is simple. The Rambam speaks of stumbling in two contexts, the first being the elucidation of Torah on the purely speculative plane. To a *ben Torah*, the possibility of error here is a critical matter, both out of commitment to truth as a universal value, and out of responsibility to the singular importance of the divine word. Secondly, there is potential for misstep in the field, possibly the minefield, of halakhic ruling, and it is to this that the second petition relates, and why it mentions the danger of rejoicing colleagues. Envious peers can, perhaps, overlook errors growing out of the free play of the mind in the course of a *shiur*; but there is nothing like a mistaken ruling to provide them instant and intense gratification.

We pray, then, simply out of our own spiritual aspirations, to attain halakhic truth in both respects. We wish to ascertain the truth of Torah, to plumb its depths and master its verities. It might seem that so long as a person has taken aim to the best of his ability, it seems to matter little, ultimately, whether or not he has hit the mark. The *Gemara* (*Kiddushin* 40a) states that a Jew is credited with full performance of a mitzva if he is intent on fulfilling a mitzva but is forcibly prevented from doing so. This, however, is only with respect to judgment of that person; at the level of accomplishment, to which a person of Halakha aspires, anyone endowed with a halakhic, as opposed to a purely Kantian, sensibility would be anguished beyond words were he suddenly to discover that his *tefillin* had been written improperly, so that, whatever his intention, he had never fulfilled the mitzva.

2. *Shabbat* 138b, *Keritut* 13b.
3. *Berakhot* 28b.

Contiguous to the area of Halakha, and yet distinct from it, is a second arena of potential error, that of *emuna*, the world of faith and doctrine. *Emuna* is both a central value in its own right, and a basis for the observance of mitzvot generally. Whether or not it is to be enumerated among the 613 mitzvot has been the subject of much debate since the time of the Rambam. What is beyond question, however, is the crucial role of faith as the substratum, both logical and psychological, of halakhic living in its totality. It is *ikkar* in the sense that Rav Yosef Albo notes in the introduction to his *Sefer Ha-ikkarim*,[4] the fundamental element out of whose premises others derive and upon which the entire system rests. In this respect, surely, *emuna* occupies, and ought to occupy, a significant place in our spiritual life. While intellectual historians may note that, comparatively, dogma plays only a minor role in Judaism, in absolute terms, dogmatic faith is deeply entrenched within Judaism, *a priori*. Religion without dogma, as Whitehead noted,[5] is unthinkable. "*Le-ovdekha be-emet*" entails, then, doctrinal truth as well. We pray that our *emuna* be steadfast and pure and that it be neither buffeted by the winds of skepticism and relativism, nor contaminated by the taints of schismatic heresy and heterodox revisionism.

The plea has particular poignancy for those who have been significantly exposed to these elements. As the French philosopher Ricoeur once remarked, the pristine innocence of naïve faith is, once lost, irrecoverable.[6] Whether or not that is indeed the case, surely, if we pray for purity of heart, striving for innocent faith is very much part of our plea. Yehoshua, in his farewell address, counsels a religiously pallid and ambivalent Jewish people, "Now, therefore, revere the Lord and serve Him with sincerity and truth (*be-tamim u-ve-emet*)" (24:14). While the scriptural use of "*tamim*" – normally an adjective – does not wholly correspond to our own, nevertheless, the conjunction of "*emet*" and "*tamim*" indicates the extent to which innocent faith is part of the request of "*le-ovdekha be-emet*."

4. *Sefer Ha-ikkarim*, p. 18, and even more explicitly in the introduction to the commentary by Gedalya Lipschitz (p. 3).
5. Alfred North Whitehead, *Religion in the Making* (Cambridge, 1926), *passim*, but especially in the second lecture, "Religion and Dogma."
6. Paul Ricoeur, *The Symbolism of Evil* (1967), p. 351.

Apart from the danger of residual skepticism or heresy, much of it socio-culturally conditioned, we are confronted by a third strain of error, one that is indigenous to the human condition as a whole. The mitzva of *emuna* – or, for that matter, the realm of divine service generally – imposes upon us a seemingly impossible mission. Let us suppose for a moment that a person were to define himself as a fervent devotee of the Almighty, whom he would then describe, Heaven forfend, as a wooden statue. His pronounced adherence notwithstanding, we would immediately regard him as a fool at best and an idolater at worst, justly deserving of the prophet Yeshayahu's scorn (*Yeshayahu* 44:16–17) against one who takes a piece of lumber and uses half for firewood and the other half as a deity. The fact that this acolyte would present himself as committed to the name of the Almighty is, of course, of little moment. The critical question is how one conceives of the Creator. Worship of anything other than the Almighty is idolatry, regardless of how it is denominated.

But is our own situation inherently different? Does not anyone who envisions God as a *rosh yeshiva* with a long beard or as a supreme general fall into the same trap? Granted, the Torah uses various terms to describe, as it were, the Almighty, because at times He is revealed, and therefore perceived, as a master fighter, and at times as a kind, elderly gentleman.[7] Nevertheless, the Almighty is by definition transcendent, a *Deus absconditus*, hidden in His numinous otherness, beyond human ken. He is, in Otto's celebrated phrase, "the wholly other," not even subject to comparison. "'To whom shall you compare Me?' says the Holy One" (*Yeshayahu* 40:25). He is "*Kadosh, kadosh, kadosh,* Transcendent, transcendent, transcendent" (*Yeshayahu* 6:3), incomprehensible, "for no man can apprehend Me and live" (*Shemot* 33:20). If so, all attempts to know Him, even in purely philosophical terms, are wide of the mark, and all our conceptions and imaginative ruminations define something else, someone else.

---

7. See, e.g., *Mekhilta* (*Ba-chodesh*, 5), paraphrased by Rashi (*Shemot* 20:2):

> Why does the verse state, "I am the Lord your God [who took you out of Egypt]"? Because He revealed Himself at the sea as a warrior, as the verse states, "The Lord is a man of war" (*Shemot* 15:3), and revealed Himself at Mount Sinai as an elder filled with compassion, as the verse states (*Shemot* 24:10), "And they perceived the God of Israel."

And here is our terrifying dilemma. We are commanded to relate to the Almighty and presumably we would seek Him even had we not been commanded; and yet we know that all our efforts are doomed to failure, that we shall always miss Him. Worse still, it is as though we direct our service to the sophisticated version, God forbid, of the wooden statue, which we have denominated as the deity. On the other hand, the more rigorously we reject anthropomorphism, the more difficult it becomes to realize the command and the aspiration to relate to Him, to love Him, and to serve Him.

On the conceptual plane, the dilemma is insoluble. Existentially and experientially, however, we live as *metzuvvim ve-osim,* commanded beings, in the knowledge that we have indeed been enjoined with two mandates. On the one hand, we know the gravity of the prohibition of idolatry and the radical difference between human and divine. This is the very heart of Judaism; it was on this point that Avraham *Avinu* parted company with the pagan world, and on this issue that we stand radically, and unalterably, opposed to Christianity. On the other hand, we are charged to relate to the Almighty, and this, at the personal level, is pervasive and perpetual: "*Shivviti Hashem le-negdi tamid,* I pose the Almighty before me at all times" (*Tehillim* 16:8). We are enjoined, then, to do our human best to transcend the apparent conflict, purify our conceptions, and serve the Almighty accordingly, secure in the knowledge that inasmuch as "The Torah was not given to the ministering angels" (*Berakhot* 25b et al.), our limited service will be accepted by God. The optimal balance is *avoda be-emet,* service of the Almighty that is both genuine and honest, and we strive constantly to achieve it as we plead, "*Ve-taher libbenu le-ovdekha be-emet.*"

EMET AS OPPOSED TO FALSEHOOD

Moving from error to falsehood, here, too, several aspects bear consideration. Proverbially, falsehood has no feet,[8] but it certainly has many tentacles. There is, first, sheer pretense, the exercise of sham divine service, with respect to which appearance bears little relation to reality. Much as we recoil from such conduct, there is, perhaps, something to

8. E.g., Rashi, *Mishlei* 12:19, s.v. *ve-ad*; *Tur, Choshen Mishpat* 1; *Beit Yosef, Orach Chayim* 36:1.

be said for it, too. A seventeenth-century pundit, Francois de la Rochefoucauld, once suggested that hypocrisy is the tribute that vice pays to virtue,[9] and the tacit recognition, at least externally, of the hegemony of truth is not without significance. Nevertheless, little needs to be said of outright hypocrisy, and those who exercise it habitually probably intend nothing of significance when they utter, "*le-ovdekha be-emet*." However, Jewish and general moralists throughout the ages have noted that deception and hypocrisy have many levels. We will all recognize the justice of a remark made by one of the chassidic masters, that if an *etrog* were taken at home rather in *shul*, people would be less concerned about the punctiliousness of fulfilling the mitzva. And even for those of us who are fundamentally sincere, the temptation of showy and pretentious piety lurks incessantly. For rabbis and for *rashei yeshiva*, this is nothing short of an occupational hazard; while few take note of how long a laborer or a lawyer stands for *Shemoneh Esrei*, the spiritual mentor is the target of surrounding eyes. Yet even for the ordinary layman, the danger is acute enough. And there is always, as the proponents of *Mussar* persistently reminded us, the prospect of self-delusion. "The heart is deceitful above all things... who can understand it?" Yirmiyahu (17:9) asked, and the presumed reply is, clearly, not even the heart's owner.

Beside the falsehood of sham, there is that of cant, religious existence that is not the real thing because it is shallow and shoddy. There is false spirituality, in the same sense that there are false notes in music; there is kitsch in serving God as there is in art – superficial emotion, stock responses, and pallid performance. This is the familiar order of "*mitzvat anashim melummada*" (*Yeshayahu* 29:13) – rote performance, of which I spoke at the outset, a world of desiccated spirit and insouciant observance. Irrespective of the extent to which it is animated by conformity, the jejune quality of this divine service is problematic by its very nature.

Akin to the *sheker* of shallowness is that of adulteration. This relates, in part, to the spiritual quality of a mitzva *per se*, and in part to its teleology, the purpose for which it is performed. But it relates primarily to the impetus of the mitzva. Granted, from a halakhic perspective,

9. *Reflections; or Sentences and Moral Maxims*, Maxim 218.

one is not inclined to accept the judgment of Thomas à Becket[10] in T. S. Eliot's "Murder in the Cathedral," to the effect that "The last temptation is the greatest treason: to do the right thing for the wrong reason." Surely *Chazal* held that not doing the right thing at all was the greater treason.

> Rav Yehuda said in the name of Rav: A person should always engage in the study of Torah or the performance of *mitzvot,* even for the wrong motives, because these ultimately bring him to the level of pure motive (*she-mitokh she-lo li-shmah ba li-shmah*).[11]

Moreover, the *Rishonim* generally assumed, with reference to this statement, that performance with ulterior motive has intrinsic merit and not just instrumental value as an initial step on the road to "*li-shmah.*"

Nevertheless, motivation is critical in establishing both the quality of an act and the worth of its agent, and our tradition has been keenly aware of this fact. Concern about the phenomenon of spiritual pride is firmly entrenched in Halakha, in the prohibition of *yuhara,* the injunction against adopting stringencies disproportionate to one's general religious level, out of a desire to inflate one's spiritual ego. In the same vein, the *Yerushalmi* (*Chagiga* 2:2) speaks of a woman who suffered unusual punishment in the netherworld, although she had presented a pious visage in the terrestrial; she had indeed fasted many times but had taken pains to publicize the fact. In the chapters devoted to the quality of *tahara,* purity, for which we pray, the *Mesillat Yesharim* (chap. 16) explains that just as there is a need for purity with regard to actions, to be certain that they are not under the wing of the *yetzer ha-ra,* so too there is a need for purity with regard to actions which, *prima facie,* belong to the Almighty. Even these may at times move away from pure divine service, which the Rambam, following both the *Gemara* in *Nedarim* (62a) and the *Sifrei,* linked with the central mitzva of loving God:

> *Chazal* said: Lest a person say, I shall learn Torah in order that I should become financially opulent, in order that I should be

10. Archbishop of Canterbury, 1163 until his assassination in 1170.
11. *Pesachim* 50b *et al.*

> called a rabbi, in order that I should get reward in the World-to-Come, so the verse says "To love God" – whatever you do, you should do solely out of love. (*Hilkhot Teshuva* 10:4)

The plea of "*Ve-taher libbenu le-ovdekha be-emet*" relates, then, to various aspects of the quest for truth: both to the discharge from error, be it halakhic, doctrinal, or iconographic, and to the emancipation from falsehood, superficiality, or adulteration.

INTEGRITY AND INTEGRATION IN THE QUEST FOR *EMET*

The quest for *emet* is not simply the discharge of error or expulsion of falsehood. It bears a positive aspect as well, one perhaps underscored by the relationship between two words in English: integrity, in the dual sense of wholeness and honesty, and integration.[12] "The Torah of the Lord is perfect"; so begins the account of Torah and *mitzvot* in the psalm (*Tehillim* 19:8). It concludes, "The judgments of the Lord are true (*emet*), righteous altogether" (verse 10). There is an *emet* that derives from the wholeness, integrity, and comprehensiveness of one's service of God. One sense of "righteous altogether" is objective, external: certain aspects of Halakha, when considered in isolation, seem difficult to understand, yet are cast into an entirely different light when seen as part of the system in its entirety. But "righteous altogether" is also at the level of the subject, of the person performing them; it is *emet* that derives from the fact that one's divine service is not simply a series of independent acts, a fragmented world, but rather a comprehensive universe of service.

This factor assumes added significance if we think of divine service in terms of a quest for some inner spiritual self. When Polonius says, "To thine own self be true, and then thou canst not be false to any man" (*Hamlet*, Act 1, Scene III), that self is presumably a unified and integrated identity. While this quest for some particular, singular self does not occupy as significant a place in our own thinking as in modern European literature, it does manifest in our world as well, for example, in the world of *Chassidut*.

12. See the chapter "The Integrity of *Teshuva*" for an expanded discussion of this idea.

Now, of course, that quest raises obvious problems, with respect to the subjective aspect of *emet*, how each individual puts it all together. *Emet* is monistic, but it is also, within certain limits, pluralistic. The character of one person's service of God does not necessarily coincide with that of another. Within our quest for *emet* in the world of divine service, we are confronted with a need to strike a balance between the sincerity of the individual, on the one hand, and, on the other, authenticity to what our tradition views as a legitimate form of *avoda*. At the extreme, the emphasis upon sincerity leads to the kind of attitude epitomized in Tennyson's famous lines, "There lies more faith, believe me, in honest doubt than in half the creeds" (*In Memoriam*, XCVI, st. 3). This, of course, we reject. But, at the same time, surely we ought to beware of going to the other extreme and thinking only in monistic terms. Would anyone today consider delegitimizing either *Chassidut* or *Mitnagdut*? The quest for the coincidence of objective and subjective *emet*, then, is a central aspect of our seeking integrity, integration, and spiritual wholeness, a significant facet of "*le-ovdekha be-emet*."

THE NEED FOR TRUTH IN *AVODA*

Like *emet*, the term "*le-ovdekha*" bears a multiple aspect. Broadly speaking, we can address the aspiration for "*le-ovdekha be-emet*" to at least three distinct realms. On one plane, *avoda* refers to the totality of one's commitment to the Almighty and observance of His *mitzvot*. When the Torah says, "You shall fear the Lord your God, and serve Him, and swear by His name" (*Devarim* 6:13), or if verses in *Tehillim* counsel, respectively, "Serve the Lord with fear" (2:11), and "Serve the Lord with joy" (100:2), clearly, they are referring to the whole range of the religious life.

But on a second level, *Chazal* singled out particular foci of *avoda*. Commenting on the term "to serve Him (*le-ovdo*)" in the second paragraph of the *Shema* (*Devarim* 11:13), the *Sifrei* (*Ekev*, 41) offers two alternative referents aside from the obvious one of sacrifices:

> "To serve Him"; this is Torah study. And just as the sacrificial order is called service, so too is Torah study called service.... "To serve Him"; this is prayer. And just as the sacrificial order is called service, so too is prayer called service.

For each, the *Sifrei* cites various proof texts, but does not explain why, indeed, these three elements have been singled out. I believe that the common denominator can be readily perceived. All three entail a relatively direct encounter with the *Shekhina*, the Divine Presence. Sacrifices are offered in the home base of the *Shekhina*, and they entail *re'iyat panim*, appearing before God in His inner sanctum. *Tefilla*, prayer, is defined halakhically as *amida lifnei Ha-melekh*, standing before the King. Torah study, quite apart from its intellectual aspect, involves, as the Rav so frequently emphasized, when one is properly motivated, a meeting with the Torah's Giver.[13]

Whatever was said earlier of the aspiration for *le-ovdekha be-emet* unquestionably applies to *avoda* in its broader sense, the totality of one's service. However, it obviously has special application to the narrower sense, in the areas enumerated in the *Sifrei*.

"A person who engages in deceit shall not sit in My house; a person who speaks untruths shall have no standing before My eyes" (*Tehillim* 101:7); so says King David of himself. The more deeply one presumes to enter the domain of *Shekhina*, the greater the degree of prerequisite probity and authenticity. If physical purification is a condition for entering the *Mikdash*, then *a fortiori* spiritual purgation: "One cannot enter the courtyard of the king in sackcloth" (Esther 4:2), whether physical or spiritual.

EMET IN PRAYER: A DIFFICULT DEMAND

The plea of "*Ve-taher libbenu le-ovdekha be-emet*" is even more acutely relevant with respect to a third realm, the last of the triad of the *Sifrei*: prayer. In part, this is because the encounter of prayer is more direct than that of sacrifices or Torah study; after all, in great measure we address the Almighty in the second person during prayer. And in part it is because "*Ve-taher libbenu le-ovdekha be-emet*" can be understood to mean that we ask that the heart be purified not just so as to infuse religious existence generally, but in order that it be able to perform its own indigenous labor, or *avoda*, particularly. That labor is, of course, *tefilla*. The heart

13. Rabbi Chalafta's view (*Avot* 3:6) that the Divine Presence abides among those – whether ten or one – who occupy themselves with Torah embodies this notion well.

needs to be pure so that a person should put on *tefillin* or take *lulav* and *etrog* properly, but all the more so in order that the *avoda she-balev*, the service of the heart, should be proper. In the words of the *Gemara*:[14] "It has been taught: 'To love the Lord your God and to serve Him with all your heart' (*Devarim* 11:13). What is service of the heart? You must say: Prayer." But the request for purity of the heart relates especially to prayer because of the particular difficulty we have, if left to our own devices, in attaining truth in *tefilla*. That difficulty is twofold – inherent in human nature, and also socio-historical.

To begin with the former, the standard of *kavvana*, proper intent, in *tefilla* is higher than with respect to *mitzvot* generally. As the Rambam explains: "What is meant by proper intention? That a person should divest himself of all other thoughts and imagine that he is standing before the *Shekhina*" (*Hilkhot Tefilla* 4:16). Moreover, the *kavvana* of *tefilla*, being more rigorously defined, is, concomitantly, more difficult to attain. The *Yerushalmi* cites *Amoraim* who confessed to counting chicks or building blocks in the course of *Shemoneh Esrei*, while another admitted to meditating upon the niceties of diplomatic protocol.[15] With reference to a much later period, Rav Amital is fond of quoting a story about students of the Ba'al Shem Tov who asked him how they could determine whether a *tzaddik* who had recently come to the area was genuine or an imposter. "Inquire of him," the Ba'al Shem Tov suggested, "whether he has a foolproof prescription against aberrant thoughts during *tefilla*. If he does, you can rest assured he's a fraud."

The problem of truth in prayer is further exacerbated by modernity, and this in several respects. For a modern person, the range of genuine relevance of prayer is generally far more limited than it was for his predecessors. As opposed to his ancient or medieval forebears, he feels less in need of divine assistance. The relatively greater degree of control over his environment which science and technology have

14. *Ta'anit* 2a (cf. *Yerushalmi Berakhot* 4:1, 29a), based on *Sifrei, Ekev* 41.

15. *Yerushalmi, Berakhot* 2:4 (end), 17b. This text, and others, became the basis of rulings by the *Rishonim* waiving the rigorous standards required according to the *Gemara* for *kavvana* in *tefilla* (see *Tur, Orach Chayim* 101, s.v. *ha-idna*, and Rema on *Orach Chayim* 101:1).

afforded him has greatly reduced the sense of dependence, which the Maharal placed at the heart of *tefilla,*[16] and Schleiermacher, after him, at the heart of religion generally.[17] Furthermore, being more secularly oriented, even when he is self-defined as religious, his genuine conviction in the efficacy of prayer is likely to be relatively attenuated. Deep down, he often has a residual sense that perhaps natural law or fortuitous chance govern his life after all. And for many, a pervasive rationalism inhibits the expression of *any* profound feeling. Matthew Arnold had a sense of modern life as being "a wintry clime" and "an iron time,"[18] and his lament of the evisceration of feeling within it obviously bears upon religious emotion in particular.

The result, within the Jewish world, is often prayer which is *pro forma* proper and yet passionless; sincere, but, in a very real sense, inauthentic. For the Modern Orthodox Jew and his community in particular, the inclination and the capacity to pray properly and with passion, with a plaintive *cri de coeur* issuing *mi-ma'amakim,* from the depths, is often sadly deficient. The essence of *tefilla* is "prayer of the impoverished when he is faint and pours forth his plea before the Lord" (*Tehillim* 102:1); but the modern Jew does not generally perceive himself as truly impoverished, and if he did, he probably would still find it difficult to shed his inhibitions and pour forth his plea. Here, surely, is an area with respect to which we need to plead, all the more urgently and passionately, "*Ve-taher libbenu le-ovdekha be-emet.*"

EMET AS A QUALITY OF OUR ENTIRE RELIGIOUS LIFE

In order to appreciate fully the import of "*le-ovdekha be-emet,*" a further point needs to be stressed. "*Le-ovdekha be-emet*" denotes a qualitative aspect of our religious existence. It does not relate to *whether* we fulfill the *mitzvot,* or how *much* we fulfill them, but simply to *how* we fulfill

16. *Netivot Ha-olam, Netiv Ha-avoda,* chap. 1.
17. Friedrich Schleiermacher, *The Christian Faith* (1821–2), Introduction, definition #3: "The common element in all howsoever diverse expressions of piety, by which these are conjointly distinguished from all other feelings, or, in other words, the self-identical essence of piety, is this: the consciousness of our absolute dependence, or which is the same thing, of our relation to God."
18. Matthew Arnold, "Memorial Verses," 1850.

them. This point is placed in bold relief in a pithy passage in which the Ramban encompasses a good deal of what we have discussed. Rejecting the Rambam's view that daily *tefilla* is to be counted as a positive biblical mitzva grounded in the verse "To serve Him with all your heart" (*Devarim* 11:13), the Ramban contends that *tefilla* is generally required rabbinically. As to the verse, it is to be understood quite differently:

> The essence of the verse "Serve Him with all your heart" is a positive commandment that the whole of our service to the Almighty be with our entire heart, to wit, with proper and complete *kavvana*, for His name (*li-shmo*), without any kind of interfering thought. Nor should we perform *mitzvot* without much thought, or to play it safe lest they have some utility, [but rather] as the verse says, "To love the Lord with all your heart, all your soul, and all your might" (*Devarim* 6:5). (Commentary on Rambam's *Sefer Ha-mitzvot*, positive commandment 5)

At the heart of *avoda she-balev*, the Ramban contends, lies the modality of all *mitzvot*, the mode in which they are experienced and expressed. This point of the qualitative nature of "*le-ovdekha be-emet*" would be noteworthy at any historical context, but I think it has particular relevance for ours. We live in an age in which *yirat Shamayim*, fear of God, at least within the Torah world, is often measured quantitatively. With respect to *shiurim*, measurements, this is literally so; if you accept the measurements of the *Chazon Ish*, you are regarded as more of a *ben Torah*, but if you rely on Rav Chayim Naeh's measurements, you are less of a *ben Torah*. This occurs in other areas as well: how many stringencies do you observe, how many halakhic positions do you take into account in your actual practice? That is the litmus test. Now, to be sure, in many cases there is indeed genuine correlation between true *yirat Shamayim* and such practices. But the correlation is hardly necessary, and the showy piety of *yuhara* previously noted might, for some, also be a significant incentive. In any event, we surely need to remind ourselves that the quantitative is not the sole definitive factor, that the key is the Ramban's prescription, "That the whole of service to the Almighty be with our entire heart, to wit, with proper and complete *kavvana*, for His name (*li-shmo*)."

This awareness of the qualitative factor in our *avodat Hashem* underscores, at the personal level, the relevance of points raised previously regarding what we mean by *emet*. The specter of various *shekarim* is not confined to outright heretics or imposters; it relates to us as well. One is not either within the camp of *sheker* or firmly ensconced within that of *emet*. There is, rather, a continuum between different levels of each. The dragon of *avodat sheker* rears its ugly head within the heart of each and every one of us, prompting our universal need for "*Ve-taher libbenu le-ovdekha be-emet*."

OVED AND *EVED*

Let us analyze further the meaning of "*le-ovdekha*." The root, *ayin-beit-dalet*, has two referents: *oved*, meaning one who serves or labors, and *eved*, meaning a servant or slave. The Maharal emphasized that *avodat Hashem*, service of God, demands both.[19] Early Christianity, from its inception, contrasted son-ship with servitude, focusing upon the former while rejecting the latter. Judaism, however, has not only accepted, but celebrated, the notion of human – and especially Jewish – bondage to the Almighty, e.g., in the verse, "They are My servants whom I brought out of the land of Egypt" (*Vayikra* 25:42). That servitude is predicated both upon man's metaphysical condition and, within the Jewish orbit, upon the Jewish people's historical circumstances. Regarding "They are My servants," Rashi says (*ibid. s.v. Ki*), "My letter of indenture takes precedence."

In no way does this servitude contravene the status of a son or daughter. When the verse asks, "If I am a Father, where is the honor due Me, and if I am a Master, where is the reverence due Me?" (*Malakhi* 1:6), it does not pose an "either-or" choice, but rather posits a dual relationship. Similarly, after each sounding of the *shofar* on Rosh Ha-shana, when we present ourselves "whether as sons or as servants," we shall certainly assume that both relationships are manifest. A Jew says "I am a servant of the Holy One, blessed be He" (*Berikh Shemeih* prayer[20]) as a mixed expression of ultimate humility and of great pride. Moreover, he senses

19. In the early chapters in *Netiv Ha-avoda*, in *Netivot Olam*.
20. Based on *Zohar, Vayak'hel* 206a.

that it is this servitude to the Almighty that releases him from all other bondage, which makes all other forms of servitude, regardless of their economic or political import, absolutely meaningless. "Rabbi Nechunya ben Ha-kaneh said: Whoever takes upon himself the yoke of the Torah, they remove from him the yoke of the government and the yoke of worldly concerns" (*Avot* 3:5), and this is to be understood not simply as an anticipatory promise, but as a matter of cardinal definition. If he has the yoke of Torah, then, at the ultimate level, there cannot be the yoke of the government and the yoke of worldly concerns. "'They are My servants,' but not servants to servants" (*Bava Metzia* 10a).

Avoda be-emet requires acceptance and attainment of this status and a focus on the true character of one's relationship to the Almighty. Exceedingly few persons attain it fully. You can count on the fingers of your hand the number of personages in *Tanakh* who merited to be described as "servant of God" (*eved Hashem*). The striving, however, is an integral element of our religious existence, incumbent upon every Jew.

PURIFICATION

Having outlined the import of "*le-ovdekha be-emet*," we turn to examining the *tahara*, purity, through which we hope to attain it. Halakhically, there are two modes of *tahara*. The most common mechanism, for both persons and implements,[21] is immersion in a body of water, either a *mikve* or a *ma'ayan*: "He shall wash his body with water" (*Bemidbar* 19:7). For earthenware utensils, however, the Torah has prescribed another mode: "And you shall break the vessel" (*Vayikra* 11:33). There are utensils so thoroughly suffused with *tum'a*, impurity, that mere immersion, which cleanses only the surface, cannot purify them. An earthenware vessel, the symbol of pervasive *beli'a*, of total absorption when it comes to forbidden foodstuffs, can be purified only by being broken down and then reconstituted as a new entity.

When we petition, "*Ve-taher libbenu*," purify our hearts, for which *tahara* do we plead to the Almighty? How do we envision that He shall purify our hearts? From an understandable, human, selfish standpoint, we hope for the purification of *tevila*, that simple, painless, antiseptic

21. Foods do not have such a means of purification.

procedure, in which surface cleansing suffices. Near the end of *viddui* on Yom Kippur we say, "May it be Your will, Lord my God and the God of my fathers, that I sin no more. In Your abundant mercy, clean away, scrape away, the sins I have committed before You, but not through afflictions and illnesses." Not too deep, not too hard. *Tevila* will be enough; who wants *shevira,* to be shattered? But if our *tefilla* and *teshuva* are genuine and sincere, if our plea, "*Ve-taher libbenu le-ovdekha be-emet,*" is, itself, an expression of *emet,* we must be ready for – nay, we must initiate – the more radical purgation as well.

Jewish tradition never shied away from acknowledging the dual, even contradictory, character of humans and their potential. It was the divine will to create us as complex, multifaceted beings: likened to angels and filled with majesty and grandeur (see *Tehillim* 8:6), but also "likened to broken earthenware," as we say in *U-netaneh Tokef.* The prayer refers to earthenware which is shattered, not only incidentally as it is buffeted by the winds of outrageous fortune, but if need be, intentionally broken, by way of being reconstituted or established anew – of being, if you will, created anew. "The heart knows its own bitterness" (*Mishlei* 14:10) – there is so much within us for which cosmetic cleansing simply will not do, so much which needs to be melted down and molded anew: our arrogance, our pride, our selfishness, our envy, our shallowness, and our sham. To the extent that we have the honesty, the *emet,* to recognize the need for reconstruction and reconstitution, painful as such radical processes may be, we pray for them, too.

The Almighty, for His part, has assured us that He is ready to purify us in both modes. One verse teaches, "I will sprinkle purifying water upon you, and you shall be purified; from all your impurities and from all your abominations will I purify you" (*Yechezkel* 36:25). But the very next verse teaches, "I shall remove the stone heart from your flesh, and give you" – after the ultimate shattering, a reconstitution – "a heart of flesh" (*Yechezkel* 36:26), one that is vibrant and pulsating. In pleading for "*Ve-taher libbenu,*" we ask, as the Almighty sees fit, for both modes. We say to Him: You, God, You know what kind of purification – *shevira* or *tahara* – we need; You know which mode to exercise and when. We thus turn to You in trust, in faith, and in truth, asking of You, hoping, that whatever *tahara* is necessary, You will provide it.

"*VE-TAHER LIBBENU*" ON THE HIGH HOLIDAYS

The request of "*Ve-taher libbenu*" has special import on Rosh Ha-shana and Yom Kippur, beyond that which it has on Shabbat and Festivals throughout the year, a point reflected in the fact that on the High Holidays we accompany the request with an explanation. "Purify our hearts to serve You in truth, for You, O God, are truth," we say on Rosh Ha-shana, "and Your word is true and endures forever," a point which explains both why we need the *tahara* – otherwise how could we, as long as we are impure, engage the God of truth? – and why we turn specifically to the *Ribbono shel Olam* to enable us to serve Him in truth, because He, after all, is the source of truth.

Beyond the distinction between the High Holidays and *Shabbatot* and Festivals there may be a further distinction, with respect to the mode of *tahara*, between Rosh Ha-shana and Yom Kippur. Rosh Ha-shana is a day of creation, "This day, on which was the beginning of Your work, is a memorial for the first day" (*Zikhronot* prayer), and hence, of re-creation. It is the day of the emergence of a new identity at both the universal level and the personal level, and this creation of a new entity may entail the dismemberment of the previous one. The purification of Rosh Ha-shana is primarily the more radical and painful mode of *shevira*, befitting a day that, as the Ramban noted, is primarily a Day of Judgment, albeit tinged with compassion.

Yom Kippur, by contrast, is a day of compassion, albeit still within the context of judgment; its mode of purification is that of "*Ve-rachatz besaro ba-mayim*," of cleansing through *tevila*. Thus *Mishna Yoma* concludes, with reference to Yom Kippur: "Rabbi Akiva said: Happy is your portion, Israel; before whom are you purified, and who purifies you? Your Father in Heaven."

The Integrity of *Teshuva*

CAN PARTIAL REPENTANCE BE GENUINE?

In the previous chapter I addressed the topic of "*Ve-taher libbenu le-ovdekha be-emet,* Purify our hearts to serve You with truth," focusing on the range of the term "*emet*" – juxtaposed to error on the one hand, and falsehood on the other – and on the thrust of the plea "purify our hearts" with respect to divine service generally and to the process of *teshuva* specifically. I would like to return now to the theme of *emet* in *teshuva,* but with a more limited focus, probing a single question concerning the integrity of repentance.

The term integrity has two primary senses. In one, it refers to wholeness as opposed to fragmentation, to something that is an entire unit and not just bits and pieces. In another, we speak of integrity in moral terms, referring to honesty and to that which is opposed to anything smacking of dissimulation or falsehood. Generally speaking, these meanings are, lexicographically and practically, distinct, but my question is: are the two, in this context, interrelated? Can *teshuva* be true while yet limited? Can it be both genuine and partial?

The question is a dual one. First, can fragmentary *teshuva* be subjectively sincere? Can one presume to be honestly remorseful with

---

Delivered at Kehillath Jeshurun, New York, in Elul 5757 (1997).

respect to one transgression while yet blandly and blindly indifferent to another? Assuming that one recognizes factually that two *mitzvot* are equally the word of God, can one repent the neglect of one but not of the other? Second, is fragmentary *teshuva* authentic on the objective plane? Does it attain halakhic legitimacy, entitling one to be designated as a "penitent"? Is it accepted by the Almighty and does it engender forgiveness and atonement?

In order to grapple with these issues, I would like to chart a dual course, first examining briefly Judaism's conception of divine service generally, and subsequently analyzing the nature and role of *teshuva* specifically.

JUDAISM'S DUAL CONCEPTION OF DIVINE SERVICE

At one of the pivotal junctures of Moshe's prolonged farewell address in *Sefer Devarim* – an amalgam of reproach and instruction – he issues a deceptively simple charge to his audience:

> Now, Israel, what does the Lord your God demand of you? Only that you revere the Lord your God, that you walk in His ways, that you love Him and that you serve the Lord your God with all your heart and with all your soul; to keep the commandments of the Lord and His statutes that I am commanding you today, for your benefit. (10:12–13)

In a notable *gemara* in *Berakhot* (33b), *Chazal* took note of the striking character of the first verse, asking whether fear of Heaven could be described as just a triviality, as though asking rhetorically: This is *all* that the Almighty asks? The *gemara* responds, "Indeed, for Moshe it is a minor matter."[1] For Moshe *Rabbeinu* – and, the *Keli Yakar* adds, not only for him personally, but for his listeners – fear of Heaven is indeed a minor matter, even though, *per se*, it is of infinite value.

1. In the *gemara*, Rabbi Chanina provides an analogue: "It is comparable to one who is asked for a large vessel and he has it – it seems like a small vessel to him. [One who is asked for] a small vessel but he does not have it – it seems to him like a large vessel."

But it seems to me that these verses are remarkable in yet another respect, if we take not only the first verse, but the second as well. The first verse speaks with reference to the cardinal aspects of religious experience and existence, the major desiderata of *homo religiosus* – to revere, to emulate, to love, to serve the Almighty. In the next verse, however, instead of these grand, cardinal values, we hear a plethora of detail: "To keep the commandments of the Lord and His statutes that I am commanding you today," to observe the whole range of *mitzvot*, everything that is being commanded in *Sefer Devarim*, which, as *Mishneh Torah*, is a capsular summary of Torah as a whole. Thus, we start with reference to major experiential goals, and then move on to the detailed observance of the *mitzvot* – a major shift.

In truth, these verses are wholly and profoundly characteristic of the mode of divine service that is endemic to Judaism. Judaism moves, and asks us to move, along a dual axis. On one plane, there are the grand, majestic concerns, the very fiber of our religious being, which serve both as a point of departure and as the ultimate *telos* of our religious experience. On another plane, we speak of a mass of detail: the multiplicity of *mitzvot*, and then the detail within each mitzva.

Now this dual focus marks our conception of the course that ideally we are obligated to chart. The world of Halakha, even at the purely normative plane of what it prescribes and proscribes, is both teleological and formalistic. It impels us to strive for the majestic, the ultimate in reaching out to the Almighty – to strive for love, awe, and clinging – and complementarily, it imposes upon us a comprehensive regimen, expressed and enmeshed in a welter of detail, relating to minutiae of daily life. On the immediate and explicit plane the latter seems far removed from the grand rhetoric and the grand reality expressed by "revere the Lord," "walk in His ways," "love Him," and "serve Him."

Nevertheless, Judaism, and Halakha as its prime vehicle, insists upon engaging the two aspects interactively, not simply in parallel. Accepting the yoke of Heaven and accepting the yoke of *mitzvot* serve as twin foci, says the Rambam,[2] of the single mitzva of the recitation of *Shema*. The peaks and the plateaus, the poetry and the prose, the

---

2. *Hilkhot Keriat Shema* 1:2.

mystique and the minutiae, are all part of an integrated religious existence within which the totality of self and of life are to be sanctified. This conjunction is at the very essence, the very core of Judaism, and it is to this music that we march.[3]

The duality in divine service is equally true with regard to how we view liability *post facto* for its violation. On the one hand, we certainly acknowledge that the ultimate goals of our religious being must rightfully be subjected to a definitive and comprehensive judgment, passed, "according to the wisdom of the Knowing God" (*Hilkhot Teshuva* 3:2), upon the total person, or, for that matter, upon a community as a whole (*Hilkhot Teshuva* 3:1). On the other hand, the selfsame Rambam takes issue with the perception that one's fate or ultimate destiny, in terms of reward and punishment, is wholly determined by the tilt of the religious scales, major deeds eclipsing, or at least overshadowing, minor commissions and omissions. He notes emphatically that Yorovam ben Nevat, who, having sinned and caused others to sin, was surely doomed to eternal perdition, will nevertheless also be held accountable for not having observed minor rabbinic decrees such as *eruvei tavshilin*.[4] One might add that the reverse is equally true – "The Holy One, blessed be He, does not deprive any creature of its reward" (*Pesachim* 118a, *Bava Kamma* 38a), and, where credit is due, be it for an isolated phenomenon, it shall be given.

THE DUALITY OF THE GRAND AND THE DETAILED IN *TESHUVA*

This dual conception, the view of the exalted and the minutiae, likewise informs our understanding and experience of *teshuva*. In the Torah, we encounter two primary, specific sources for *teshuva*, in addition to the numerous general admonitions for turning and returning to the Almighty.

The first source, cited by the Rambam in his *Sefer Ha-mitzvot*, and in the first chapter of *Hilkhot Teshuva*, consists of the verses in *parashat Naso*, which, as *Chazal* interpret them, address the case of *gezel ha-ger*, theft from a convert who died leaving no heirs:

---

3. The conjunction can be similarly found in other verses, e.g., *Devarim* 13:5: "You shall follow the Lord your God, fear Him, observe His commandments, hearken to His voice, worship Him, and cleave to Him."
4. In *Iggeret Ha-shemad* (in the Rambam La-am edition, *Iggerot Ha-Rambam*, p. 63).

> Speak to the children of Israel: Any man or woman who commits any wrong toward a fellow man by acting treacherously against the Lord, and that person realizes his guilt: They shall confess their wrongdoing that they did, and he shall make restitution of the principal amount and add one-fifth to it, and he shall give it to him who was wronged. (*Bemidbar* 5:6–7)

The phrase "They shall confess their wrongdoing" might have been taken to be part of the contingent scenario; if a person misappropriated or stole an object from a convert,[5] took an oath to that effect, and subsequently owned up to the fact that he did so and confessed, then he must pay restitution and a fine. But *Chazal* take the confession as prescriptive: "They shall confess" indicates it is something he must do, and it serves as a paradigm for sins generally, that confession is necessary as the central component of *teshuva.*

The second specific source for *teshuva,* more familiar to most of us, is drawn from the latter part of the passage in *parashat Acharei Mot* concerning the Temple service for Yom Kippur: "For on this day He shall atone for you to purify you of all your sins; you shall be purified before the Lord" (*Vayikra* 16:30). In light of the ending, "you shall be purified before the Lord," this verse is understandably often taken as a promise rather than as a command. Nevertheless, for our purposes I would like to adopt, be it only instrumentally, Rabbeinu Yona's view that "you shall be purified" in this context is normative, meaning that there is a special mitzva of *teshuva* on, or in anticipation of, Yom Kippur (*Sha'arei Teshuva* 2:14). Moreover, I would like to treat the verse as Rabbeinu Yona understood it, as relating not only to Yom Kippur, but as being paradigmatic of a certain mode of *teshuva,* a way of thinking about, approaching, and implementing *teshuva,* and, as such, to compare and contrast this mode with the mode embodied in the phrase "They shall confess their wrongdoing" in the passage of *gezel ha-ger.*

Indeed, there is a marked contrast. The confession in *Naso* constitutes one aspect of a specific, halakhically mandated response to a very

5. The Rambam adds the situation in which someone denied a debt to a convert (*Hilkhot Gezeila Va-aveida* 7:2).

particular act. In objective terms, that act may appear to be of limited import. The amount stolen can be minuscule, as small as a *peruta,* as the *Mishna* in *Bava Kamma* (103a) tells us. The aggrieved is a convert, who may have been viewed as being on the periphery of the community. The incidence may be singular, having happened just once, in a moment of frailty or under difficult circumstances, and is not necessarily characteristic of one's moral and religious lassitude in general. Nevertheless, "They shall confess their wrongdoing."

The call in *Acharei Mot* for "You shall be purified," on the other hand, is issued within a wholly different context. No particular sin is cited, and, perhaps, no detailed confession is envisioned. Today we are very much accustomed to the alphabetical catalog of *Ashamnu,* expanded, in the times of the *Ge'onim,* to the dual alphabetical listing of the *Al Chet,* embellished still further by the *Chayei Adam,* and more so by latter-day successors. But these lists appear to have been very foreign to *Chazal.*

A *gemara* in *Yoma* (87b) addresses the confession to be recited on Yom Kippur. First it discusses the part of the service in which the confession is recited, and then examines what is said. After offering a catalog of various versions of confession, the *gemara* adds:

> Mar Zutra said: [The preceding confessions are necessary] only if he did not say, "*Aval anachnu chatanu,* But we have sinned." But if he said "*Aval anachnu chatanu,*" no more is necessary.

The various texts that this or that *Amora* prescribed are relevant only if a person has not said "But we have sinned." You don't have to sing *Ashamnu,* you don't have to recite the *Al Chet*; this short phrase is enough. The *gemara* concludes:

> As Bar Hamdudi said: Once I stood before Shemuel, who was sitting, and when the prayer leader came up and said "*Aval anachnu chatanu,*" he rose. We learn from here that those words are the quintessential *viddui.*

There is no reference to a particular sin, no presentation of any detail of sins, just a very general acknowledgement of being in a state of sin:

"We have sinned." In contrast with the passage of "They shall confess their wrongdoing," where specificity and detail are required, here the general recognition of guilt and sin is the quintessential confession of Yom Kippur. And, as the verse in *Acharei Mot* indicated, the correlative quest for purgative regeneration – "you shall be purified before the Lord" – is, presumably, its quintessential *teshuva.*

The contrast between the respective sources is clearly reflected in the Rambam's writing. He begins *Hilkhot Teshuva* by referring to the case of an individual who, having committed a particular sin, wants to do *teshuva.* Citing our verse from *gezel ha-ger,* the Rambam states that the penitent must confess the wrong that he did. Then the Rambam delineates the confession:

> How does one confess? One states: "I implore You, God; I sinned, I transgressed, I committed iniquity before You by doing the following. Behold, I regret and am embarrassed for my deeds, and I promise never to repeat this act again." This is the essence of the confession. (1:1)

For the *teshuva* to be total and the *viddui* complete, the sin needs to be denominated specifically.

On the other hand, when the Rambam begins to speak of the *teshuva* and confession of Yom Kippur, he writes:

> Yom Kippur is a time of *teshuva* for all, individuals and community alike.... Accordingly, everyone is obligated to repent and confess on Yom Kippur.... And what is the confession here? The confessional prayer customarily recited by all Israel is: "*Aval anachnu chatanu,* But we have sinned"; this is the essence of confession. (2:7–8)

Here one does not focus upon a particular action, nor even mention it. The conception of *teshuva* is not of correcting a particular sin, but of seeking out the Almighty: "Seek out the Lord when He may be found" (*Yeshayahu* 55:6). To the extent that the confession is the basis of that quest, it is simple and comprehensive – not by enumerating, but by failing to enumerate.

We have, then, two very different modes of *teshuva*: one specific and detailed, relating to a particular action, and another which is indigenous to Yom Kippur – the general searching and yearning for the Almighty, and a molding of the self, so as to be worthy of, and animated by, that quest. Of course, each kind of *teshuva* addresses itself to a different aspect of sin.

FIVE ASPECTS OF SIN

Sin is multifaceted; we can designate at least five major elements. There is, first, the wrong itself, the abomination in its own terms. Second, there is the fact that any sin assigns priority to our desires, as opposed to deferring to God's authority. Third, there is the impact upon the self – sin defiles, contaminating one's innermost being. Fourth, you have acted against the Almighty, damaging, as it were, the divine dominion by doing something that is against His will. Finally, there is the rupture in our relationship to the Almighty, illustrated by the verse "Your iniquities have been a barrier between you and your God" (*Yeshayahu* 59:2).

We have here, in sum, five aspects, which might be broken down into two major classifications: the moral and the religious. By "moral" I do not mean that which we would have arrived at on our own, being of ethical import – for these purposes, I include also *mitzvot* between man and God, even statutes, with no obvious, independent justification. Rather, by "moral" I am referring to that aspect of sin that is the wrong as such, irrespective of the interrelation to the Almighty. On the other hand, by the "religious" I mean to focus on the dimensions of the sinful act that have to do with our relationship with the Almighty.

This latter aspect could certainly be construed as being of universal significance – every sinner, whoever and wherever he may be, has, by his deeds, in effect interposed between himself and the Almighty. But it has additional significance both with respect to the Jewish people at one level and the individual Jew at another, precisely because the relationship is more intimate. Explaining why God refers to Himself as being "a jealous God" (*Shemot* 20:4) with regard to idolatry, the Ramban (in his commentary, *ad loc.*) states that this term is applied only with reference to idol worship by the Jewish people, not by the nations of the world. Though the prohibition against idolatry is one of the seven Noachide laws, the element of betrayal, and, as it were, the jealousy in response (however that is understood),[6] is specific to the Jewish people.[7] What is true of idolatry is true of the whole of our religious existence. Since a Jew is more intimately, covenantally engaged with the Almighty, then anything that attenuates or ruptures that relationship is to be regarded that much more seriously.

Of course, if sin is multifaceted, then *teshuva* is multifaceted. There is moral *teshuva*, which relates to the wrong *per se*, corresponding to the contamination, the defilement of the self – the *teshuva* of "they shall confess." And there is religious *teshuva*, which reasserts the authority of Heaven and tries to make up with the Almighty – the *teshuva* of "You shall be purified before the Lord."

PARTIAL *TESHUVA* CONSIDERED IN THE MORAL AND RELIGIOUS DIMENSIONS

Against this background, let us return to our initial query: what do we make of partial *teshuva* – repentance that is fragmentary, sporadic, or inconsistent? I believe the presumptive answer should be clear: with respect to the passage of "They shall confess their wrongdoing," which relates to a particular sin, partial *teshuva* – call it even selective *teshuva* – is indeed feasible. While, obviously, the optimal goal is always total and ultimate *teshuva*, the absence of that level of *teshuva* is no barrier, in halakhic terms, to either *teshuva* or atonement.

The *Gemara* (*Chullin* 5b) records a dispute as to whether a person who normally transgresses by eating forbidden fats is allowed to bring

---

6. The rich imagery in *Tanakh* describing the relationship of the Jewish people and the Almighty in terms of betrothal, marriage, and lover and beloved reinforces this concept of divine jealousy, rendering its correlative metaphor of betrayal as fornication extremely apt. See the chapter, "Renunciation, Divorce, and Rehabilitation," for development of this theme in greater detail.
7. There might very well be halakhic ramifications to this distinction. It would appear from the Rambam (*Hilkhot Avoda Zara* 3:1, 5–6; *cf. Hilkhot Melakhim* 9:4) that the prohibition against idol worship is dual for Jews: one transgresses whether the worship is conducted the way that the idol is normally worshipped, or one diverted modes of divine service to idol worship, even if the idol is not normally worshipped that way. However, with regard to other nations, the prohibition is only against worshipping an idol in its normal manner.

a sin offering for unwittingly eating blood. The Rambam rules (*Hilkhot Ma'aseh Ha-korbanot* 3:4) that with the exception of idolatry and public desecration of Shabbat, a flagrant violator in one regard may indeed achieve atonement with respect to a different transgression. Moreover, even with respect to the very same sin – if Reuven has stolen from both Shimon and Levi, and seeks to recant from one but not the other – the *teshuva* is efficacious. The only exception is one who has become so habituated to the sin that any confession or *teshuva* becomes a sham:

> If he was a blatant violator with regard to a transgression, and it is public knowledge that he commits it, and he has become accustomed to doing so – whether to anger God or out of desire – a sacrifice for that transgression is not accepted. (*Ibid.* 3:5)

Barring those provisos, partial recantation, even of the same sin, is indeed possible.

With regard to religious *teshuva*, however, our intuitive response is quite different. Return and reconciliation focus upon one's relationship to the Almighty. We must therefore ask ourselves: Can the regeneration and renascence of that relationship be willfully selective? Can a husband who has abused his wife decide to stop beating her but continue to berate her? Can a wife who has betrayed her husband break off with one paramour only to arrange a tryst with another? Are love and fidelity divisible, quantitatively or qualitatively?

Thus, so long as we speak of the moral side of *teshuva*, correcting a particular wrongdoing, even correcting ourselves with respect to that wrongdoing, some measure of selectivity, while certainly not desirable, is nevertheless acknowledged. But if we speak of mending fences, reestablishing our interactive relation with the Almighty, then either we are committed or we are not.

QUALIFYING THE DISTINCTION

These intuitive responses, which I think are fundamentally sound, should nevertheless be qualified, and this in both directions. The legitimacy and validity of a given act, be it a primary mitzva or a facet of *teshuva* when one already has violated a mitzva, may, notwithstanding my earlier comments, be conditioned upon a basic moral and spiritual level – not necessarily total *teshuva* but a sound base upon which even minimal *teshuva* can and ought to be grounded. For instance, while one who blatantly eats forbidden fat can seek atonement regarding blood, this point may very well apply if he violates out of desire, but *not* if he seeks to anger God.[8] Another example is in the Rambam's encomium to *teshuva* in chapter 7 of *Hilkhot Teshuva*, in the course of which the Rambam makes a very striking point:

> How exalted is the level of *teshuva*! Only yesterday this sinner was divided from God, the Lord of Israel, as the verse states, "Your iniquities have been a barrier between you and your God" (*Yeshayahu* 59:2).... He would perform *mitzvot*, only to have them thrown back in his face, as the verses state, "Who asked that of you, to trample My courts?" (*ibid.* 1:12), and "If only you would lock My doors, and not kindle fire on My altar to no purpose! I have no pleasure in you, says the Lord of Hosts, nor will I accept an offering from your hand" (*Malakhi* 1:10). Today, [after having repented,] he clings to the Divine Presence.... He performs *mitzvot*, and these are accepted with grace and joy, as the verses state (*Kohelet* 9:7): "God has already accepted your works," and (*Malakhi* 3:4), "And the offering of Yehuda and Yerushalayim shall be pleasing to the Lord, as in days of old and the earliest years." (7:7)

According to the Rambam, part of the contrast between the situation before and after *teshuva* is how this person's *mitzvot* are regarded. Before *teshuva*, he does *mitzvot* and the Almighty throws them back at him, as though saying, "Who needs your *mitzvot*?" The Rambam draws support from verses in *Yeshayahu*, but he significantly expands their implication in the process. Yeshayahu speaks there particularly of sacrificial offerings and of prayer, and one might have suggested that he makes his harsh critique since we are talking about presenting

8. Admittedly, the Rambam (*ad loc.*) makes no such distinction.

oneself in the innermost chambers of the Almighty.[9] But the Rambam says this applies to *mitzvot* generally.

More broadly, we have the sense that the validity and the value of a mitzva may be contingent upon the individual's basic moral and spiritual level. We intuit that, beyond a certain point, if a sinner wants to fulfill a mitzva, the act is not only not positive, but actually abominable. This sensibility is reflected in the verses that the Rambam cites – those in the first chapter in *Yeshayahu*, famously read as the *haftara* on *Shabbat Chazon*, and those in the *haftara* of Yom Kippur, from chapter 58. With stinging rhetoric, these passages focus to a considerable extent on the contrast between moral rot and presumed religious performance, and clearly postulate the principle that there can be *mitzvot* that are not only not "pleasing to the Lord" but are even detestable.

In an even sharper vein, we may qualify my original position by citing a remarkable, and awfully frightening, statement, drawn from the *Yerushalmi* in *Kiddushin* (1:9). With reference to the verse "Dead flies putrefy the perfumer's oil" (*Kohelet* 10:1), Ben Azzai expounded:

> Just as if a single dead fly gets into fine oil that was used for anointment, does it not spoil it? So, too, an individual – by one sin that he sinned, he loses all merits in his hands.

It is possible for a sin to be so grievous that it wipes out all of a person's merits. There could be extreme situations in which, even at the plane of individual action, the *teshuva* mode of "They shall confess their wrongdoing" eclipses all other modes and determines the value and validity of every other moral or religious act. But these situations are, Jewishly and halakhically speaking, extreme and extremely rare, and I mention them only by way of qualification. The basic postulation that partial *teshuva* is both possible and efficacious is, I think, correct.

---

9. This theme can be seen in *halakhot* that apply specifically to those aspects of religious experience that are most intimate: e.g., "The offering of the wicked is an abomination" (*Mishlei* 21:27), and prayer, which, under certain conditions, can be deemed abominable (see *Berakhot* 22b–23a; *Shabbat* 10a; *Eruvin* 64a).

Possibly of even greater moment is the reverse qualification: that there is room for the partial, for the selective, even with regard to the aspect of *teshuva* characterized by "You shall be purified." Theoretically, the postulate that the *teshuva* of purification must be total makes logical and spiritual sense. We recoil – and properly so – at the thought that a person will implore the Almighty for forgiveness and atonement, trying to repair a ruptured relation and to place it on new footing, while leaving whole areas of sin and corruption untended. If we speak of *teshuva* in terms of *tevila,* of purifying immersion, we would say that just as immersion cannot be piecemeal (*Shulchan Arukh, Yoreh De'a* 201:1), so too *teshuva* cannot be. The object or the individual to be purified has to be completely immersed.[10]

Nevertheless, existentially, the demand for totality and comprehensiveness is simply awesome, even overwhelming. Can we merit the fulfillment of the promise, "For on this day He shall atone for you to purify you of all your sins," only if we have attained near perfection? Will our normal, stumbling selves, willing of spirit but weak and incontinent of flesh, plugging a hole here and leaving another there, be barred at the door? If few of us ever get beyond selective and fragmentary *teshuva,* will that *teshuva* then be dismissed peremptorily as inadequate? We only hope and pray that the answer is no.

"BEING OVERPOWERED BY ONE'S STUDIES" VS. "UPROOTING FROM ONE'S HEART"

What, then, of our sound intuition that purity cannot be partial, that the religious aspect of *teshuva* must be complete? I believe that our intuitions and our hopes can be reconciled in light of an analogy drawn from a different, yet related, area. The *Mishna* in *Avot* states:

> Rabbi Dostai son of Rabbi Yannai says in the name of Rabbi Meir: If a person has forgotten a single thing from what he has learned, the verse regards him as if he has, in effect, abandoned his own being [or, brought judgment to bear upon himself], as the verse

10. See the radical, chilling interpretation of the last *mishna* in *Yoma* (85b) cited in the section "Annual *Teshuva*" in the chapter, "*La-kol Zeman*."

> states, "Beware very much, and watch your soul very much, lest you forget the things which your eyes saw" (*Devarim* 4:9). Are we to understand that this [very severe statement] applies even to one whose studies have overpowered him, [exceeding his cognitive abilities]? The verse concludes, "And lest they depart from your heart all the days of your life." A person is only liable if he sits down and uproots them from his heart. (3:10)[11]

What is the meaning of "if he sits down and uproots them from his heart"? According to Rabbeinu Yona, this applies not only when a person tries consciously to forget, such as when Rabbi Zeira fasted upon arriving in Israel from Babylonia, in order to forget what he learned previously (*Bava Metzia* 85a). It includes even the failure to review adequately, given the natural human propensity to forget – a thought that should frighten yeshiva students who don't review adequately. But setting aside, for the moment, Rabbeinu Yona's addendum, it is clear that there is a cardinal difference between "sitting down and uprooting them from your heart" and "one's studies overpowering him." What characterizes this distinction?

"Sitting down and uprooting from your heart" refers to a person who forgets not with grief but with indifference, not with a sense of loss but with insouciance. Whether he remembers or doesn't remember is not so important to him. This is a person to whom ignorance of a certain tract of Torah is of little moment, a person whose commitment to learning and knowing Torah is partial, not only in terms of accomplishment but in terms of aspiration and value. "Being overpowered by one's studies" is the opposite of this; the pressure of circumstances, new material he learned, or other factors brought about the forgetfulness. Unable, as he sees it, to do more, he finds himself with limited knowledge and limited engagement, but he also thirsts for more and is concerned that his achievement is inadequate or at least incomplete.

Analogously, with regard to partial *teshuva*, I believe we need to distinguish between falling short and actively uprooting. If a person strives, out of a sense of commitment and engagement, for totality of

11. 3:8 in the Kehati edition.

teshuva, but moves on that path slowly and incrementally, encountering various difficulties such that he is unable to realize the whole of his aspiration – this is *teshuva* which strives for purification and thus, in a meaningful sense, attains purity. But a person who works toward *teshuva* only in certain areas and who is unperturbed by the fact that other areas are untended may be said to be "uprooting" himself from those other areas. He may correct a particular sin and attain the *teshuva* of "they shall confess their wrongdoing." But purity, under those circumstances, certainly cannot be attained.

There is, then, meaning and value to partial *teshuva*. First, at the level of "they shall confess their wrongdoing," Judaism recognizes the value even of the piecemeal; every day, every action, every moment, is of significance. Second, even at the level of purity, provided the partial *teshuva* is the result not of lack of concern but of one's perceived inability to achieve, as long as the striving – the sense that "God desires the heart" (*Sanhedrin* 106b) – is there, then there can be partial purity as well.

THE DESIRABILITY OF SELECTIVITY

I would go a step further. I submit that in purity, as in serving God generally, a measure of selectivity is not only licit but desirable. Given a fundamental faith commitment to accepting the yoke of Heaven and *mitzvot,* given our responsibility to adhere to the word of God and to Him, I believe that, at the level of implementation, some degree of selectivity, of assignation of priority, is inevitable and even desirable. Surely we must not be indifferent to any sin. We cannot immerse with a single impurity in hand. But to eradicate not just the impurity *per se* but the roots of evil, to attempt to restructure our personality and regenerate our spiritual being – we do best to proceed with concentrated and chosen emphases. We cannot press with equal vigor on all fronts. Even if we could, there is much to be said – with respect to divine service generally, and the regenerative aspect of *teshuva* specifically – for channeling energies into particular areas.

This point is brought home forcefully by the *Orchot Chayim,* citing several Provençal *Rishonim.* After noting that the early pious men consistently and faultlessly fulfilled all 613 commandments, he writes:

> It was also taught in the *Mishna* (*Kiddushin* 39b): "Anyone who performs one mitzva has goodness bestowed upon him, his life is lengthened, and he inherits the World-to-Come." And the *Yerushalmi* (1:9) teaches: To whom does this refer? To him who singled out a particular mitzva and never violated it his entire life.[12]

In support, he cites examples from the *Gemara* where later *Amoraim* would specify the *mitzvot* that they were especially careful to perform – such as *tzitzit, tefillin,* or three meals on Shabbat. He then remarkably links this notion to the famous *gemara* (*Makkot* 23b–24a) where the 613 commandments were "compressed" to general principles – to eleven, to six, to three, and to one:

> This is the meaning of "David came and established them on eleven," that if one fulfills them precisely and as they were commanded, and takes great care never to violate anything regarding them throughout his days, he is called righteous, and he inherits the World-to-Come. The same holds for "Chabakuk came and established them on one," [as the verse states,] "The righteous man shall live by his faith" (*Chabakuk* 2:4): that if he fulfills it as it was commanded, and assiduously, even though he cannot be that assiduous with all the *mitzvot,* with all their commands and precision, with that alone he is called pious, and he inherits the World-to-Come. Thus the Sages *z"l* taught (*Kiddushin* 39b): "Anyone who performs one mitzva above his merits has goodness bestowed upon him," and the *Yerushalmi* explains that this is one who set aside a mitzva and never violated it in his life.[13]

---

12. *Hilkhot Rosh Ha-shana, chelek* 1, *ot* 25 – *inyanim acherim mi-teshuva* (Stitzberg ed., 1957, p. 227).
13. This *gemara* in *Kiddushin* is usually understood in quantitative terms, that if a person has one mitzva *over and above* his other merits, i.e., the scales are perfectly even and he adds one mitzva, then "goodness is bestowed upon him." But the author of the *Orchot Chayim* explains this differently, linking it to the *Yerushalmi* about an individual's zealous regard for a single mitzva.

The twelfth-century Provençal sage he quotes, Rabbi Meshullam ben Ya'akov, does not spell out the basis for these views, but the import can be readily perceived. Fulfilling a single mitzva "as it was commanded" lends a qualitative dimension to one's service of God that pursuing 613 *mitzvot* equally and concurrently does not permit. It increases awareness, sharpens commitment, intensifies attentiveness and alacrity, and energizes one's total spiritual self to the performance of that chosen mitzva. As a result, not only is that particular mitzva fulfilled at a higher level, but the whole of one's divine service is enhanced, extending to *mitzvot* which have not been the beneficiaries of that specific attention. Previously untapped inner strength, hitherto unattained, perhaps undreamt of, as well as religious identity and experience, are forged in the crucible of that mitzva fulfilled "as it was commanded."

All this is with regard to one's divine service at the primary plane, before he sins. Likewise, after he sins, imagine the quality and level of his *teshuva* if he performs certain aspects of it "as it was commanded," assiduously. Even if his performance of *teshuva* is relatively less intense and comprehensive in other areas, there is room to regard it as not unacceptable.

TESHUVA BI-BEKI'UT AND *TESHUVA BE-IYYUN*

In an additional analogy to the world of Torah study, let us draw a comparison between modes of learning and modes of *teshuva*. In many *yeshivot* today – and there are analogues in the academic world – the day is divided between learning *be-iyyun* and learning *bi-beki'ut*. The latter is learning whose goal is to cover ground and provide more comprehensive, albeit superficial, knowledge, while the former, learning in depth, is that which is geared to sharpening skills, developing a method, and probing minute detail.[14]

14. The distinction, well known to *Chazal*, has halakhic implications. The *Gemara* in *Sukka* (28b), when discussing whether a person should study Torah in the *sukka* or not, concludes conditionally: if one is learning *bi-beki'ut*, which does not require a great deal of concentration, one may do so in the *sukka*, notwithstanding the disturbances one might encounter there. But if one learns *be-iyyun*, one should do so at home. Similarly, the *Gemara* in *Ta'anit* (10b) raises the question of whether Torah scholars should engage in intricate and complex Torah discussion while they are traveling. Again, the

Both types of Torah study, of course, are essential: on the one hand, you want to touch base, to the extent possible, with the entire Torah and to know the fundamental principles. You want to ensure that in terms of attitude, no area is foreign and nothing strikes you as being irrelevant. On the other hand, if you want to become a Torah scholar, then you must also engage in the kind of learning that enables you to develop skills, mold an approach, sharpen yourself, and be able to understand in depth; this is a qualitative, as opposed to a quantitative, aspect. The balance of partly extensive and partly intensive learning will help you move on both fronts.

Just as there is learning *bi-beki'ut* and *be-iyyun*, there is *teshuva bi-beki'ut* and *be-iyyun*. Certainly, on a basic level, one must bring searching and examination to bear upon the whole range of one's life, all facets of one's activity, and all aspects of one's personality, values, and self. One needs to be certain that with regard to no area is one "uprooting them from his heart"; of nothing does one say, "Well, it's not important, it doesn't matter." If it's a *halakha*, if it's a moral value – it matters! But at the same time, there is indeed to be commended and recommended *teshuva* that is *be-iyyun*, by focusing upon certain areas. These are selected partly on the basis of their objective significance, and partly, as with regard to the statement cited in the *Orchot Chayim*, on the basis of personal predilection. With regard to these areas one walks the extra mile, attains a higher level, reaches further, and probes deeper; one seeks there to fulfill *teshuva* "as it was commanded," assiduously. Here again, to the extent that one has aspired to and consequently attained *teshuva* of higher quality in one specific area, particularly on what we have termed the religious plane, then from there one's link to the Almighty will be realized at a higher plane.

THE *TESHUVA* OF ROSH HA-SHANA AND THE *TESHUVA* OF YOM KIPPUR

As we look to Yom Kippur, to what do we strive, what do we anticipate? At one level, we seek the *teshuva* of "they shall confess their wrongdoing," ridding ourselves of various impurities, ferreting out and correcting

---

response is to distinguish: if the topic is relatively superficial and won't reduce their attentiveness to the road or alertness to their surroundings, they may discuss it. But they are not permitted to get deeply involved in learning, in a very serious way.

failings. We do this with an eye to comprehensiveness, if we can; but to the extent that we find ourselves honestly unable to attain comprehensive *teshuva,* we recognize the value of partial, even selective, *teshuva.* Still, this is always on the condition that we are never – never! – in the situation of "uprooting it from our hearts." We confront the Almighty on Yom Kippur, having spent a year trying, in some way, to be a servant of God, having spent Elul and the *Aseret Yemei Teshuva* trying, and yet acknowledging that after all that, we are imperfect and incomplete; and out of our imperfection, we plead and implore, hope and aspire. But we should be able to say, honestly, that if we are imperfect, it pains us. If we are incomplete, it grieves us. If we lapse and say to the Almighty that circumstances overpowered us, due to various pressures, problems, and difficulties, we cannot be indifferent. If we can achieve these feelings and attitudes, we can present ourselves as pure in one sense, even though we are not fully pure in another sense.

In this respect, there is a difference between Rosh Ha-shana and Yom Kippur. Rosh Ha-shana, apart from its own unique character, is also a day of *teshuva;* it is the beginning of the Ten Days of Repentance. But the *teshuva* of Rosh Ha-shana differs from that of Yom Kippur. The *Midrash* (*Midrash Tehillim* 27, sec. 4) interprets the opening verse of *mizmor* 27, "*Le-David, Hashem ori ve-yish'i,* The Lord is my light and my salvation," as follows:

> The Rabbis interpreted the entire psalm as referring to Rosh Ha-shana and Yom Kippur. "My light" is on Rosh Ha-shana, which is a day of judgment, as the verse states, "He shall bring forth your righteousness as the light, and your judgment as the noon day" (*Tehillim* 37:6); "my salvation" is on Yom Kippur, when He saves us and forgives all our sins.

The *Midrash* speaks more in terms of the resolution of sin on the part of the Almighty, though "my light and my salvation" refers and applies also to our own activity and attitude. The *teshuva* of "they shall confess their wrongdoing," of correcting individual sins, is a *teshuva* of light; there is illumination and recantation, and the sin is corrected. That is the *teshuva* of Rosh Ha-shana. On the other hand, on Yom Kippur we strive for a measure of reconciliation with the Almighty, a salvation even when the light is not complete. "Indeed, You are," says Yeshayahu (45:15), "a God who conceals Himself; the God of Israel, the Savior." At times, even a concealed God, a *Deus absconditus*, is a Savior: when due to our incessant sin, illumination and enlightenment are not yet our lot, yet due to God's mercy, salvation for which we pray and yearn is indeed available – provided our prayer, our yearning, and our striving are present and sincere.

In the *Gemara*, there is a dispute between Rabbi Yehuda Ha-nasi (Rebbi) and the Sages as to whether Yom Kippur atones only along with *teshuva*, or even without *teshuva*. Normally this is understood to mean that for Rebbi, Yom Kippur is a day of pure grace, effecting atonement even though we are totally unworthy, and even if we have not performed *teshuva*. It atones for those who perform *teshuva* and for those who do not; it simply falls as the rain, as the manna from heaven! According to the Sages, Yom Kippur is a day that relates to merit, to worth; if we have made the effort, the day atones.

But the truth, I think, is different. While the *Mishna* in *Yoma* (85b) indeed speaks of Yom Kippur atoning along with *teshuva*, and the *Gemara* (85b) says that this *mishna* is to be understood according to the Sages, the *Gemara* in *Shevuot* (13a) and the *baraita* in *Torat Kohanim* (11:14) both say that Yom Kippur "atones for those who are returning," who are in a process of returning. That means that according to the Sages, too, Yom Kippur is a day of grace and not just a response to merit. It is indeed a gift – the greatest gift – and is given to us not when we are fully accomplished, but when we are fully striving. We receive it not when we have attained perfection, but when we aspire for it and recognize its worth. In order to attain that atonement of "you shall be purified before the Lord," we seek to rid ourselves of impurities and acknowledge what our ultimate duty is in terms of its scope and depth. We present ourselves before the Almighty, trying, qualitatively, to intensify our connection to Him by focusing upon certain specific areas.

One further element deserves to be added. Yom Kippur comes annually, and annually we make the effort; we have Elul, we have the Ten Days of Repentance, we pray and perform *teshuva* every year. But we have to ask ourselves another question – apart from what happens each year, what happens *over* the years? To what extent is there process or progress; what is the incremental element from year to year? Many are troubled by the presumed Sisyphean aspect of *teshuva*; people work themselves up to a fevered pitch, and the day following Yom Kippur they are back where they started. Even when this is so, one should still treasure *teshuva* and treasure Yom Kippur; there are times one needs to run quickly just in order to avoid losing ground. But, of course, the hope and the aspiration, and the test of purity on a lifelong basis, is the fact that we strive to grow incrementally over the years. We strive for a purity that applies not only "where we are," but that enables us to approach and strive for the ultimate purity. "You shall be purified before the Lord" on this Yom Kippur, and "You shall be purified before the Lord" at the final Yom Kippur.

Teshuva: Impetus and Motive

Most of us today have come into contact with *ba'alei teshuva,* those individuals who have radically altered their credo and lifestyle, crossing the Rubicon between a secular and a religious Weltanschauung. But classical *teshuva,* the *teshuva* ordinarily intended by prophets, *Chazal,* and the *Rishonim,* takes place within the context of faith, within a pre-existing relation to the Almighty and to Torah. Whence does that spring? What, broadly speaking, impels a person toward *teshuva*?

Predictably, the impulses to *teshuva* have been classified by *Rishonim.* In *Sha'arei Teshuva,* Rabbeinu Yona lists six factors that motivate *teshuva*: if a person is beset by tribulations (2:1); comes upon old age (2:7); is exposed to *mussar* from various sources of wisdom and inspiration (2:10); reads directly from the Torah and the prophets (2:13); anticipates the Ten Days of Repentance (2:14); and more generally, whenever a person is confronted by *memento mori,* the prospect of death,

Delivered as the Hausman/Stern *Kinnus Teshuva* lecture at the Gruss Institute in Jerusalem, Tishrei 5754 (1993).

which might hang over him at any time (2:15). The Meiri,[1] after referring obliquely to Rabbeinu Yona, expands the list to nine, listing them in what he takes to be an order of ascending or descending worth. Both lists, by and large, are confined to the immediate stimulus that bears its message to a sinner; the content of *teshuva* would probably be little affected by whether the person has received the message visually or orally, or whether from a *mussar* book or an instructor and role model.

But it is precisely the question of the quality of the *teshuva* and the impact of impulse upon content that I wish to address. In this connection, we are better served by the familiar distinction in the *Gemara* between *teshuva* that springs from love (*ahava*) or from fear or awe (*yira*). In the *Gemara* in *Yoma* (86b), the distinction relates primarily to the result of *teshuva* rather than to its impulse:

> Reish Lakish said: Great is *teshuva,* for one's intentional sins are counted as unwitting transgressions.... Is that so? Did not Reish Lakish say: Great is *teshuva,* for one's intentional sins are counted as merits?... This is not difficult; one is out of love, the other out of fear (*yira*).

If *teshuva* is motivated by love, then sins become regarded as merits, while if *teshuva* is motivated by fear, then intentional sins are considered only as unintentional. To be sure, the questions of the result and the impetus are related at least indirectly, and perhaps directly: the fruits of *teshuva* are a function of its character. And yet, with reference to motivation for *teshuva,* the differentiation of fear and love hardly covers the topic, especially if we take the term "*yira*" to refer to awe, rather than to the fear of possible punishment. Even a cursory survey of the impulse of *teshuva* leads us beyond this *gemara* to discern and describe at least three principal tracks of *teshuva,* each with its own *primo mobile,* initiating force.

THE MOTIVE OF MITZVA

The first impetus is normative, the fact that *teshuva* is a mitzva. As an aside, whether *teshuva* is to be numbered as an independent unit within

1. *Chibbur Ha-teshuva* 1:2.

the 613 *mitzvot* is questionable. Some *Rishonim* – notably the *Semak* and possibly the Ramban[2] – counted it, while the Rambam possibly did not.[3] The Rambam opens *Hilkhot Teshuva* with a conditional formulation:

> If a person transgresses any of the *mitzvot* of the Torah, whether a positive commandment or a prohibition, whether willingly or inadvertently, when he repents, and returns from his sin, he must confess before God, blessed be He, as the verse states, "Any man or woman who commits any wrong toward a fellow man.... They shall confess their wrongdoing" (*Bemidbar* 5:6–7). This refers to verbal confession (*viddui*), and this confession is a positive commandment.

Since the Rambam avoids a categorical statement, the *Minchat Chinnukh* (mitzva 364) infers that, in the Rambam's view, one is not commanded to perform *teshuva* at all. One who fails to do so is liable for the initial sin that he has failed to redress, yet he incurs no additional liability for abjuring *teshuva*, as he might, for instance, for eschewing the consumption of *matza*.

At this point, suffice it to say that this is a highly novel position, one which, both halakhically and hashkafically, the Rav *z"l* regarded as absolutely untenable. Even were we to subscribe to the thesis of the *Minchat Chinnukh* on the purely formal, halakhic plane, surely no one can view *teshuva* as entirely optional.

Frequently, the *Gemara* insists that whenever the Torah prescribes a punishment for an action, there must also be a separate, concomitant source for a prohibition.[4] The *Sefer Ha-chinnukh* (mitzva 69) explains that this is to preclude a person's thinking that a punishment may be regarded as the price extracted for a sin, but that if a person is willing to pay the price, it is perfectly licit for him to indulge himself.

2. Albeit in his Commentary on the Torah to *Devarim* 30:11, not in his commentary on Rambam's *Sefer Ha-mitzvot*.
3. For a fuller treatment of the Rambam's position, see the chapter "*Teshuva*: Obligation and Opportunity," in the section "*Teshuva* as Obligation."
4. E.g., "There is no punishment without warning" (*Sifrei Devarim* 173, *Sanhedrin* 56b), or "This teaches the punishment; whence do we derive the prohibition?" (*Sanhedrin* 54a).

The apocryphal Litvak is reported to have suggested, "To talk *lashon ha-ra* is so enjoyable that it's worth the punishment!" This, the *Sefer Hachinnukh* says, *Chazal* took for granted as being inconceivable; hence, if we have learned of punishment, there must be a prohibition somewhere behind it. How much more so will we say that so central a value as *teshuva* cannot be regarded as a matter of preference or a question of taste! Indeed, the prophets repeatedly issue clarion calls for repentance, whether addressing the community: "Return, Israel, to the Lord your God, for you have stumbled in your iniquity" (*Hoshea* 14:2), or individuals: "Seek out the Lord when He may be found, call upon Him when He is near. Let the wicked one forsake his way, and the iniquitous man his thoughts; let him return to the Lord, and He will show him mercy, to our God, for He is abundantly forgiving" (*Yeshayahu* 55:6–7). These are not suggestions; these are demands. The response to them, to the normative word of God as expressed through them, therefore reflects one impetus to *teshuva*.

TWO TRACKS OF *TESHUVA*: MORAL AND RELIGIOUS

There is also the sinner's reaction to one of two realities that are complementary, and even coincident, yet clearly differentiable: his relation to his sin on the one hand, and his relation to the Almighty on the other. They can be readily described as moral and religious *teshuva*, respectively.

The moral aspect of *teshuva* focuses on the sinful act as an incarnate, evil reality. In this sense, sin's impact is multiple. There is, first, the specific wrong in its naked isolation. Second, it has a contaminating effect upon the world, either in the rational sense that evil radiates socially, or in the metaphysical sense that even a single mitzva or sin affects the fabric of the entire cosmic order (as Rav Chaim Volozhiner says in the *Nefesh Ha-chayim* and elsewhere). Third, the sin has a contaminating effect upon the sinner's soul, again, whether on the rational, psychological plane, or the mystical.

The religious impact of sin, with reference not to the act but to our relationship to the Almighty, also has multiple aspects. First, every sin, by definition, is an affront to the Almighty, as one assigns priority to one's own will as opposed to His. Second, there is, *salva reverentia*, an impact upon divine majesty, the existence of sin truncating and reducing, as it were, the inherent Presence of the *Shekhina* as reflected in this world. Third, sin establishes a divisive barrier that interposes between the sinner and the Almighty, illustrated by the celebrated phrasing of the Rambam (*Hilkhot Teshuva* 7:7), as he contrasts the sinner's renewed status with his previous one:

> Only yesterday this sinner was divided from God, the Lord of Israel, as the verse states, "Your iniquities have been a barrier between you and your God" (*Yeshayahu* 59:2). He would call out [to God] without being answered.... He would perform *mitzvot,* only to have them thrown back in his face.

Thus, there are two broad categories of sin – moral and religious – each multifaceted, and there are, correspondingly, two tracks, apart from the first already mentioned, to *teshuva.*[5]

These two aspects of *teshuva* reflect different orientations, and they are dominated by different elements. Moral *teshuva* is rooted in the past, as it is anchored in a desire to break with previous modes of existence and experience. As such, it is aroused by guilt and recognition of sin. This includes both an awareness of a particular sin, and also the compelling sense of sin as a reality, as a pervasive force that has infected one's being and from which one needs to be purified.

Religious *teshuva,* on the other hand, is future-oriented, animated by yearning and longing. As such, it is motivated by aspiration, but also by a sense of shame – that one has let the Almighty down and has let oneself down.[6] *Chazal* note the significance of shame as a factor within

---

5. These two tracks correspond to the two prepositions with which the Prophets speak of *teshuva*: movement "from," as in "Turn, turn from your evil ways" (*Yechezkel* 33:11), which reflects moral *teshuva,* and movement "to," as in "Return, Israel, to the Lord your God, for you have stumbled in your iniquity" (*Hoshea* 14:2), which reflects religious *teshuva.* See the chapters "*Teshuva:* Ferment and Repose" and "*Teshuva* of Norm and of Crisis" for an expanded discussion of these themes.
6. Some sociologists, from Ruth Benedict down, speak of "shame cultures" and "guilt cultures," and, given Judaism's emphasis upon sin, atonement, and sin offering, they see Judaism as being primarily a guilt culture. This notion is thoroughly erroneous, as will be explained.

the process of *teshuva*, both in deterring an individual from sin[7] and as a motivator for repentance after one sins.[8] Shame is a vital force within the context of *teshuva*.

MUST *TESHUVA* BE COMMANDED?

With respect to both moral and religious *teshuva*, we are confronted by a gnawing question connected to their relation to the first element, *teshuva* as mitzva.

On the moral plane, is it possible that a committed Jew would remain mired neck-deep in excremental filth, continuing to choke on his own pollution, were *teshuva* not a mitzva? Need the dung heap's denizens be *commanded* to move, shower, and change?[9]

The question is equally valid with respect to the religious plane, the sin's impact with respect to the divine. Rav Yitzchak of Corbeil, the *Semak*, states (*siman* 51) that there is a mitzva of *teshuva*, based on the verse, "And you shall return to the Lord your God and listen to His voice" (*Devarim* 30:2). Similarly, with reference to the verse, "For this mitzva that I enjoin upon you today, it is not too hard for you, nor is it beyond

7. The *Gemara* (*Nedarim* 20a) defines the very purpose of Revelation of the Torah in terms of shame:

> It was taught in a *baraita*: "That His fear may be upon your faces" (*Shemot* 20:17) – this refers to shame; [continuing in the verse:] "so that you not sin" – this teaches that shame leads to fear of sin. From here the Sages said: It is a good sign that a person experiences shame. Others say: Any person who experiences shame will not quickly sin, and one who is not shamefaced, it is known that his forefathers did not stand at Mount Sinai.

It is presumably in this sense that *Chazal* (*Yevamot* 79a) speak of one of the signs of Jewish peoplehood, i.e., that Jews are shamefaced.

8. "And Rabba bar Chinnana Sava said in the name of Rav: One who sins and is ashamed of it, all his sins are forgiven" (*Berakhot* 12b). Rabbeinu Yona, in *Iggeret Ha-teshuva*, writes, "And the light of shame shall be visible at all times on one's countenance," and he quotes the verse cited by the *Gemara* in *Nedarim* (see prev. note), "That His fear may be upon your faces so that you not sin."

9. If one rejects the thesis of the *Minchat Chinnukh*, and focuses, as did the Rav *z"l*, upon the caption to *Hilkhot Teshuva*, "There is one positive commandment herein, namely, that a sinner should repent from his sin before God and confess," one could say that the Rambam here sets down a mitzva of moral *teshuva*.

reach" (*Devarim* 30:11), the Ramban understood the term "this mitzva" to refer to the specific obligation of *teshuva*.[10]

Indeed, the normative question might even be more acute on the plane of religious *teshuva*. Moral *teshuva* is presumably valid even piecemeal. One can make confessional statements as part of rectifying one sin, while remaining oblivious to another. We rule, in light of the *Gemara* in *Chullin* (5b), that if a person disregards one food prohibition he can bring a sin offering with regard to another; this offering is accepted, for it is not designated as "the offering of the wicked," which "is an abomination" (*Mishlei* 21:27; see *Shevuot* 12b, *Zevachim* 7b). On the religious level, however, this kind of piecemeal treatment is problematic. After all, only one sovereign can prevail. Either a person acknowledges the yoke of Heavenly reign, and "negates his own will before His" (*Avot* 2:4), or he does not. In this context, we take note of the analogy between immersion and *teshuva* that appears in the last *mishna* in *Yoma* (85b), where Rabbi Akiva consoles the nation after the destruction of the Temple, assuring them: "Just as a ritual bath purifies the impure, so too, the Holy One, blessed be He, purifies Israel." The Rav *z"l* noted that just as immersion must be total, as one cannot immerse one organ at a time, so too *teshuva* needs to be total and comprehensive.

The religious stakes are, patently, quite high. If refraining from *teshuva* entails continued existential catastrophe, perpetual divorce, God forbid, from the Ground of all Being, need a devoted Jew be commanded to seize the moment of *teshuva*?

Perhaps an even more rigorous objection might be raised. Oughtn't we give the position of the *Minchat Chinnukh* a fairer hearing? Might a command here be not only superfluous but damaging? Given such critical experiential concerns, might not a normative element, which would direct *teshuva* into routinized channels and implementation,

10. Ramban, Commentary to the Torah *ad loc.*:

> But the correct interpretation is that when the term "mitzva" refers to the totality of Torah, it says, "all the mitzva that I enjoin upon you today" (*Devarim* 8:1). Rather, "this mitzva" refers to the aforementioned mitzva of repentance, for the verses "You shall return in your heart" (30:1) and "You shall return to the Lord your God" (30:2) constitute the mitzva wherein He commands us to do so.

transmute existential confrontation into dutiful performance? These are valid considerations, and I think we ignore them at our peril.

DIVINE SERVICE AS BEING COMMANDED

At bottom, however, they relate not so much to the phenomenon of *teshuva* specifically, but to our divine service generally – and especially to Halakha. Essentially, these contentions hinge upon the critique, familiar from early Christianity to contemporary existentialism, of normative mandate as the basis of the spiritual life. The criticism is that inflexible rules cannot cope with malleable, contextual reality, and that legalism both constricts spiritual liberty and deadens the inner self with which religion is ultimately concerned.

But the Torah – the very term bespeaks the normative – has held otherwise. It has regarded man in general, and, *a fortiori*, the Jew in particular, as a called and commanded being. The central category of Judaism is mitzva – the divine imperative. Even a so-called *devar reshut*, the optional, assumes its character within the context of commandment, and with reference to it. When the Torah describes in *Bereishit* the human mandate to partake of the Creator's world, it couches it in terms of mitzva: "And the Lord God commanded the man saying: Of every tree of the garden you may eat. But of the tree of the knowledge of good and evil, you shall not eat of it, for on the day that you eat of it, you shall be worthy of death" (2:16–17). The commandment here precedes both the license and the prohibition, intimating that not only the proscription against eating of the tree of the knowledge of good and evil, but the license to indulge in the fruit of all other trees, is part of a normative order which characterizes man's relation to the Creator.

If this is true at the universal plane, then all the more so at the Jewish plane. Covenantal relation, we hold, is not attained through epiphanous revelation alone, but through the revealed norm. Of course, *Chazal* recognize, in the words of the *Gemara* in *Sanhedrin* (106b), that ultimately the Almighty seeks the heart. They hold, however, that being commanded does not undermine inwardness, but rather enriches it. Contrary to current popular morality, which holds, with the Kantians, that voluntary, autonomous moral behavior is superior to submission to normative constraint, *Chazal* determined that "One who is commanded and performs a mitzva is greater than one who is not commanded and performs it" (e.g., *Bava Kamma* 38a). This is both because the commanded one is more likely to mind his task assiduously, as some *Rishonim* noted, and because the element of responsiveness to the divine will adds a spiritual dimension not otherwise attainable.

So it is with *teshuva*. It is part of a dialogue with the Almighty, as in "Return to Me, and I will return to you" (*Malakhi* 3:7), or "Bring us back to You, O Lord, and we shall return" (*Eikha* 5:21), and it is a response to what is both a command and an entreaty: "Return, wayward sons; I shall cure the recalcitrance" (*Yirmiyahu* 3:22). The dialogue poses a challenge and opens a channel not otherwise extant. Nevertheless, the danger of legalism, the prospect that religious existence may not be ennobled by the normative element but reduced to it, clearly exists, both in the realm of *teshuva* and in general. *Chazal* were keenly aware of the danger, which they expressed with regard to two central axes of the religious life: prayer and Torah.

THE DANGER OF THE NORM IN PRAYER AND TORAH STUDY

Regarding prayer, Rabbi Eliezer states factually in a *mishna*, "One whose prayer is fixed (*keva*), his prayer is not supplication" (*Berakhot* 28b). In an effort to explain the word "*keva*" in this context, the *Gemara* (*Berakhot* 29b) offers: "Rabbi Ya'akov bar Idi said in the name of Rabbi Oshaya: Anyone whose prayer is like a heavy burden upon him." In the *Mishna* in *Avot* (2:13), Rabbi Shimon posits normatively, "Do not make your prayer a fixed duty (*keva*), but a plea for mercy and an entreaty before God." Clearly, there exists a danger of prayer being transformed from pleading to a fixed duty.

Similarly, there exists the possibility of relating to Torah study as a burden to be unloaded. The *Gemara* (*Menachot* 99b) cites the dictum of the school of Rabbi Yishmael: "The words of the Torah should not be like a debt to you, and you are not at liberty to desist from them." Rashi explains the statement:

> "They should not be like a debt to you" – like a person who has incurred a debt, who says: "When will I pay it off and be rid of it?" Similarly a person, with regard to Torah, should not say: "I will learn one chapter and exempt myself," for you have no right to feel that you have exempted yourself [from Torah study].

Evidently *Chazal* and *Rishonim* recognized the danger. But the resolution of the danger lies not in rejection of the norm but in its internalization to the point that we strive to forgo our wishes in favor of the Almighty's. This is the gist of Rabbi Yehuda Ha-nasi's counsel, "Do His will as if it were your will" (*Avot* 2:4), and, to the extent that it is realized, the element of command serves to deepen religious consciousness and sensibility. Yet there may be some who do not attain this lofty orientation, for whom command indeed may constrict their total religious self; and as we reject antinomianism in all its forms, the avoidance of such a fate must be part of our deeper spiritual charge.

WHAT FACTORS ENABLE *TESHUVA*?

A lingering question persists: What enables these factors to take hold at the practical level? How and why does a person who had paid no heed to the mitzva of *teshuva*, who hitherto had been perfectly comfortable with himself, his lifestyle, his values, and his relation to the Almighty, now come to seek, to aspire, and to transmute them? I believe we can identify three factors.

The first is that which was emphasized by Rabbeinu Yona, a phalanx of external stimuli that have brought the message of *teshuva*, verbally or scripturally, whether by exhortation or imprecation, to the previously complacent sinner: for example, he reads the works of the prophets, hears penetrating rebuke, or the Ten Days of Repentance impress him.

The second is the factor Rabbeinu Yona had listed first, which the Torah itself cites: the pressure of crisis. The Torah in *Va'etchanan* puts it as follows:

> The Lord shall scatter you among the nations, and you shall remain few in number among the nations where the Lord shall lead you.... You shall seek from there the Lord your God, and you shall find Him, if only you seek Him with all your heart and with all your soul. When you are in distress and all these things have befallen you, in the latter days, you shall turn to the Lord your God and obey His voice. (*Devarim* 4:27–30)

When you are in dire straits, from there – *de profundis* – you will return to the Almighty and hearken to His voice. A similar factor, with slightly differing emphases, is also found in *parashat Nitzavim*:

> And it shall be, that when all these things happen to you, the blessing and the curse, which I have set before you, you shall return in your heart, among all the nations where the Lord your God has banished you. And you shall return to the Lord your God and listen to His voice, in accordance with all that I am commanding you today; you and your children, with all your heart and all your soul. (*Devarim* 30:1–2)

This second efficient cause, distress, strikes a pessimistic note – not only due to the fear of apostasy and retribution prior to *teshuva*, but due to the intimation that the road to *teshuva* is ordinarily paved with adversity. Unsettling as the intimation may be, *Chazal* evidently came to terms with it. "Rabbi Abba bar Kahana said: The act of the removal of the ring," whereby Achashverosh indicated that Haman had total hegemony, "was more powerful [an inducement to *teshuva*] than were forty-eight prophets and seven prophetesses" whom the Almighty sent to *Klal Yisrael* (*Megilla* 14a).

Yet, as pessimistic as the tone may be, the verses and the talmudic passages also resonate with a very reassuring note. Even if one's *teshuva* is, in effect, foxhole *teshuva*, it is accepted by the Almighty. It is, to be sure, an inferior *teshuva*, presumably attaining lesser results.[11] But it is accepted. Moreover, whatever its catalyst,

11. The inferiority of such *teshuva* is clearly indicated by a distinction set out in *Yoma* 86a:

> Rav Yehuda asked: One verse states: "Return, wayward sons, I shall cure the recalcitrance" (*Yirmiyahu* 3:22). Another verse states: "For I shall be your Master, and I shall take you, even one from a city, and two from a family" (*Yirmiyahu* 3:14)! Here it is referring to repentance out of love or awe, and there, through suffering.

As Rashi explains, the first verse regards penitents as children when the *teshuva* is motivated by love and awe, while the second verse, when they repented only when made to suffer, regards them as servants who have simply carried out their mandate. Of course, let us bear in mind that, from a Jewish perspective, servitude to the Almighty, too, is an exalted state.

if the *teshuva* gathers momentum and becomes wholly genuine, it too may lead to hitherto unattained spiritual heights. The *Gemara* (*Shabbat* 88a) asserts that at the time of the miracle of salvation from Haman the Jews undertook a renewed and wholly volitional acceptance of the Torah. In the same vein, after the foretold calamities in *Nitzavim*, the subsequent verses (*Devarim* 30:6) promise a quasi-messianic total commitment which, in the Ramban's view (s.v. *u-mal*), signifies the very excision of the evil inclination and a return to the primal state of radical innocence within which man serves the Almighty wholly and intuitively.

THE FACTOR OF HUMAN FREEDOM

The third explanatory factor is of a wholly different order. The first two are, in a limited vein, deterministic, relating to response to external stimuli. The essence of *teshuva*, however, whether it entails repentance for a single peccadillo or the reorientation of one's total personality, is human freedom, free will.[12] To believe in human freedom is to hold that change within, initiated by the gestalt of will, intellect, or emotion, may be independent of change without. Change may result from the contemplation of factors that, by dint of inertia, indolence, or inattentiveness have been previously ignored. These may cover a broad spectrum, being not only widely divergent but even antithetical.

With respect to the related phenomenon of how to avoid sin in the first place, two *Tannaim* offer sharply contrasted counsel.

> Akavia ben Mahalalel said: Consider three things, and you will not fall into the hands of sin. Know whence you came, and whither you are going, and before whom you will need to give account and reckoning. Whence you came – from a putrid drop; and whither you are going – to a place of dust, worm, and maggot; and before whom you will need to give account and reckoning – before the King of Kings, the Holy One, blessed be He. (*Avot* 3:1)

12. It is no accident that the most vigorously eloquent assertion of free will in our Torah world appears in the middle chapters of the Rambam's *Hilkhot Teshuva*.

The first *mishna* in the preceding chapter in *Avot* opens and concludes as follows:

> Rebbi [Yehuda Ha-nasi] said: Which is the right course that a man should choose for himself? That which brings honor to him who adopts it, and brings him honor from men.... Consider three things and you will not stray into sin: Know what is above you – a seeing eye, a listening ear, and all your deeds are written in a book. (*Avot* 2:1)

These are, of course, two very different prescriptions. As Rabbeinu Yona noted (*Sha'arei Teshuva* 2:20), Akavia ben Mahalalel's prescription is in the spirit of the radical pessimism of the first chapters in *Kohelet,* and focuses upon the insignificance of man and the vacuity of human life. It is described by the skeptical interlocutor of Tennyson's *The Two Voices* as "a life of nothings, nothing-worth, from that first nothing ere his birth, to that last nothing under earth." Rabbi Yehuda Ha-nasi, by contrast, addresses majestic man – an individual who has the capacity of magisterially selecting the proper course, a course which, as some *Rishonim* interpret, brings glory to himself, to the Almighty, to his fellow man. His prescription envisions man as the worthy object of the Almighty's perpetual regard, as living and working, in terms of Milton's autobiographical sonnet, "as ever in my great Taskmaster's eye." Very different from "a putrid drop," from "worm and maggot," yet the ultimate goal is similar.

The call to attentive contemplation has a normative ring. The critical initial step is taking heed and taking stock. The opening to *teshuva* is the recognition, common to Socrates and the *Mussar* masters, that the unexamined life is not worth living, or at least that the examined life would be far richer and purer. Although attention to a fact that was previously ignored may be the result of another's persistent urging, the resultant *teshuva* nevertheless may be accurately described as reflexive *hit'orerut,* a self-awakening. The *Or Ha-chayim* (*Devarim* 4:29) describes the people's penitential search for God as "repentance which is self-induced, when people become aware that they have sinned and want to rehabilitate themselves to be in good standing with their Creator."

Teshuva may also be induced by distress – not the fear of enemy persecution, but the inner crisis, the angst resulting from the loss of anchor and identity. Without any external pressure, the recognition of the vacuity of life, of a life devoid of a transcendental dimension, impels one to the Almighty. This, too, is a *teshuva* that is *hit'orerut*. As Rabbeinu Bachya explains in his *Kad Ha-kemach*, in the section on *teshuva*:

> You should know that repentance requires that man should realize his lowliness and insignificance, for he is dust and ashes in his life and worms and maggots in his death. By bearing this in mind, one's effort to repent will be successful and he will achieve perfect contrition with proper and pure intent.

Contemplating the "worms and maggots" not only helps avoid sin prospectively, as Akavia ben Mahalalel proposed, but helps one perform *teshuva* subsequent to sin.

Conversely, *hit'orerut* may come about in the spirit of *Tefilla Zaka*, which views sin against the backdrop of human majesty and the human capacity for good – a capacity that has been defiled and now needs to be purified. For students of the Rav *z"l*, self-awakening is more likely to be heightened by the awareness of man's latent spiritual greatness and his potential for attaining the grandest of creative gestures, the regeneration of self, delineated in the concluding chapter of *Halakhic Man* and elsewhere. Whatever the specific content, the respective messages of human worthlessness and potential grandeur are not mutually exclusive, and the same individual may, successively or concurrently, have recourse to both. The basic message is the same: bethink thyself and bestir thyself.

This third explanation for what brings a person suddenly to be impelled to *teshuva* may simply be that there need be no explanation, none beyond the vagaries of the convolutions of the human spirit. It is here, in the explanation without explanation, that the challenge and the promise of *teshuva* inheres, in the realization of our own capacity and our own responsibility. This is encapsulated in the famous *gemara* in *Avoda Zara* (17a) about Elazar ben Dordaya, who sought aid in his defense from multiple sources in nature, and was turned away by each. He finally concluded:

> "*Ein ha-davar talui ela bi,* This matter is dependent only on me." He placed his head between his knees, and he broke out crying, until his soul left him. A voice from on High went out and stated, "R. Elazar ben Dordaya is destined for life in the World-to-Come."

Indeed, *ein ha-davar talui ela banu* – this matter depends only on us.

MEASURING OUR OWN COMMUNITY: SPIRITUAL INATTENTIVENESS

How do we, the so-called Modern Orthodox or Religious-Zionist community, measure up to the challenge and the promise? The demand of *teshuva* is dual: confront and respond. I am afraid that we leave much to be desired on both counts.

With respect to the first, the external stimuli impelling us both to come to grips with sin and to connect to the Almighty are often sadly deficient. The sense of distress, of impending external danger, is, by and large, fortunately absent. Most of us, thank God, know little of "removal of the ring"; so that factor is weak. As to the impact of the Word of God and the awareness of His message from external sources, that voice, too, is often muted. The babble of competing cultural messages permeates the general scene and hence the Jewish world, which, by dint of its modernity, is often in close contact with the broader ambience and suffused with some of its elements.

In this setting, the prospect for self-generated *hit'orerut* also dips very often. In a modern world marked by self-reliance, and flooded by consumerist diversions of all sorts, the soil is often not ripe for the growth of spirituality in general, and divine service in particular. To be sure, as a matter of personal concern, there is much existential confrontation and ferment; people may be dissatisfied with their spiritual status quo and searching for deeper meaning in their lives. But on a mass basis, it is often constricted.

This is not, in and of itself, reason for opting out of this community. But it certainly is reason for being fully and deeply aware of its problems and for coping with those problems. Every generation, the *Chafetz Chayim* once suggested, has its own besetting sin – as does, one might add, each community within that generation. Addressing our own community, I need to focus upon the besetting sin, the inherent danger, of the Modern Orthodox community, the danger against which we need to be on our perpetual guard. That danger is, quite clearly, *heise'ach ha-da'at*, spiritual and religious inattentiveness.

The Almighty can be failed in three different ways. One can rebel against Him, one can distort Him, and one can ignore Him. The danger indigenous to the modern world is clearly the last – it is that *heise'ach ha-da'at* which is indigenous to the society of success, real or imagined. We read in *Ha'azinu*:

> Yeshurun waxed fat and kicked out; you grew fat, you grew thick, you became obese. He forsook God, his Maker, and scorned the Rock of his salvation .... You disregarded the Rock that bore you, and you forgot God, your Maker. (*Devarim* 32:15, 18)

You became successful, secure, and self-reliant, and then you forgot the Creator who had molded you and given you life. It is this danger – *heise'ach ha-da'at* or forgetfulness – against which Moshe *Rabbeinu* particularly enjoins to a *Kenesset Yisrael* on the verge of attaining a pinnacle of success: conquering and settling *Eretz Yisrael*.[13] *Heise'ach ha-da'at*, religiously speaking, is the tragic flaw, the Achilles' heel of a modern world, general and Jewish, which has attained a measure of success in enlarging, in Bacon's famed phrase, "the bounds of human empire," in asserting a degree of presumed control over its environment and beyond.

This is not total obliviousness, but rather inattentiveness, a degree of neglect. The message that needs to be hammered home to this kind of environment is that of the verse in *Kohelet* (12:1): "So remember your Creator in the days of your youth." Even in the midst of vibrant youth and heady success – remember your Creator! It is against this *heise'ach ha-da'at* that we need to guard and to fight, inwardly and outwardly, personally and communally. We must combat this danger by deepening our own religious awareness and spiritual sensibility, by expanding and intensifying the Torah education of our children, by enriching the

13. *Devarim* 8:10–14 notes the same sequence of material success breeding arrogance and the forgetting of God.

Jewish character of our culture, and by saturating our world with a far greater measure of God-consciousness and Torah-consciousness.

RESPONDING TO OUR SPIRITUAL INATTENTIVENESS

Having confronted our inattentiveness, what of our response? Here too we are in difficult straits. R. Elazar ben Dordaya said: This matter is dependent only on me, and he broke out crying. The supposedly rationalistic and philosophic Rambam writes: "Among the paths of repentance is for the penitent to constantly call out before God, crying and entreating" (*Hilkhot Teshuva* 2:4). But where do *we* stand in relation to crying? Our gut instinct is that crying is for the ignorant and the superstitious; but we are sophisticated and intellectual, and therefore decorous and restrained. *Ribbono shel Olam!* Amidst all this decorum and restraint, can't we, at least at *Ne'ila*, shed some genuine tears? Wordsworth, in a celebrated line, spoke of "thoughts that lie too deep for tears." In the typical Modern Orthodox community or synagogue, do the thoughts lie too deep for tears or too shallow for tears? Referring to Himself, God says: "My soul will cry in its inner chambers" (*Yirmiyahu* 13:17; *Chagiga* 5b); do we at least cry where decorum and restraint are not a consideration, in the inner chambers?

We once had a great ancestor, a man urbane and successful, but he found his ultimate spiritual redemption and return, his ultimate spiritual peace, only through tears: "Yosef could not contain himself among all those standing around him, and he called out: Get every man out of my presence. No man stood with him when Yosef made himself known to his brothers. He cried out loud and the Egyptians heard; it was heard even in Pharaoh's house" (*Bereishit* 45:1–2). Only after the great, cultured, urbane second-in-command to Pharaoh was able to break down was he able to find himself again within the bosom of his family, even within his own bosom. And again, after Ya'akov's death, it was the crying of Yosef, of all the brothers, that the Torah singled out: "Yosef fell upon his father's face; he wept upon him and kissed him" (50:1). If one makes peace with a father of flesh and blood so, then *a fortiori* in relation to our Father in Heaven! So may the image of the righteous Yosef animate us – if not to be totally dissolved in tears, at least to open somewhat that terrible dam which inhibits our moral response to sin, or our religious response to the Almighty. This terrible dam inhibits our giving vent to our sense of shame and guilt, and inhibits our relating to the past or aspiring to the future.

GOD AS THE CRUCIAL ELEMENT IN *TESHUVA*

Up to now, we have spoken of different impulses to *teshuva*: the normative, the moral, and the religious. We have tried to point out factors that prod us toward each of these tracks. Employing and unifying all three tracks is a daunting task, and, despite our failings and weaknesses, we cannot lose hope or become fainthearted. For in the course of our discussion heretofore, we have omitted one critical element – God Himself.

The Rambam starts his *Hilkhot Teshuva* with the mitzva of *teshuva*, in all its basic elements and procedures, and in the concluding chapter he speaks both of pure moral idealism:

> One who serves God out of love occupies himself in the Torah and the *mitzvot* and walks in the paths of wisdom for no ulterior motive, not because of fear that evil will occur, nor in order to acquire benefit. Rather, he does what is true because it is true, and ultimately, good will come because of it (10:2),

and then of total passionate devotion:

> What is the proper degree of love? That a person should love God with a very great and exceeding love until his soul is bound up in the love of God. Thus, he will always be obsessed with this love as though he is lovesick. (10:3)

The norm at the beginning, and the moral idealism and the passionate devotion at the end – these cover the whole gamut, but for unique individuals. What of everyone else; what of one who is not able to travel these three paths, perhaps not even one of them? For him there is a lesser order of *teshuva*, and there is a factor which impels that *teshuva*, too, and accepts it. It is the Almighty who effects *teshuva*. Within the full equation of *teshuva*, He is central, absolutely critical.

In this respect, it is useful to differentiate between Rosh Ha-shana and Yom Kippur. Rosh Ha-shana, to the extent that it is the first of the Ten Days of Repentance, relates primarily to moral *teshuva*, to the return *from* our sins; as such, it sets the high standard of the pristine perfection of the proto-historical creation: "For this day is the opening of all Your works, a remembrance of the very first day" (*Zikhronot* prayer on Rosh Ha-shana). Yom Kippur, by contrast, is preeminently the day of religious *teshuva*, of regeneration through reconciliation. It is the day of return *to* the Almighty, and His standards are less exacting. Rosh Ha-shana is the day of the completely righteous, those who have already performed *teshuva*. Yom Kippur, on the other hand, is the day, as *Chazal* tell us (*Rosh Ha-shana* 16b), of *beinonim*, the intermediate people. It is the day of penitents.

Rabbi Yehuda Ha-nasi claims that Yom Kippur atones even for those who are unrepentant. Yet even the Sages, who disagree with Rabbi Yehuda Ha-nasi, do not say that it atones only for those who perform complete *teshuva* by the deadline (see *Yoma* 85b, 87a). All they require is that one be among those returning, among those who are in the process of *teshuva*, aspiring toward rectitude and reconciliation, but not necessarily having achieved them. A person's aspiration to *teshuva* is not only something that the Almighty accepts, but is something toward which He impels, which He helps us mold. He is an efficient cause of the aspiration. He accords us the *chesed* of graciously accepting the *teshuva* we have wrought, in the spirit of "Bring us back to You, O Lord, and we shall return, renew our days as of old" (*Eikha* 5:21). In addition, we may even envision Him as actively engaged in helping us on the road to reaching Him.

"If one comes to purify himself," *Chazal* say (*Shabbat* 104a), "he receives assistance." If a person is among the penitents and the aspiring, if that is his direction, then he is helped by the Almighty Himself. And never is there a day of greater coming to purify and never a day of greater assistance than on Yom Kippur, a day epitomized by the phrase: "To purify you of all your sins; you shall be purified before the Lord" (*Vayikra* 16:30). So, on "the great and awesome day of the Lord" (*Malakhi* 3:23), as we stand before the Almighty, intoning, "Open us a gate, at the time of the locking of the gate, for day is passing"

(Yom Kippur liturgy, *Ne'ila*), we will be mindful of our imperfections, our weaknesses and the flaws of our *teshuva*; and yet we will aspire to a better day and a better self. May we merit to give praise and thanksgiving to the Almighty, not only for accepting our *teshuva* but for impelling it, for aiding us in the realization of Rabbi Akiva's exclamation:

> How fortunate are you, Israel; before whom are you purified, and who purifies you? It is your Father in Heaven, as it is stated, "And I will sprinkle purifying water upon you, and you shall be purified" (*Yechezkel* 36:25). And it says: "The Lord is the ritual bath of Israel" (*Yirmiyahu* 17:13). Just as a ritual bath purifies the impure, so too, the Holy One, blessed be He, purifies Israel. (*Yoma* 85b)

Kallot Va-chamurot: Gradation of Sins in Repentance

DIFFERENTIATED AND UNDIFFERENTIATED REPENTANCE

Many sources note the existence of different levels of severity or importance within the world of mitzva observance. I wish to examine the extent, if any, to which we are sensitive to these gradations within the context of *teshuva*. Let me open by citing two classic texts. Rambam opens his *Hilkhot Teshuva* as follows:

> If a person transgresses any of the *mitzvot* of the Torah, whether a positive commandment or a prohibition, whether willingly or inadvertently, when he repents, and returns from his sin, he must confess before God, blessed be He, as the verse states, "Any man or woman who commits any wrong toward a fellow man, by acting treacherously against the Lord, and that person realizes his guilt. They shall confess their wrongdoing" (*Bemidbar* 5:6–7).

Delivered as the Hausman/Stern *Kinnus Teshuva* lecture at the Gruss Institute in Jerusalem, Tishrei 5762 (2001).

> This refers to verbal confession, and this confession is a positive commandment.
>
> How does one confess? One states: "I implore You, God; I sinned, I transgressed, I committed iniquity before You by doing the following. Behold, I regret and am embarrassed for my deeds, and I promise never to repeat this act again." This is the essence of the confession. Whoever confesses profusely and elaborates on this matter is praiseworthy.

The Rambam's presentation here is comprehensive and undifferentiated. He makes a sweeping statement about "any of the *mitzvot* of the Torah, whether a positive commandment or a prohibition." There is no hint of weighing the significance or substance of a particular sin. The process is more or less uniform, the formulation identical, except for the fact that a person must mention exactly what he has done – slandered someone, shaved with a razor, lent with interest, etc.

In contrast, the third section of Rabbeinu Yona's *Sha'arei Teshuva* opens with an exhortation for penitents to distinguish between the various levels of commandments and prohibitions:

> The penitent is exhorted to search his ways to discover how many transgressions and sins he is guilty of; and after having performed a diligent examination, he is further exhorted to determine the severity of each of his sins, as it is said, "Let us search and examine our ways" (*Eikha* 3:40). He must do this to appraise himself of the degree of sin involved in every one of his misdeeds. There are cases of guilt so great that they approach Heaven, and instances of evil that are as weighty as many great sins. The magnitude of one's repentance will be commensurate with the magnitude of his soul-searching. His spirit will be broken to the extent of his awareness of the magnitude and gravity of his transgression – and then his uncircumcised heart will be humbled and he will requite his transgression.

According to Rabbeinu Yona, it is important to distinguish between gradations of sin for a number of reasons. First, this is necessary in order that the requisite repentance be commensurate with the misdeed.

Second, it is required so that the sense of guilt and the sense of shame – two different yet interactive responses[1] – be of the proper dimensions.

Clearly, Rabbeinu Yona's presentation differs substantially from the Rambam's. The Rambam, whether discussing the *viddui* (confession) as quoted above, or discussing the stages of *teshuva*, in his second chapter, does not highlight the need for inquiry into the different grades of sin. Rabbeinu Yona, on the other hand, devotes the third section of his book to a very detailed catalog of different levels of sin, listed in ascending order.

In terms of our own experience, goals, and directions, should we assume, like the Rambam, that there is a uniform sense of *teshuva*, or, like Rabbeinu Yona, that differentiation is critical in order to engage in *teshuva* properly? If the latter, what kind of differentiation do we have in mind, and what kind of categories can we think of?

SINS AGAINST GOD AND AGAINST MAN

Let us start with the familiar distinction between *aveirot bein adam la-Makom*, sins a person commits against God, and *aveirot bein adam le-chavero*, interpersonal sins. The *Mishna* at the end of *Yoma* (8:9) speaks of the need to attain forgiveness from the person one sinned against in order for Yom Kippur to atone for an interpersonal sin, whereas with regard to *aveirot bein adam la-Makom*, it is sufficient if someone makes his peace, as it were, with the Almighty. This distinction can be variously understood.

In a pragmatic sense, the Rosh (*Yoma* 8:17) and others say that interpersonal sins undermine the solidarity of *Klal Yisrael*. If this is the case, then interpersonal forgiveness is valuable in its own right, but is not directly related to the quality of the *teshuva* involved. Rather, in addition to the person repenting, something else can be attained – Jewish unity.

The *Gemara* in *Rosh Ha-shana* (17b) suggests a different explanation:

> Beloria the convert once asked Rabban Gamliel: "It is written in your Torah [that God] 'does not show favor' (*Devarim* 10:17). Yet it is also written, 'May God show favor to you' (*Bemidbar* 6:26)!"

1. See the chapter "*Teshuva*: Impetus and Motive" for elaboration on this idea, at the end of the subsection "Two Tracks of *Teshuva*: Moral and Religious" and in footnote 6 there.

> R. Yosei Ha-kohen joined the conversation and said to her, "I will give you a parable that will illustrate the matter. A man lent his neighbor an amount of money and fixed a time for payment in the presence of the king, while the other swore to pay him by the life of the king. When the time arrived, he did not pay him, and he went to excuse himself to the king. The king, however, said to him, '[For] the wrong done to me I excuse you, but go and obtain forgiveness from your neighbor.' So, too, here: one verse speaks of offences committed by man against God, and the other of offences committed by man against his fellow man."

With regard to our transgressions that are *bein adam la-Makom,* God is willing to shower His grace upon us. However, forgiveness for *aveirot bein adam le-chavero* is not up to God. The reason one must placate the other person is that God is not the proper address; you have to pay the person from whom you borrowed or placate the person against whom you transgressed.

Perhaps the most obvious interpretation is that without placating the other person, there is a problem with the quality of your *teshuva.* The most basic premise of *teshuva* is *azivat ha-chet,* abandoning the sin. If one does not do this, it is like plunging into a *mikve* while gripping a continuous source of impurity. With regard to *aveirot bein adam la-Makom,* one confesses to God, and that constitutes abandonment of the sin. But if a person has offended another and has not taken pains to placate him, then the offense is continuing; it is a festering sore. That being the case, the *teshuva* is inadequate to attain the communal atonement offered by Yom Kippur, because one has not repented properly.

INTENTION AND MITIGATING CIRCUMSTANCES

Apart from the classification of *mitzvot* and, consequently, transgressions, there are additional factors that affect the quality of a transgression. The *Gemara* in *Yoma* (36b) speaks about the multiple confession of "*chatati, aviti, pashati,*" which distinguishes between different levels of rebelliousness. Though the Rabbis and Rabbi Meir disagree regarding the sequence and the interpretation of this confession, they agree that one should distinguish between sins committed rebelliously, sins committed willfully but not out of a sense of rebellion, and sins committed through carelessness.

Similarly, in other contexts a contrast is drawn between transgressions done *le-hakh'is*, to spite God, and those done *le-te'avon*, to quench a desire. If a person commits a sin in order to anger God or rebel against Him, then, apart from the particular sin, he also transgresses the prohibition of *chillul Hashem*, desecration of God's name (see Rambam, *Hilkhot Yesodei Ha-Torah* 5:10). But if a person is impelled by appetite, not rebellion, then, although his sin may be intentional, it is not committed out of a desire to fight God, but rather out of weakness of the flesh, and is consequently less severe.

In addition to these factors, there is the question of habituation. In certain contexts, if a person commits a sin repeatedly, the punishment is commensurate.

Then there is the matter of mitigating circumstances. *Chazal*, by and large, did not take the view of many modern penologists, criminologists, sociologists, and psychologists that somehow everything can be ascribed to nurture or nature, and that, to a great extent, one can be divested of personal responsibility. The sense of personal responsibility and liability is central for us, and it is related to our faith in humanity, our belief in free will, and our conviction in a person's ability to act if he so desires. Nonetheless, there is some recognition of circumstances that can promote certain actions or mitigate particular transgressions. The *Gemara* in *Berakhot* (32a) offers the example of a father who grooms his son and leaves him with a purse of money in front of a brothel. In such circumstances, the sin is much harder to avoid than under normal conditions.

SEVERITY OF THE ACT

Beyond all this, we have the distinction, addressed by Rabbeinu Yona, between different levels of severity of the transgression itself, differentiating between *kallot*, lighter infractions, and *chamurot*, more severe sins. The *Gemara* in *Yoma* (83a) says that if a person is suddenly seized on Yom Kippur with a consuming passion to eat, and that otherwise his health will be in danger, then you must feed him. But what do you feed him if no kosher food is available? You feed him whatever constitutes a lesser degree of transgression. For instance, if you have *tevel*, untithed produce, or a *neveila*, an animal that died without proper slaughtering, you feed him the latter, because eating it violates a prohibition punishable by lashes, while the former prohibition entails death at the hands of Heaven. The *sugya* goes on to elaborate what is more severe and less severe, and Rabbeinu Yona expands upon this.

This kind of "*kallot* and *chamurot*" refers to different gradations along the same continuum, but other distinctions exist as well. For example, within the realm of prohibitions, there are those punished by lashes and those punished by death. Nevertheless, the Rambam (*Hilkhot Teshuva* 1:2) describes the sin of taking a false oath as being among the *chamurot*, even though it is only punished with lashes, because it entails the desecration of God's name. Similarly, some positive precepts are singled out as being particularly weighty, as in the statement, "The mitzva of *tzitzit* is equivalent to the entire Torah" (*Nedarim* 25a, *Shevuot* 29a). To take another example, the Rambam (*Hilkhot Mattenot Aniyyim* 10:1) says that a person needs to observe the mitzva of *tzedaka*, charity, more than any other positive commandment. And he also describes redemption of captives as a "*mitzva rabba*," a great mitzva (*Hilkhot Mattenot Aniyyim* 8:10).

Yet there is another kind of distinction between *kallot* and *chamurot*. The *Mishna* in *Yoma* (85b) teaches:

> The sin offering and the guilt offering [for the] undoubted commission of certain offenses procure atonement.
>
> Death and the Day of Atonement procure atonement together with repentance.
>
> Repentance [by itself] procures atonement for lighter transgressions (*kallot*): [the failure to fulfill] positive *mitzvot* and [the violation of] prohibitions.
>
> In the case of more severe transgressions (*chamurot*), repentance suspends [the divine punishment], until the Day of Atonement comes to procure atonement.

The *Gemara* (*Yoma* 86a), the *Mekhilta* (*Yitro, Ba-chodesh*, 7), and the *Yerushalmi* (*Yoma* 8:7 and elsewhere) cite the famous classification of *chilukei kappara*, levels of atonement:

> R. Mattia ben Charash asked R. Elazar ben Azarya in Rome: Have you heard about the four kinds of sins, concerning which R. Yishmael has lectured?
>
> He answered: They are three, and repentance is connected with each. If one transgressed a positive commandment, and repented, then he is forgiven on the spot…
>
> If he has transgressed a prohibition and repented, then repentance suspends [the punishment] and the Day of Atonement procures atonement…
>
> If he has committed [a sin to be punished with] excision or death at the hands of the court, and repented, then repentance and the Day of Atonement suspend [the punishment], and suffering finishes the atonement…
>
> But if he has been guilty of the profanation of God's name, then penitence has no power to suspend punishment, nor the Day of Atonement to procure atonement, nor suffering to finish it, but all of them together suspend the punishment and only death finishes it…

The Rambam (*Hilkhot Teshuva* 1:2) cites this *gemara*, stating that the scapegoat sent to the wilderness provides atonement for all sins accompanied by repentance; but if one does not repent, the scapegoat provides atonement only for *kallot*. He then provides a definition of *kallot* and *chamurot*:

> Which are the light sins, and which are the severe ones? The severe sins are those for which one is liable for execution by the court or for *karet* (excision). False and unnecessary oaths are also considered severe sins, even though they are not [punished by] *karet*. [The violation of] the other prohibitions, and [the failure to perform] positive commandments that are not punishable by *karet* are considered light [sins].

The Rambam explains that *chamurot* are sins punished by *karet* or death, and false oaths, which entail a *chillul Hashem*; *kallot* are all other sins. There is not a continuum of sin, but rather two groups starkly separated in terms of atonement. The group of *kallot* achieves atonement by means of the scapegoat alone, even without repentance; and where there is repentance, *kallot* receive atonement immediately, while *chamurot* must wait.

Are we to regard *kallot* and *chamurot* as fundamentally different categories, as would seem implicit in the *Mishna* and in the Rambam's statement, or as different points along a spectrum of severity, along the lines of the *Gemara* (*Yoma* 83a) that distinguishes between the different foods to feed someone on Yom Kippur? We can get guidance on this from a striking statement of the Ramban.

RAMBAN: TWO ELEMENTS OF ATONEMENT

Regarding a person who brings a *korban ola*, a freewill offering wholly burnt on the altar, a verse (*Vayikra* 1:4) states, "*Ve-nirtza lo le-khapper alav*, It shall be favorably accepted, to atone for him." *Chazal* ask: we know for which sins a *chatat* (sin offering) or *asham* (guilt offering) atone, but for which sins does an *ola* atone? Rashi (*ad loc.*) quotes the answer found in *Torat Kohanim* (*Nedava, parasha* 3, 4:8):

> For what kind of sins does [the freewill burnt offering] effect atonement? Should you say, for sins [where the punishment if willfully committed] is excision, or any of the [four] deaths imposed by a court, or death at the hands of Heaven, or lashes, [this is difficult, as] the punishment for all these sins is already stated, [and atonement is effected by those punishments, and not by this offering]! You must conclude that [the freewill burnt offering] effects atonement only for transgressions of a positive mitzva, and for the violation of a prohibition that is juxtaposed to a positive mitzva.

The Ramban (*ad loc.*) explains why *Chazal* were motivated to give this explanation. Regarding capital crimes and sins entailing *karet*, the Torah specified the punishments for willful commission and the sacrifices brought for unintentional commission. But the Torah does not mention that any sacrifice needs to be brought for unintentional commission of certain sins: those punishable by lashes or by death at the hands of Heaven if committed willfully. On the surface, it does not make sense for the Torah to mention the punishments for willful and unintentional commission of some sins, and the punishment only for willful commission of other sins. Therefore, the Ramban concludes that, regarding the latter category of sins, "there is no burden of sin at all if they are committed unintentionally, and they do not need any atonement." Finally, there is a third category, for which the Torah mentions no punishment even for willful commission. This category includes transgression of a positive mitzva and violation of a prohibition juxtaposed to a positive mitzva. Since it is impossible that no atonement is needed for willful commission of these sins, *Chazal* conclude that the freewill burnt offering atones for these.

The Ramban himself goes beyond this approach:

> It is possible to say that because in the case of the freewill offering, [God] did not use the expression "to make atonement for him concerning the error which he committed," as He said with reference to the offering brought for other sins committed unintentionally (*Vayikra* 5:18), and instead He said, "it shall be favorably accepted," it appeared to our Rabbis that [the burnt offering] effects atonement for those who willfully commit certain sins, seeing that these persons are not [hitherto] "favorably accepted" by Him. For he who commits a sin unintentionally is yet, in spite of the sin, considered "favorably accepted" by God. If, then, [the burnt offering procures atonement for willful sinners,] it must refer to those who willfully transgress a positive mitzva or a prohibition that is juxtaposed to a positive mitzva. For regarding these transgressions, no punishment is mentioned in the Torah; yet those who violate them are not pleasing to God, because they have violated His commandment. How, then, shall these people become favorably accepted by their Master? By bringing this gift [i.e., the freewill burnt offering].

In other words, if a person sins in error, he is nevertheless favored by God (*retzui Hashem*); but if he sins intentionally, he is not favored. Therefore, the verse "it shall be favorably accepted (*ve-nirtza lo*)" cannot refer to sin committed in error, for such a person is *retzui Hashem* even without bringing an offering. The verse must, then, refer to one who sins intentionally. Since we already know the punishments meted out to those who sin intentionally, it must be that the verse refers to an intentional sinner who receives no punishment but is nevertheless not favored by God, i.e., those who transgress a positive mitzva or a prohibition that is juxtaposed to a positive mitzva.

Ramban's comment is remarkable in two respects. First, it invites the obvious question which Rav Meir Dan Plotzki asked (*Keli Chemda, Vayetze* 38b): Are we to understand that someone who sins in error, unwittingly, is *retzui Hashem,* and that he does not require repentance or atonement? Second, we know that one must offer a sin offering if one unintentionally commits a sin that would be punished with *karet* if it were performed intentionally. But if we adopt what seems to be the Ramban's assumption, that an unintentional sinner does not require atonement because he is *retzui Hashem,* then why does someone who unintentionally transgresses a sin punishable by *karet* have to bring a sin offering? Isn't he *retzui Hashem*?

We can suggest two explanations for the Ramban's comment. One is that the second question answers the first. The extent to which we would say that negligence renders one culpable depends on how serious the infraction is. If it is a relatively minor matter, so that even if done willfully it isn't much of a sin, then it can be overlooked if it is done through negligence. Yet a graver infraction entails a greater degree of responsibility and culpability, and one would not be considered *retzui Hashem* if he committed these acts unintentionally.

I believe we can offer another explanation if we take into account a different purpose of the sacrifice, apart from its function in regaining divine favor for the sinner. The Ramban draws a sharp line between *kallot* and *chamurot.* When one unintentionally commits an ordinary prohibition, it does not require atonement. But severe prohibitions, which would require *karet* or death if committed intentionally, require atonement even when one commits them unintentionally. This distinction has important implications.

With regard to *kallot,* i.e., ordinary prohibitions, the seriousness of the transgression has less to do with the nature of the deed than with the character of the person who is sinning. In his willful confrontation with the Almighty, he chose to prioritize his own desire over God's. Leaving aside certain moral considerations, it is not the deed that needs to be redeemed, but the person. Consequently, if the person has not been pervaded by sinful desire but rather committed the deed in error, he himself does not require redemption, and he remains a *retzui Hashem*. However, with regard to *chamurot*, i.e., severe prohibitions, it is not only the person who requires redemption; the event needs to be redeemed, and the world within which that sin has been committed needs to be redeemed.

We need, therefore, to consider the nature of *teshuva* in two separate contexts. In *teshuva* for *aveirot kallot*, what is critical and central is the redemption and purgation of the self. With regard to *chamurot*, however, it is not sufficient that a person repent and thereby regain the status of *retzui Hashem*; rather, a sacrificial offering is required to cleanse the social and metaphysical orders of the consequences of that sin. The quality of an *aveira chamura* is that it defiles. Therefore, this defilement needs to be confronted. The *teshuva* of *chamurot* needs to incorporate both one's personal redemption and the righting of that which one has defiled.

NULLIFYING OUR WILL BEFORE GOD'S

Coming back to our original question of the Rambam's approach versus Rabbeinu Yona's, are we to think of sin as a uniform phenomenon, or are we to differentiate and classify categories and circumstances of sin? This question applies to divine service generally and *teshuva* particularly. I think the answer is clear: we need both Rambam's formulation and Rabbeinu Yona's.

On the one hand, there is a common denominator to all sins, and we need to confront this if we want to improve ourselves. Every time a person fails in the realm of Torah, Halakha, and morality, he stands before the question of what kind of person he is and what kind of life he leads. Does he give preference to his own will or to God's? Does he think in egocentric or theocentric terms? Every time a person is confronted by God's will, Prospero's question arises: "My foot, my tutor?" (*The Tempest*, Act 1, Scene 2); will he be led by his head or by his foot?

At this plane, when one considers the question of nullifying one's will before God's (see *Avot* 2:4), the differentiations of *kallot* and *chamurot* fall away. All sins, in this sense, are severe. In his *Life of Solon* (XVII, 4),

Plutarch writes: "Draco himself, when asked why he had decreed the death penalty for the great majority of offenses, replied that he considered that the minor ones deserved it, and for the major ones no heavier punishment was left." There is substance to this approach. The *Yerushalmi* (*Makkot* 2:6) recounts, "Prophecy was asked, 'A sinner – what is his punishment?' It answered, 'The soul that sins shall die' (*Yechezkel* 18:4, 20)." No question is raised as to which sin it was, whether major or minor, *kallot* or *chamurot*. If a person sheds the role of *metzuveh*, one who is commanded, and instead usurps the role of *metzaveh*, commander, that is the ultimate rebellion! Though sometimes the severity is mitigated by circumstances and some sins are committed through weakness rather than rebellion, nevertheless, the bottom line is one gave preference to one's own will over the Almighty's.

In this sense, when a person confronts not just a particular *aveira* but the critical existential question of whose will is to prevail, his or God's, the proper confession is simply to recognize one's rebelliousness: "*Chatati, aviti, pashati lefanekha*!" I was rebellious before You on several levels; I stood before You, I was at that juncture, and I took the wrong turn. This is one aspect of *teshuva*.

DETAIL AND RELATIONSHIP

But it is not the only one. *Teshuva* entails a plethora of aspects because sin is multifaceted. At least five different aspects of sin can be singled out. One is the wrong *per se*, the choice of doing evil. Second is the fact that the evil a person has done transgresses the will of God; over and above murder being murder, it is also something which God has proscribed. Third, one must consider the ramifications of sin, the contamination of the self and the impurity. Fourth, defying God's will is a "personal" affront to Him; it is spitting in His face, so to speak. That being the case, there is a fifth result: one's relationship to God has been impaired. Sin opens a chasm or sets up a barrier between oneself and the Almighty. "Your iniquities have been a barrier between you and your God" (*Yeshayahu* 59:2).

If a person wants to engage in *teshuva*, he needs to relate to all these elements and effect a *tikkun* (repair) in each. There needs to be a *tikkun ha-chet* (repair of the sin), a *tikkun* of one's relationship with God, and a *tikkun* of the self. Each of these three types of *tikkun* should be examined independently, and in order to do so, we need to distinguish between two veins of *teshuva*: *teshuva* "from" and *teshuva* "to." The former is exemplified by the verses, "Turn, turn from your evil ways" (*Yechezkel* 33:11), and "Let the wicked one forsake his way, and the iniquitous man his thoughts" (*Yeshayahu* 55:7). The latter is exemplified by verses that discuss not what a person is leaving, but where he is headed: "Return to Me, and I will return to you" (*Malakhi* 3:7), and "Return, Israel, to the Lord your God" (*Hoshea* 14:2).

Tikkun ha-chet is a matter of "turn[ing] from your evil ways." As such, one must consider, along the lines of Rabbeinu Yona, the gravity and specifics of his sin, and, as Ramban implied, how to repair the damage that the sin brought upon the world. This requires great attention to detail.

There are religious traditions and schools of thought that not only neglect attention to detail, but even scorn it. The Lutheran tradition, for example, believes that one is so suffused with sin that the only thing to do is to try to make peace with God, whether actively or passively, waiting for divine grace or seeking it. But acting to fix minor or major failings is not relevant. Some call this a "religious," as opposed to a "moral," view of divine service, where "religious" refers to focusing upon one's relationship with God, and "moral" refers to the righting of wrongs. If one adopts this focus, then indeed one does not need to differentiate among sins. Neither the quality nor the quantity of sin is as important as the existence of a barrier between God and oneself, and one must focus on transcending that barrier, pleading for grace, throwing oneself at God's mercy.

There is something to be said for an approach that does not content itself solely with picking up the pieces, with trying to adjust and repair, but rather seeks rehabilitation by establishing anew a bridge to the Almighty, a bridge allowing one to find his way to God and enabling God to come to him. Yet, though we understand that one cannot focus *solely* on detail in our divine service generally, and in *teshuva* particularly, surely we believe that there is a "moral" element of *teshuva* and of divine service, a need to right the wrong and terminate its perpetuation. Our whole conception of divine service, *avodat Hashem*, rests upon two pillars: one is awareness of the overpowering importance of our relationship with God, as in the verses, "But as for me, the nearness of God is my good" (*Tehillim* 73:28), and "As the hart yearns for water brooks, so my soul yearns for You, O God" (*Tehillim* 42:2). The other pillar is attention to a disciplined life and its minute details, which suffuses the world of Halakha.

We reject totally the view that when one pursues the overarching relationship and the quest for intimacy and rehabilitation, all of the minutiae simply disappear into insignificance. On the other hand, we also reject the view that the specific actions and details will suffice. We do not – we dare not – focus exclusively on one of these two pillars. Our world is built in a multifaceted and multi-planed way by relating to and integrating both aspects. The ability to relate to God is the most fundamental and basic aspect of human existence, and also its overarching, ultimate, beatific attainment. At the same time, the attention to the detail of every *halakha,* and the ability to integrate the poetry and the prose of *avodat Hashem,* is central to our conception and our experience.

This dual focus is, consequently, central to our view of *teshuva,* and can lead us to a different way of distinguishing between *kallot* and *chamurot*: not as signifying types of sin, but rather as signifying different approaches to *teshuva.* The *teshuva* of *chamurot,* which concentrates on actions and the desire to right them, requires that we weigh, grade, and prioritize. The *teshuva* of *kallot,* which concentrates not on what we have done but on trying to reestablish our relationship with God, allows a focus on overarching goals, expressed in universal categories and uniform *viddui.*

While *tikkun ha-chet* and *tikkun* of one's damaged relationship with God are characterized by different approaches to *teshuva* – the *chamurot* mode and the *kallot* mode, respectively – the two approaches interact and coalesce in the third element of repair, namely, *tikkun* of the self, which has been contaminated by sin. To repair and purify oneself means to reaffirm and reestablish one's relationship with God, as well as to engage in a spiritual and moral purgation that takes into account actions and details.

TWO CONFESSIONS

Historically, we encounter two types of confession. The *Gemara* in *Yoma* (87b) speaks of various formulae of *viddui* stated by a number of *Amoraim*, and then adds:

> Mar Zutra said: [The preceding confessions are necessary] only if he did not say, "*Aval anachnu chatanu,* But we have sinned." But if he said "*Aval anachnu chatanu,*" no more is necessary. As Bar Hamdudi said, Once I stood before Shemuel, who was sitting, and when the prayer leader came up and said "*Aval anachnu chatanu,*" he rose. We learn from here that those words are the quintessential *viddui.*

Aval anachnu chatanu: simple, uniform, undifferentiated confession. It is simply an acknowledgment, with bowed head, with shame and guilt, that we have gone astray. Whether our sin is minor or major, it is still a sin: "But we have sinned."

Today, however, we have expanded this simple confession into an entire *alef-beit* of sin: *ashamnu, bagadnu, gazalnu,* etc. The *Ge'onim* added even more: a double *alef-beit* of *Al Chet,* concluding with a list of sins categorized according to the gravity of their punishment: "sins punishable by the court, sins punishable by *karet,*" etc. And if that isn't enough, some people have taken each line of *Al Chet* and elaborated much further. The Rambam's *viddui* was enough for the *Gemara,* but Rabbeinu Yona's *viddui* entered the mainstream of our life and our experience on Yom Kippur.

Yet that experience on Yom Kippur is itself differentiated. Broadly speaking, we stand on Yom Kippur with a dual charge. We stand with the Rambam, trying to eradicate the roots of sin, to eliminate the tendency and desire for sin. Reciting the confession of *aval anachnu chatanu,* we confront where we are and where the Almighty is, and try to reach out to Him, hoping that He will reach out to us. At the same time, we stand with Rabbeinu Yona in following the advice of *Eikha* (3:40), "Let us search and examine our ways." Detailing our sins one after another, we examine what we have done and how we have done it, weighing the severity of each transgression, so that we know not just whether we are sinners, but exactly what kind of sinners we are. On Yom Kippur, we engage in a highly religious enterprise and a highly moral enterprise; that is Yom Kippur as a whole.

But at the end of the day, when we come to *Ne'ila*, we change our tune a bit. In the first four prayer services of Yom Kippur, we say *aval anachnu chatanu* and then go through the whole list of *Al Chet*. However, as dusk approaches, when the conclusion of the day and its atonement is on the horizon, we turn to God and say: Master of the Universe, we have been working on ourselves all year and especially since the beginning of Elul, weighing and measuring our sins, and all of Yom Kippur we have been striving and groping and hoping. But now, at the end of the day, we have only one thing left, and that is to cast our hopes and prayers upon You. We look to You after we have gone the extra mile, and maybe it isn't enough. Now it is too late in the day, and we cannot involve ourselves again in this calculus, identifying and grading sins, pinning down each one. Now it is our very selves encountering You, and we implore You, we beg for Your forgiveness, for *selicha, mechila, kappara*!

At *Ne'ila*, we do not say *Al Chet*. We content ourselves with saying *Aval anachnu chatanu*, followed by *Ashamnu*. We do so in the hope that what we have done over the course of the year, what we have done during Elul, during *Selichot*, during *Aseret Yemei Teshuva*, during the first four prayers of Yom Kippur – following Rabbeinu Yona, trying to right wrongs as best as we could, trying to examine and to inquire – makes us worthy and deserving of forgiveness. But now we look for something more: for *tahara*, purification, to fulfill the verse, "*Lifnei Hashem tit'haru*, You shall be purified before the Lord" (*Vayikra* 16:30).

This purification has a dual character. When a person is purified in a *mikve*, each part of him is immersed in the *mikve*, and the whole of him is immersed in the *mikve*. Similarly, on Yom Kippur we strive for both types of purification. There is the type that comes from moral purgation, from the confrontation with sin, from the attempt to eradicate and overcome it. This is an aspect of *tikkun atzmi*, self-correction, and of *tikkun ha-chet*. We also strive for the purification of "*Mikve Yisrael Hashem*" (*Yirmiyahu* 17:13), translated homiletically as "The Lord is the *mikve* of Israel." This second type of purification refers to our rehabilitation and to the reestablishment of our relationship with God, which springs not solely from below, but also from above.

"*Lifnei Hashem tit'haru,*" Rabbeinu Yona said, means that there is a special mitzva to repent on Yom Kippur (*Sha'arei Teshuva* 4:17). Here we encounter purification as a charge, a mandate, which entails examining and investigating our ways; this is the specific and detailed aspect of *teshuva*. Yet "*Lifnei Hashem tit'haru*" is also to be understood as an aspiration and a promise that if we have confronted "*mi-kol chatoteikhem,*" all our sins, then God, for His part, will proclaim, "*Tit'haru,* You shall be purified!"

Mediocre *Teshuva* and the *Teshuva* of the Mediocre

TESHUVA FOR THE FEW AND *TESHUVA* FOR THE MANY

The concept of *teshuva* encompasses two seemingly contradictory aspects. On the one hand, when *teshuva* is successfully completed, it can have an elitist tinge. As *Chazal* say, "In the place where *ba'alei teshuva* (penitents) stand, even the completely righteous cannot stand" (*Berakhot* 34b, *Sanhedrin* 99a). In this respect, *ba'alei teshuva* constitute a sort of spiritual aristocracy. And as *Chazal* say elsewhere, "I have seen the sons of Heaven," those who will bask in the Divine Presence in the World-to-Come, "and they are but few" (*Sukka* 45b). Presumably *ba'alei teshuva* are among these "sons of Heaven," few though they are.

On the other hand, *teshuva* has a very democratic, exoteric cast. It is necessary for all, as Kohelet declares, "For there is no man who is wholly righteous on earth, who shall do only good and not sin" (*Kohelet* 7:20), and it is also accessible to all.

Chazal highlight a number of historical figures and events from the Bible in order to convey the message of the universality of *teshuva*. The *Gemara* (*Sanhedrin* 103a–b) presents different views on how to evaluate

Delivered as the Hausman/Stern *Kinnus Teshuva* lecture at the Gruss Institute in Jerusalem, Tishrei 5764 (2003).

the character of Menashe, the son of Chizkiyahu. Some consider him so dastardly that they include him in the short list of people who have no share in the World-to-Come. Others base their assessment on the account in II *Divrei Ha-yamim* 33:12–19, which describes how, toward the end of his days, Menashe began to pray to God in his time of crisis. In light of this, one view in that *gemara* states, "He who asserts that Menashe has no portion in the World-to-Come weakens the hands [i.e., the resolve] of *ba'alei teshuva*" (103a). In an even more daring statement, the *Gemara* (*Avoda Zara* 4b–5a) posits that from a certain ideal perspective the story of David and Bat-Sheva was not meant to occur. Neither he nor she was originally destined for that kind of an encounter, and yet God caused the encounter to occur in order to establish a model of *teshuva* for all.

What is the nature of this model? First, there is a clear connection of cause and effect between *teshuva* and forgiveness. But beyond forgiveness, *teshuva* represents a leveling element. The Rambam stresses that because everyone has free will, *teshuva* imposes an obligation on all and provides an opportunity to all:

> Since free choice is granted to all people, as explained, a person should always strive to do *teshuva* and to confess verbally for his sins, striving to cleanse his hands from his sins in order that he may die as one who has performed *teshuva*[1] and [thereby] merit the life of the World-to-Come. (*Hilkhot Teshuva* 7:1)

Since *teshuva* is centrally important, the goal of attaining the status of "one who has performed *teshuva*" and thereby merits "the life of the World-to-Come" is not limited to a particular class or group, nor to those who are outstanding or deviant in some respect. It is a universal goal.[2]

1. Although the Rambam uses the term *ba'al teshuva* here, he is using it differently from the way it is used in our nomenclature. Today, a *ba'al teshuva* is one who was previously not committed to Torah and *mitzvot*, but then repented, adopting a life of commitment to those ideals. By contrast, the Rambam's *ba'al teshuva* is one who was committed all along to Torah and *mitzvot* but would sin on occasion, and who then sought to perfect himself by engaging in *teshuva*.
2. For the Rambam, the goal is universal in the broadest sense of the term, as he states, "free choice is granted to all people," but for our purposes we will confine ourselves to universality within the Jewish people.

Thus on the one hand, *teshuva* rings of aristocracy, and, on the other hand, it is characterized as comprehensive, universal, and even democratic. It is to this duality that we will relate, particularly with regard to the relationship of *teshuva* to mediocrity. While the word "mediocrity" has a very pallid ring, if not an outright negative one, the equivalent word *beinoniyut* as it is used in *Chazal* and in traditional Jewish literature seems to have no such connotation. In fact, as the point of departure of his seminal work, the *Tanya,* Rav Schneur Zalman of Liadi quotes a *baraita* that discusses the fate of a *beinoni,* a mediocre person (*Nidda* 30b). He goes on to quote a *gemara* in which one of the greatest of the *Amoraim* cites himself as an example of a *beinoni* (*Berakhot* 60b). Despite this, for our purposes, we will assume that a *beinoni* is no more than what the literal meaning of the word suggests: a middling, mediocre person.

It is particularly important to focus on the fate and the destiny of the *beinoni* during the Ten Days of Repentance. The *Gemara* says:

> Three books are opened in Heaven on Rosh Ha-shana, one for the thoroughly wicked, one for the thoroughly righteous, and one for the *beinoni.* The thoroughly righteous are inscribed definitively in the book of life; the thoroughly wicked are inscribed definitively in the book of death; the *beinonim* remain suspended until Yom Kippur. If they merit, they are inscribed for life; if they do not so merit, they are inscribed for death. (*Rosh Ha-shana* 16b)

According to this passage, the Ten Days of Repentance, the days of "Seek out the Lord when He may be found; call upon Him when He is near" (*Yeshayahu* 55:6), represent the hour of decision for the *beinoni.* The obvious issues raised by this classification by righteousness notwithstanding,[3]

3. Do we indeed observe empirically that all the righteous, having been written positively on Rosh Ha-shana, survive the upcoming year? Do all the wicked die in the course of the upcoming year? The *Gemara*'s dichotomy does not seem to be borne out in reality. Furthermore, the Rambam (*Hilkhot Teshuva* 3:1) defines a *beinoni* as a person who is in a position of exact equipoise. If he is mostly wicked, he is a *rasha*; if he is mostly righteous, he is a *tzaddik*. One good deed or one sin can tip the scales in either direction; a *beinoni* is exactly in the middle. This strikes us as a difficult idea, and we question: who is exactly in the middle? The Rambam seems somewhat troubled by these issues in his presentation at the

we observe here an awareness of the significance of *teshuva* specifically during this holy period to the average people, the *beinonim,* who "remain suspended" from Rosh Ha-shana until Yom Kippur. As presumably all of us are among the *beinonim,* this subject is particularly relevant.

THE ELITISM OF PURITY

Let us begin our analysis with a text that does not relate directly to *teshuva,* but which still relates to the central issue of elitism versus democracy. In the sixteenth chapter of *Mesillat Yesharim,* the Ramchal, R. Moshe Chaim Luzzatto, opens with a discussion of the quality of *tahara* (purity): "Purity entails the reparation of one's heart and thoughts." He goes on to clarify that *tahara* is purity of action and motive, to the point that one's soul contains no impurity whatsoever that could serve to adulterate one's heart and thoughts. He says that if one engages in a fundamentally positive action – perhaps even a mitzva – but there is even the slightest aspect of impurity within one's motive or attitude, then one can no longer speak of that action as being characterized by *tahara.* "Thus," he continues, "even if the impure motive plays only an insignificant part, the action to which it leads can no longer be absolutely pure." The Ramchal then introduces an essential halakhic analogy:

> In the same way that a meal offering on the altar had to consist only of the finest flour that had been sifted thirteen times in order to remove from it all impurities (*Menachot* 76b), so should we offer on the altar of the divine will only the choicest deeds, wholly free from the slightest taint of impurity.
>
> I do not say that all conduct which falls short of this standard is to be entirely discountenanced. God withholds His deserts from no one, and rewards each deed according to its worth. But I speak of perfect worship which is expected from those who truly love the Lord. It can be called perfect only when it is pure and is rendered for no reason except that of serving God.

---

beginning of the third chapter of *Hilkhot Teshuva,* and the Ra'avad adamantly objects to his approach.

Purity, says the Ramchal, cannot be partial; it must be completely and utterly pure. Just as before a meal offering is brought to the altar it must be sifted thirteen times, ensuring that every impurity has been thoroughly removed, one must similarly achieve total purity in one's person and actions in order to attain the quality of *tahara*. The Ramchal does not go so far as to say that in the absence of this total purity a person or an action cannot be deemed virtuous. Indeed, every person is rewarded for his good deeds in a manner that is commensurate with the nature of those deeds; a small impurity in the motive behind a particular action certainly does not nullify it altogether. But according to the Ramchal, that person or action cannot be considered truly pure.

Before assessing this seemingly elitist approach to self-perfection, it is important to provide some background information regarding the context in which the Ramchal's statement appears. In the preface of *Mesillat Yesharim* the Ramchal cites a *baraita* brought by R. Pinchas ben Ya'ir, which presents a scale of qualities and values in ascending order:

> The knowledge of Torah leads to watchfulness, watchfulness to zeal, zeal to cleanliness, cleanliness to abstinence, abstinence to purity, purity to piety, piety to humility, humility to the fear of sin, and the fear of sin to holiness. (*Avoda Zara* 20b)

The Ramchal examines each of these qualities in order over the course of *Mesillat Yesharim*, defining its nature and character, outlining the modes of its implementation, and warning of possible obstacles in the way of achieving it.

Mesillat Yesharim can be divided into two parts. Roughly speaking, the first half addresses the qualities that one must possess in order to be what we may term a *tzaddik*. This requires following the law carefully; one must do what is expected of him and refrain from doing what he should not do. By contrast, the second half of the book is directed at one who aspires to be a *chassid* (pious person), defined by the Rambam as one who goes beyond the letter of the law in his deeds (*Hilkhot De'ot* 1:5). Thus, one can be defined as a *tzaddik* even if he is marked by a minor impurity, and even if he does not meet the spiritual standards that correspond to the physical *kashrut* standards of a meal offering. But *tahara* goes beyond the level of the *tzaddik*; it is a step on the way to becoming a *chassid*, a member of the spiritual elite. *Tahara* has no middle point, no spectrum; one is either pure or impure. The moment that the slightest imperfection exists, one has in effect missed the boat and cannot be regarded as a *tahor*.

One might very well be satisfied not to be among the elite, among those of whom the verse says, "Bring in My pious (*chassidai*), who made a covenant with Me over sacrifice!" (*Tehillim* 50:5). One might be content not to benefit from God's special protection attested to by the verse, "He guards the steps of His pious (*chassidav*)" (I *Shemuel* 2:9). One might be a fine person, an upstanding Jew, at peace with his exclusion from the select few *chassidim* in our midst. Nevertheless, the thrust of the elitism of the *chassid* is quite troubling, even depressing. Since one must be completely pure in order to be considered *tahor*, there are effectively no intermediate steps. This is an incredibly daunting prospect.

To some extent this notion is morally troubling as well. One might invest great effort in attempting to attain the level of *tahara*, only to slip up on some minor misdeed or impure intention, some peccadillo of thought or action. While this misstep may seem trifling, it is enough to disqualify one from the ranks of the pure. It is also distressing from a religious perspective, in terms of one's *avodat Hashem*, that this classification should be so rigorous; such rigid classification feels almost oppressive. Finally, the standard of perfection here is so high that it is likely to deter many people from pursuing *tahara* in the first place. They may reasonably argue that while *tahara* is attainable for the *Chafetz Chayim* and those of his stature, it is far beyond their own grasp.

It is entirely understandable that the kind of total purity that the Ramchal discusses here indeed exists in certain areas of *avodat Hashem*, and that such a standard is even necessary in those arenas. Even a minor blemish can render an item disqualified. A red heifer is halakhically invalid if it has even two hairs that are not red. An animal that has some minor scratch, such as a withered spot in the eye, is similarly invalid for sacrifice. Additionally, even when the high standards of blemishes do not apply – such as regarding bird offerings,[4]

4. A bird offering is invalidated only if a whole organ is missing, not if it has a less severe blemish.

wood for the altar, and meal offerings – there is still the ideal of being *tamim*, perfect: "They and their libations shall be perfect (*temimim*)" (*Bemidbar* 28:31).

In the physical world – in particular with regard to the standards of purity that apply in the Temple – this level of punctiliousness is certainly understandable.[5] But even in ordinary circumstances, can the same degree of rigor, the same in-or-out binary dichotomy truly apply at the human plane as well, particularly at the human spiritual plane? The saying goes that in certain contexts, "a miss is as good as a mile." But is that applicable in the spiritual world as well? And if so, just how high is the bar for entrance into the realm of *tahara*?

From a halakhic perspective, one who performs *tevila* (ritual immersion) is either *tahor* or *tamei*, with no status between the two. Either one's *tevila* is successful or it is not, whether this is due to a *chatzitza* (separation between the water and one's body) or for a different reason. Can we apply the same standard to the quest for *tahara* that R. Pinchas ben Ya'ir outlines, asserting that the slightest *chatzitza* disqualifies the total process and denudes it of significance or substance? The prospect of such a reality is frightening.

THE ELITISM OF *TESHUVA*

One special type of *tahara* is the purity that seekers of *teshuva* pursue as part of the process of atonement: "For on this day He shall atone for you to purify you of all your sins; you shall be purified before the Lord" (*Vayikra* 16:30). Does this level of *tahara* apply only to those who experience a perfect immersion, who have not only cast the *sheretz* (impure animal) out of their

5. There is also a suggestion that it can, in certain circumstances, be harmful. The *Gemara* (*Gittin* 56a) famously relates a story in which the fate of the Temple itself hinged upon R. Zekharia ben Avkulas' dogged adherence to this standard of purity. Certain people, in an attempt to sow discord between the Romans and the Jews, suggested that the emperor send a calf to the Jews to offer at the Temple in order to test their loyalty. A very minor blemish was inflicted on the calf, one that seemed insignificant to the Romans but which rendered the offering impure by halakhic standards. R. Zekharia ben Avkulas refused to compromise and allow the calf to be offered, infuriating the Romans and causing R. Yochanan to declare, "Through the scrupulousness of R. Zekharia ben Avkulas our House has been destroyed."

hand but who subsequently avoided any invalidating *chatzitza*? It seems inconceivable that they are the only ones who merit *tahara* on Yom Kippur.

Furthermore, if we indeed reach this conclusion, exalting and idealizing the process of *teshuva* and raising its demands to heights that are beyond the reach of the ordinary *beinoni*, there may be no greater way to weaken the resolve and determination of *ba'alei teshuva*. If one indeed asserts that *tahara* is the prerogative of the elect, and if there is indeed no middle ground between being blemished and unblemished, should the *beinoni* simply lower his spiritual standards, contenting himself with a middling spiritual life in general and a middling *teshuva* in particular? The idealization of elite *teshuva* can have an adverse effect on the *beinoni*, leading him not to intensify his spiritual effort, but to relax it.

To summarize the two problems raised by the idealization of *teshuva*: On the one hand, we are troubled that we cannot attain such a noble and grand ideal; on the other hand, we may resign ourselves to the understanding that if we cannot attain elite *teshuva*, we will lower our expectations and efforts, contenting ourselves with a low-key form of *teshuva*. While the Ramchal admits, regarding *tahara* at least, that even a lesser version of this quality is still virtuous and still rewarded, it belongs to a different plane and is of a different order.

IT IS NOT IN THE HEAVENS

In a sense, the solution to both problems lies in several verses from *parashat Nitzavim*:

> For this mitzva that I enjoin upon you today, it is not too hard for you, nor is it beyond reach. It is not in the heavens, that you should say, "Who among us can ascend to the heavens and take it for us and impart it to us, that we may do it?" Neither is it beyond the sea, that you should say, "Who among us can cross to the other side of the sea and take it for us and impart it to us, that we may do it?" For the matter is very close to you, in your mouth and in your heart, to do it. (*Devarim* 30:11–14)

What is this mitzva of which the Torah speaks? Commenting on the concluding verse, Rashi states that it refers not to one specific mitzva, but to the whole complex of *mitzvot*, the totality of the world of divine service (30:14, s.v. *ki karov elekha*). The Ramban, however, takes issue with this. After quoting Rashi, he says:

> The truth is that when it refers to the entire Torah, it says, "all the mitzva that I enjoin upon you today" (*Devarim* 8:1). But "this mitzva" refers to the aforementioned mitzva of *teshuva*, for the verses "You shall return in your heart" (30:1) and "You shall return to the Lord your God" (30:2) constitute the mitzva wherein He commands us to do so. And it is stated in the indicative mood [rather than the imperative] to suggest that it is a promise; this is something that will happen in the future. (30:11, s.v. *ve-ta'am*)

According to the Ramban, this verse refers specifically to *teshuva*, and it is *teshuva* that the Torah says here "is not too hard for you, nor is it beyond reach."

If we accept the Ramban's interpretation, what is the message of this passage? The content and the tone of the passage are, almost explicitly, intended to be reassuring. Don't be concerned that attaining *teshuva* will be too difficult. On the contrary, it is "close to you"; you will manage. And yet, alongside the reassurance, the message is also very demanding.

First, the passage anticipates the inevitable rationalization of the *beinoni*, rejecting it out of hand. The *beinoni* may feel that although he would like to learn Torah, pray with better focus, and engage in spiritual regeneration, he is simply unable. It's too hard, beyond his powers. He wasn't raised in the proper home; he didn't receive the proper education; he doesn't live in the right kind of society; he doesn't have the necessary intellectual or moral powers – he just can't do it. Invoking the principle that "the Torah exempts in a case of compulsion" (*Bava Kama* 28b), the *beinoni* claims that more or better could not possibly be expected of him; it is beyond his ken. Anticipating this response, the Torah insists that the *beinoni* persevere nonetheless. Thus, when the Torah says not to worry, since *teshuva* is within a person's reach, this is not just a form of reassurance, a way of giving psychological support. There is a demand that accompanies the reassurance, namely, that there is no room to rationalize that achieving *teshuva* is impossible. No matter how mediocre a person may be, the Torah avers, *teshuva* is always within one's reach.

There is also an additional dimension to the Torah's demand here. Reading between the lines of the verses, *Chazal* perceived a second message that is both implicit and possibly contradictory:

> What is the significance of the text: "It is not in the heavens… neither is it beyond the sea"? "It is not in the heavens" [indicates] that if it were in the heavens, you would have to ascend after it, and if it were beyond the sea, you would have to cross after it. (*Eruvin* 55a)

Contrary to the literal meaning of the verse, which implies that theoretically one would be exempt from *teshuva* if it were beyond one's abilities, this passage indicates that there is no excuse for not pursuing *teshuva* – even if it is "in the heavens" or "beyond the sea." In light of this understanding, the verse constitutes a factual statement that carries with it both an element of reassurance and a persistent and total demand. If it is in the heavens, you must strap on a parachute and retrieve it. If it is beyond the sea, you must likewise go to the necessary lengths to reach the goals that the Torah has set forth.

What we previously understood as a very reassuring passage in the Torah is now, in light of the interpretation in *Eruvin*, extremely and powerfully demanding. In this reading, the manifest thrust of the verses is that difficulty is no excuse – not with respect to observing the *mitzvot* generally, and not, in light of the Ramban's interpretation, with respect to *teshuva*. We are told, on the one hand, that the limited spiritual talents of the *beinoni* are sufficient to achieve a satisfactory level of *teshuva* from the Torah's point of view. *Teshuva* is attainable. Will it be perfect? Will it compare to the *teshuva* of the *Chafetz Chayim*? Certainly not. But the *teshuva* of the *beinoni* is also a form of *avodat Hashem*. God accepts this kind of *teshuva* as well, and it too has religious and spiritual significance. But the concurrent message is that one must do all that one can, exerting all the effort at one's disposal, harnessing all of one's energies and all of one's capacities in order to attain the noblest religious end. If we read these two messages together, they assert that we may be granted a compassionate discount with regard to accomplishment and attainment – God will be satisfied with whatever you are able to achieve – but not with regard to effort and exertion. We are not held responsible for our output, but we are strictly accountable for our input.

THE ETHOS OF EFFORT IN THE TORAH

In contrast to certain foreign religious orientations that are wholly subjective, Halakha is a system in which objective elements count for a great deal. But by encouraging us to try our hardest to reach the highest level of *teshuva*, the Torah here seems to promote an ethos of effort within this highly objective system. This has great subjective significance. Suppose one tries and cannot reach the heavens or beyond the sea. The Torah insists that one's effort was not for naught; on the contrary, it had a great deal of meaning. This ethos is central to our perception of the spiritual world.

Chazal maintained that the ethos of effort and intent partly reflects certain details of Halakha at the level of *ta'amei ha-mitzvot* (reasons for the commandments). The final *mishna* in *Menachot* points out that the phrase "a sweet savor (*rei'ach nicho'ach*)" appears in the Torah with regard to various gradations of offerings, including those of cattle, birds, and flour. Objectively, these types of offerings differ significantly from one another in a number of ways, not least in terms of the financial sacrifice made by the person bringing the offering. But the Torah uses the same phrase for each offering to communicate the message that "It is the same whether one offers much or little, so long as he directs his heart to Heaven" (*Menachot* 110a). While this is not to suggest that one may relate to religious observance in a completely subjective manner, there is, at the very least, a recognition of the value of effort, irrespective of results.[6]

6. Of course, one may not simply invoke the principle that "God desires the heart" (*Sanhedrin* 106b) and imagine that having one's heart in the right place is sufficient. It is certainly not immaterial whether one does more or does less when serving God. In discussing the relationship between Torah scholars and laymen, the *Gemara* (*Berakhot* 17a) states that a Torah scholar should not be haughty because he sits in the *beit midrash* and the other person sits at his job. And yet, the *Gemara* continues, one might protest, arguing that while the layman may come home at night and look a little bit at the *daf*

In this respect, the stress upon effort is reassuring for us, the *beinonim*, in our mediocrity. The flip side is that while the results become less critical, the exertion becomes much more critical.

To some extent, this ethos of effort and intent has a universal aspect; *Chazal* perceived it as relevant not only to the narrow world of Torah and *mitzvot*, but in a much broader sense to the human condition in general. In this connection, there is a remarkable talmudic passage that I never tire of quoting to my students:

> Our Rabbis taught: Four things require strengthening (*chizzuk*), namely, Torah [study], good deeds, praying, and one's worldly occupation...
>
> From where do we know this of Torah and good deeds? Because it says, "But you must be very strong and resolute to observe faithfully all the Teaching" (*Yehoshua* 1:7). "Be strong" – in Torah; "and resolute" – in good deeds.
>
> From where [do we know this of] prayer? Because it says, "Look to the Lord; be strong and of good courage! O look to the Lord!" (*Tehillim* 27:14). From where [do we know this of] one's worldly occupation? Because it says (II *Shemuel* 10:12), "Let us be strong and resolute for the sake of our people." (*Berakhot* 32b)

Rashi explains the import of this passage:

> "Require strengthening" – so that one will strengthen himself in them, constantly and with all his might. "Worldly occupation" – if he is an artisan, toward his craft; if he is a merchant, toward his merchandise; if he is a soldier, toward his battle.

---

yomi, the Torah scholar sits studying Torah the whole day and should be rewarded accordingly. Thus, the *Gemara* continues, one must bear in mind the *mishna* in *Menachot* cited above: "It is the same whether one offers much or little, so long as he directs his heart to Heaven" (110a). *Chazal* were not suggesting that whether a person learns a little or a lot is irrelevant; on the contrary, it is very relevant! But the message is that it is all a function of opportunity, ability, and sometimes circumstance. The result of a person's actions in divine service may be objectively deficient, but their subjective content has the potential to elevate those actions to great heights in the eyes of God.

Chizzuk here does not refer to external strengthening but to internal reinforcement; according to Rashi, this means that one must exert maximal effort and invest maximal time. This, of course, is quite a tall order. But again, we find reassurance in the recognition that results are not the only thing that counts. We gave it a good try, played the game by its rules, and are rewarded in kind. At the same time, playing the game by its rules means going all out.

The application of this ethos of effort to *teshuva* is clear, particularly for the *beinoni* during the Ten Days of Repentance. He can be reassured by the fact that the effort he exerts in achieving even the paltriest measure of *teshuva* is recognized and rewarded. But he is also charged with going all out, with doing his best to attain the very highest level of *teshuva*, even if it seems obviously beyond his ability.

THE TORAH'S VIEW OF MEDIOCRITY

Broadly speaking, Jewish thought and Halakha do not contain the kind of disdain for mediocrity, or for the middle class as its representative, that is a pervasive theme in much of nineteenth-century literature. Neither does one find the kind of admiration and idealization of the animal, the primitive, and the unschooled that pervades a good deal of Romantic literature, nor the idealization of power found in much late nineteenth-century writing, including that of Nietzsche. In those sources, the mediocre were disdained for being bourgeois and philistine, "a nation of small shopkeepers," as Napoleon said of England dismissively. The narrator in Dostoyevsky's *Notes from the Underground* stated that he wanted to be "either hero or dirt – there was no middle ground." That is not an attitude to which we can relate; indeed, this approach is not endemic to our world.

In fact, at times, traditional Jewish literature seemingly idealizes the average. We read in the *haftara* of the first day of Rosh Ha-shana that Chana requested "*zera anashim*" (I *Shemuel* 1:11) from God. As these words mean literally "seed of men," the straightforward meaning of the phrase is "a male child"; Chana wanted to have a boy. But according to one view in the *Gemara* (*Berakhot* 31b), Chana was requesting "a child that is swallowed up among men" because he is so average and inconspicuous – not too tall and not too short, not too strong and not too weak, not too smart and not too stupid – completely average! But even when our literature promotes a vision of greatness, it is not accompanied by disdain for the mediocre, for the day-to-day life of ordinary people. Still, it does not necessarily follow from this that mediocrity in the spiritual realm can be accepted, let alone admired as such.

What, then, is the role of mediocrity in the world of *teshuva*? Let us first explain what we mean when we refer to "mediocre *teshuva*." Mediocre *teshuva* may be emotionally flaccid, halakhically pallid, spiritually insipid, limited in aspiration, lacking animation, and not driven by a sharp sense of guilt. It may be characterized by a yearning to come close to God, but in a very low-key manner, involving no great emotional or spiritual exertion internally and no great effort to make amends and try to chart a new path externally.

This kind of mediocre *teshuva* cannot fulfill the demanding standard that the Torah sets forth charging us to go into the heavens and beyond the sea in pursuit of *teshuva,* if need be. While it is not totally worthless, it is grievously inadequate. Even if we assume, counter to the Rambam's assertion (*Hilkhot Teshuva* 2:4), that one does not need to completely reinvent oneself in order to attain *teshuva,* and that it is enough to look at oneself and seek to rebuild and regenerate while maintaining one's identity, this still requires copious effort, engagement, and involvement. Where that is lacking, the pallid result hardly conforms with the ideals or the standards of *teshuva.*

In light of this, we can be neither halakhically nor philosophically content with a *teshuva* that is born of convenience and limited by convenience. Nor is it wise, just, or acceptable to expect that God should be content with this kind of *teshuva.* If, however, we try our best with our own talents and our own intellectual and moral powers, but we nevertheless fall short because of our confined ability, our constricted horizons, or inimical circumstances, our *teshuva* is wholly acceptable. "It is the same whether one offers much or little"; there is a regard for effort as opposed to results, not only in the realm of Torah study or sacrificial offerings, but in the realm of *teshuva* as well.

"LET US SEARCH AND EXAMINE OUR WAYS"

The "*teshuva shelema,*" complete repentance, for which we pray in the *Amida* and in *Avinu Malkenu* is defined, fundamentally, by spiritual input, and not solely, or primarily, by the level of results. When a *beinoni*, a mediocre person, engages in *teshuva*, the objective result will inevitably be mediocre as well, as it proceeds from a mediocre mind and a mediocre soul. It is limited by the abilities and horizons of its agent. But this kind of mediocrity is much less critical in defining complete *teshuva*. Where there is mediocrity in attainment and achievement but no mediocrity in exertion and intent, that is, indeed, *teshuva shelema*.

There are three tests that can be used to ascertain whether *teshuva shelema* has been achieved: the question of initiative, the question of concomitant attitude, and the question of aspiration.

The first question, which I will call the question of initiative, i.e., to undertake in-depth examination, serves to determine whether we are on the right track and whether our efforts are being directed properly. The verse in *Eikha* says: "Let us search and examine our ways and return to the Lord" (3:40). This is the point of departure for *teshuva*: "If a person sees that painful sufferings visit him, let him examine his conduct" (*Berakhot* 5a). If one is a religious person, he does not regard his trials and tribulations simply as a matter of accident, but as being in some sense providentially ordained. So he looks into himself, to see if altering his conduct might improve his situation. That application of the verse seems to circumscribe the need for us to "search and examine our ways" to times of crisis. In the context of the verse, this understanding is very reasonable; the book of *Eikha* mourns the national crisis of the destruction of the Temple, the slaughter of the people, and the devastation of the country. This was indeed a case of "If a person sees that painful suffering visits him," not on the individual level, but at the collective plane.

But the verse can be taken in a broader sense as well, as the Rambam indeed does in his discussion of free will and its scope: "Every human being is free to become righteous like Moshe *Rabbeinu* or wicked like Yorovam" (*Hilkhot Teshuva* 5:2). This is a remarkable, almost incredible statement. The idea that a person has the freedom to reach either extreme of virtue and of sin runs quite contrary to our self-image. We do not imagine that we will reach the spiritual heights of Moshe *Rabbeinu*, nor do we imagine that we will set up golden calves like Yorovam ben Nevat. But the Rambam, in fighting against advocates of the philosophy of predetermination, is conveying the message that our spiritual achievements and failings – even to the extremes of Moshe or Yorovam – are never set in stone. Thus, the Rambam continues:

> Since free choice is in our hands and our own decision [caused us to] commit all these wrongs, it is proper for us to repent and abandon our wickedness, for this choice is presently in our hand. This is implied by the following verse: "Let us search and examine our ways, and return to the Lord."

For the Rambam, *teshuva*, turning back to the Lord, is not just for those who find themselves in anxiety and tribulation; it is for everyone.

Rav Yosef Dov Soloveitchik used an analogy of *chametz* (leaven) to explain how one should relate to *teshuva*. On Pesach, no *chametz* may be found in one's home. But it is not enough simply to throw away the bread in one's pantry in the time leading up to the holiday; one is halakhically obligated to engage in *bedikat chametz*, a formal, intensive search for *chametz* throughout one's home. Rav Soloveitchik explained that this idea is at the root of the difference between *teshuva* throughout the year and *teshuva* during the Ten Days of Repentance and Yom Kippur. All year, if one realizes that he sinned, he is obligated to repent. This is a narrow, specific obligation whose goal is to remedy an immediate spiritual crisis. This *teshuva* is not meant to advance and enrich one's spiritual life in any broad, overarching way. It does not entail an obligation to wake up each morning and give oneself a thorough spiritual self-examination. But during the Ten Days of Repentance, that is precisely what one is obligated to do. One must engage in a kind of spiritual *bedikat chametz*: "Let us search and examine our ways."

In this context, two points should be stressed. First, the verse does not limit the requirement to search and examine ourselves to our actions alone. Action-centric *teshuva* does exist; indeed, the Rambam speaks of a very narrowly focused form of *teshuva*, where one addresses each individual transgression that he has committed, in the first and second chapters of *Hilkhot Teshuva*. Later on, however, from the fifth chapter and on, the Rambam speaks not of this narrowly focused *teshuva*, but of *teshuva* in the broad sense, of self-examination and self-regeneration. The language of the verse alludes to this broad scope: "Let us search and examine our ways (*darkeinu*)," and not only our actions.

The term *derekh* appears in the context of *teshuva* in various other verses as well. Rav Soloveitchik expanded on this, citing the first verse in *Tehillim*: "Happy is the man who has not followed the counsel of the wicked, or taken the path of sinners (*derekh chatta'im*)." The verse is not referring only to the actions of sinners, but to the path they take, their lifestyle, their scale of values, their order of priorities – the very mode of their existence. The same is true in a quote from *Yeshayahu*, in a passage that epitomizes the essence of the Ten Days of Repentance: "Seek out the Lord when He may be found.... Let the wicked one forsake his way (*darko*), and the iniquitous man his thoughts" (55:6–7).

We need to examine not only if we ate non-kosher food or were involved in prohibited relationships, if we committed one particular transgression or another. In the *Zikhronot* (remembrances) prayer on Rosh Ha-shana, we state that God takes note of "each person's works, his purpose...the thoughts and plans of all mankind, and the impulses behind each person's acts." God remembers not only our actions, but the thoughts and the element of self-deceit behind these actions that lead us astray – and we need to relate to these as well. The spiritual perspective does not confine itself to a person's external actions, judging, purifying, or even repairing them, but demands a concern with correcting the totality of one's personality.

We note further that there are two separate verbs in this verse: searching and examining. Searching refers to gathering the data, while examining is analyzing that data. The process of searching ourselves is often unpleasant. Once one begins to scrape the surface of his self-image, he may discover that while his actions pass muster, the motives behind these actions are not as proper as they should be. He may then come to the realization that he is not at the spiritual level that he had previously thought. Despite this challenge, meaningful *teshuva* must involve search. The verse states: "The life breath of man is the lamp of the Lord, revealing all his inmost parts" (*Mishlei* 20:27). Just as God searches the "inmost parts" of man, we are charged with doing the same for ourselves. We must search ourselves, scrutinizing not only what we do with our hands, with our mouth, and with our feet, but also what is in our heart of hearts. Only after we search can we examine, trying to understand and evaluate what we have seen.

There is an analogue to this in the field of medicine. Before a person undergoes a medical procedure or begins a treatment regimen, doctors must first arrive at a proper diagnosis. Before we can repair our spiritual selves, we must first understand the scope and the details of our failings. This is true of the *teshuva* of the mediocre no less than of the *teshuva* of the most adept. Of course, cognoscenti with great sensitivity and knowledge will probe more deeply, understand more richly, and be more sensitive to nuances. Their searching and examining will perhaps produce better objective results. But the process of searching and examining as such, as well as the awareness of its significance and its imperative need, is common to the educated and the boorish, to the mediocre and the superior. The critical aspect is not how well we assess ourselves, in terms of what we put on the table when the process is complete, but how we understand the process itself and to what extent we are engaged and committed to it.

It is a truism of religious philosophy that we are, in effect, *shomerim*, custodians. On the one hand, we are custodians of the world at large; God placed Adam in the Garden of Eden "to cultivate it and to guard it" (*Bereishit* 2:15). But first and foremost we are custodians of ourselves, and the injunction "to cultivate it and to guard it" applies equally to this domain. The Talmud speaks of four different types of *shomerim*: the unpaid guardian, the paid guardian, the renter, and the borrower. The paid guardian must remunerate the owner if the object is stolen or lost, while the unpaid guardian is not held liable in such cases. But according to the Talmud (*Bava Metzia* 93b), there is also a difference in the quality and the level of the service that the guardian is expected to provide. One position in the *Gemara* states that it is sufficient for an unpaid guardian to guard the item "as people do," i.e., as people do with respect to their own possessions – in a relatively relaxed manner. A normal person does not stand at the door of his home all day with a gun, or keep his money in an armored car, so an unpaid guardian is held to the same standard. However, a paid guardian is providing a professional service and is thus expected to carry out this service professionally. Similarly, if we are custodians of ourselves, and "Let us search and examine our ways" is one facet of that custodianship, then we must regard ourselves not as unpaid guardians but as paid guardians. It is not enough to assess ourselves "as people do"; it is not enough to do the bare minimum, taking it easy as long as we are not positively negligent. We are paid guardians and "Let us search and examine our ways" is the high standard that is expected of us as a result.

This is the essence of the element of initiative that is so critical to *teshuva* generally conceived and applicable to the *teshuva* of the mediocre no less than the *teshuva* of the elite. It means plumbing the depths, exploring our inner being, and acting on this exploration to the best of our abilities. While a more sophisticated person may reach a little more deeply than his less advanced counterpart, the critical factor is that every person at every stratum must search and examine.

KEVA VERSUS *TACHANUNIM*

The second element of *teshuva shelema* is the element of attitude. The Talmud (*Berakhot* 29b) discusses the *Mishna*'s statement that prayer should resemble *tachanunim* (supplications). It is a kind of imploring, involving not just presentation of a list of demands, but genuine supplication. The *Mishna* continues that if, on the other hand, one's prayer is *keva* (fixed), it cannot be *tachanunim*. The *Gemara* presents various interpretations for the word *keva*, which seems to be presented as the opposite of *tachanunim*. One of these interpretations is especially relevant, not just to prayer but to *avodat Hashem* generally, and to *teshuva* particularly: "Anyone whose prayer is like a heavy burden on him." Such a person is observant and totally committed to the Halakha; it would be unthinkable for him to forgo the fulfillment of a mitzva such as prayer. But what does he bring to bear to that fulfillment? Is there a sense of excitement? Does he, a man of flesh and blood, feel the incredible merit of being able to stand before the Master of the Universe in prayer? Does he recognize the emotional and spiritual need to pray, beyond the technical halakhic requirement? Or perhaps it is all a burden: three times a day the bell tolls and he has to pray – so he prays.

Rav Soloveitchik once commented that a certain type of American Jew "doesn't want to *daven*; he wants to have *davened*." While such a person indeed considers prayer a duty that must be fulfilled, he does not feel the spiritual urge to pray; he simply wants the task to be over with. He would never shirk his responsibility to go to pray at the synagogue, nor would he miss Torah reading. But he is not charged by it and he is not charged for it.

Teshuva is sometimes approached as a cold duty as well, including the element of searching and examining that we discussed above. When the Ten Days of Repentance begin, one might consult the Rambam and the *Shulchan Arukh* and find the law stating that one must do *teshuva* during this period. If one considers himself a halakhic Jew and a good soldier, he will do it – but it is a burden. He would rather not have to get up early for *Selichot* and undergo the various unpleasant ordeals inherent in the process of searching and examining himself. He does it, almost against his will, because he feels that he must. But *teshuva shelema* must be genuinely meaningful, in terms of one's attitude. Most importantly for our discussion, this quality of *teshuva* is just as pertinent for the mediocre as it is for the exceptional. There is no reason that a person who is mediocre in religious talents should be less genuinely driven by the religious impetus for *teshuva* than a person who is religiously sharp and sensitive. If the *teshuva* of one possessed of less potential comes from a place of pure motivation and earnestness, it is fully acceptable.

TESHUVA "FROM" AND *TESHUVA* "TO"

The third element of complete *teshuva* is the element of aspiration. What is one's vision? What does one dream about in bed at night and in the course of his daily activity? *Teshuva* can be truly mediocre if it is devoid of aspiration. Such *teshuva* lacks vision: One might search and examine himself, perhaps with the proper motivation as well; but it is not part of any grand vision or continuous process. His acts of *teshuva* are a series of islands – a whole archipelago, perhaps – but there is no yearning, and that is what makes his *teshuva* mediocre. So much of *teshuva* is about yearning. Yearning is both the *terminus a quo* and the *terminus ad quem* of *teshuva*, both its point of departure and its destination.

Teshuva has two fundamental channels: the moral and the religious. These two channels can be seen in the linguistic presentation of *teshuva* in our traditional texts as being *teshuva* "from" or *teshuva* "to." The moral channel is "*teshuva* from," the impetus to respond to sin and evil in their broadest sense and to rid oneself of them, expressed in, "Turn, turn from your evil ways" (*Yechezkel* 33:11). Similarly, the Rambam's introductory title for his *Hilkhot Teshuva* reads, "That a sinner should repent from his sin." There is a recoil, a revulsion from sin and from evil in all shapes and forms. However, this recoil has a positive side to it as well. It is a desire to get away from being soiled by sin and to achieve a life of purity and perfection, in which one has left behind his "evil ways" and has assumed a new lifestyle and possibly a new identity. That is the *teshuva* of the first two chapters of *Hilkhot Teshuva* and of many verses in the *Tanakh*. This moral *teshuva* is not satisfied with simply cleaning one's hands of sin and leaving it at that. It must also be conjoined by a desire and a vision to attain spiritual good, purity, and integrity.

The religious channel of *teshuva* is being drawn "to" something or Someone – "*el Hashem*" or "*ad Hashem*," as in, "Come, let us turn back to the Lord" (*Hoshea* 6:1). Here too, many biblical verses call on one to strengthen his connection with God. To engage in this type of *teshuva*, one must yearn to repair his relationship with God and once more enjoy His favor and His grace. One must aspire to have access to Him and feel close to Him.

Both channels, the moral and the religious, include the element of aspiration that is critical to complete *teshuva*, albeit perhaps in different proportions. This element of aspiration, like the elements of initiative and attitude, is wholly endemic to, fully accessible to, and ultimately, it is hoped, thoroughly characteristic of the *teshuva* of the mediocre. Even the most mediocre spiritual pilgrim can and must transcend the bounds of his mediocrity and attain previously unscaled heights, perhaps developing a fresh identity in the process.

CONSTANT STRIVING

In a sense, one might say that the only fundamental aspiration of the *teshuva* of the *beinoni* is to leave the ranks of the mediocre. He has been a *beinoni* for a long time and desires that his spiritual self will undergo a revolution; he will no longer be a *beinoni* but a different person entirely, as the Rambam says. He will join the aristocratic elite; he will be one of the "sons of Heaven" who are "but few," as explained in the beginning of the chapter. He will stand where the completely righteous cannot stand. That is, indeed, one aspect. But realistically, this kind of total transformation, this transmutation of the self, is a rarity. It is not easily achieved and not generally common. It may be one's goal or intended destination, but it cannot be considered thoroughly characteristic of the ordinary process of *teshuva*.

Nevertheless, for a person who recognizes that he is a *beinoni* and will remain a *beinoni*, the element of aspiration can still be conceived, albeit in more limited terms. Indeed, there are many different levels of mediocrity, both quantitatively and qualitatively. Part of the element of aspiration in *teshuva* is a recognition of this spectrum, contrary to the perspective of *Mesillat Yesharim* that one is either in or out, with no gradation in between. We must recognize that *teshuva* is not simply a destination attained; it is a direction pursued.[7]

There is a remarkable word that appears in *Hilkhot Teshuva*, in a *halakha* that we cited above:

> Since free choice is granted to all people, as explained, a person should always strive (*yishtadel*) to do *teshuva* and to confess verbally for his sins, striving to cleanse his hands from sins in order that he may die as one who has performed *teshuva* and [thereby] merit the life of the World-to-Come. (7:1)

What does it mean that a person should strive? The Rambam never says that a person must "strive" to eat *matza* on Pesach, or that one should "strive" to eat in the *sukka* on Sukkot. These are obligations, period. Indeed, the Rambam uses that exact terminology in the first chapter of *Hilkhot Teshuva*, stating that when one discovers that he has sinned, he is *obligated* to follow a certain process of atonement. But here in chapter 7 the Rambam is speaking of the overall spiritual direction of a person's life, and in this context it is the striving that is crucial and central. It is a reflection of the fact that *teshuva* is a process and not necessarily a Rubicon that one must cross.

7. There are, of course, certain halakhic elements in *teshuva* that we must be able to define concretely for various purposes. Has a person done *teshuva* or not? Can he bring an offering or is he forbidden to do so? Is he considered an apostate or not? It is important that we answer these and other local and specific questions. But broadly conceived, in more general, spiritual terms, we can leave aside those definitions and speak of *teshuva* as a process, orientation, or direction.

The Rambam's injunction to strive to do *teshuva* also throws down the gauntlet before us. Even when we are not engaged in a specific, narrowly focused element of *teshuva,* the impetus to move along that path, to leave "the path of sinners" and "turn, turn from your evil ways" in pursuit of new paths and new directions is indeed central to *teshuva*. Moreover, it is central not just to the *teshuva* of the cognoscenti and the sophisticated; it is crucial to the *teshuva* of the average person, the average Jew. These people may be mediocre in certain respects, but their *teshuva* – in terms of effort and intent – need in no way be mediocre. "A person should always strive": Even when that *teshuva* itself is mediocre in terms of its objective results, that mediocre *teshuva,* too, has great potential for being accepted and for helping one achieve atonement. It can be meaningful and vital both for him and in the eyes of God Himself.

YOU SHALL BE PURIFIED BEFORE THE LORD

During the Ten Days of Repentance we stand with anticipation and trepidation, a mixture of awe bordering on terror knowing that the books of life and death are open before Him (*Rosh Ha-shana* 32b). We feel excitement that this marvelous day, Yom Kippur, not only charges us to purify ourselves, but in turn purifies us as well. We are told that none other than God Himself – *Mikve Yisrael* – will purify us. In the midst of these heady emotions, we start asking ourselves where we stand and if we are indeed worthy of atonement and purification. Have we, out of the depths of our own mediocrity, done all that we could?

The Rambam speaks of the wonders of *teshuva*:

> How exalted is the level of *teshuva*! Only yesterday this sinner was divided from God, the Lord of Israel.... He would call out [to God] without being answered.... He would perform *mitzvot,* only to have them thrown back in his face. (*Hilkhot Teshuva* 7:7)

He was despised and despicable; God did not want to hear of him or from him. But that was yesterday.

> Today, [after having repented,] he clings to the Divine Presence.... He calls out [to God] and is answered immediately.... He performs *mitzvot*, and these are accepted with pleasure and joy, as it states: "God has already accepted your works" (*Kohelet* 9:7), and it states: "And the offering of Yehuda and Yerushalayim shall be pleasing to the Lord, as in days of old and the earliest years" (*Malakhi* 3:4).

This passage speaks not only to the philosopher or the person with profound insight and wisdom; it speaks to the average person.

Particularly during the Ten Days of Repentance, the *beinoni* must ask himself if he has done enough and exerted enough effort to merit this sublime state, this intimate connection with God that the Rambam declares is the bounty of *teshuva*. If we can indeed exert ourselves, within the context of all our limitations, we can stand before the Creator on Yom Kippur and, in all humility, say that we did what we could and we tried our best. In the language of *Selichot* of *erev* Rosh Ha-shana, we have acted "as is our craft (*ke-umanuteinu*)"; now we ask You to act "as is Your craft" (*ke-umanutekha*), namely, to see that the nation of Israel as a whole is purified and worthy to enjoy the blessing of "the whole Israelite community shall be forgiven" (*Bemidbar* 15:26, 11:50). When God fulfills our request, we will be worthy of the purity and sanctity described in the verse: "For on this day He shall atone for you to purify you of all your sins; you shall be purified before the Lord" (*Vayikra* 16:30).

Teshuva of Norm and of Crisis

TESHUVA OF NORM

I would like to examine two types of *teshuva* (repentance), their respective sources and characters, and the interaction between them. The first type, which I will call the "*teshuva* of norm," has a dual connotation, suggesting both normal and normative. On one plane, it might simply be depicted as ongoing spiritual maintenance. If one visits his doctor for a checkup, or has his car checked routinely, may one do less in the spiritual realm? The spiritual realm is far more crucial, impinging, as it does, on eternal life. It is, moreover, far more susceptible to breakdown: "For there is no man who is wholly righteous on earth, who shall do only good and not sin" (*Kohelet* 7:20).

Given the frailty of both flesh and spirit, our constitution is such that sin is inevitable. The need to confront it is a constant staple of our temporal existence. This is not a Christian concept, a guilt-ridden preoccupation with original sin. "The inclination of man's heart is evil from his youth" (*Bereishit* 8:21) is, after all, a verse in the Torah. *Chazal* (*Bereishit Rabba* 34:10) interpret the verse as meaning that "the evil inclination commences when one stirs to leave his mother's womb," while the positive

Delivered as the Hausman/Stern *Kinnus Teshuva* lecture at the Gruss Institute in Jerusalem, Tishrei 5766 (2005).

inclination commences only at age thirteen, and the gap is difficult to close. They put it more sharply when attesting, "Man's evil inclination is perpetually strengthening" (*Sukka* 52b; *Kiddushin* 30b), and when stating that were it not for divine assistance for those properly motivated, one would be hard put to triumph over that evil inclination, which renews itself daily.

At this level, *teshuva* is normal, a routine part of our spiritual maintenance. Yet it is also normative, in both a timeless and a timely fashion. It is timeless in the sense that introspection is expected and demanded of a person simply as a function of his existence as a spiritual being, having been created in the image of God: "It would have been easier for man not to have been created, but now that he has been created, he should investigate his actions; some say he should examine his actions" (*Eruvin* 13b). It is also time bound, varying with the temporal cycle; there is always a basic level of spiritual responsibility, and there are also periods that require more than usual.

The Ten Days of Repentance are such a time. The *Gemara* explains that although God answers the community "whenever we call out to Him" (*Devarim* 4:7), the individual should "seek out the Lord when He may be found" (*Yeshayahu* 55:6), namely, during "the ten days from Rosh Ha-shana until Yom Kippur" (*Rosh Ha-shana* 18a; *Yevamot* 49b). While the *Gemara* understands this period as a window of opportunity, the Rambam (*Hilkhot Teshuva* 2:6) translates it into a responsibility: inasmuch as this is a time when "repentance and calling out to God… are even more desirable and will be accepted immediately," the obligation of *teshuva* devolves upon each of us.[1]

FOCUS ON SPECIFIC ACTIONS

If we ask ourselves about the character and range of *teshuva* as a norm, I think it would be fair to suggest that it bears a moral cast, rather than a religious one. By this I mean that it focuses on the wrong that has been done, and not on the damage to one's relationship with God. In order to understand this, let us enumerate five ramifications of sin.

---

1. While the Rambam applies this logic to Yom Kippur (2:7), his rationale would apply to the Ten Days of Repentance as well (2:6); if this is "when He is near," then seize the day and make the most of the opportunity.

The first three components relate to the sinful act and to the sinner. First, by sinning you wrong yourself by damaging your personality, be it a moral wrong or a religious wrong; you do yourself an injustice, aside from the spiritual or religious consequences of the act. Second, sin impacts the soul of the performer. *Chazal* speak in certain contexts of sins being "*metamtem*"; they defile, confuse, and abuse the soul. Third, sin precipitates punishment.

The remaining aspects address the sin as it relates to God. The sin is an affront to God Himself. Apart from the evil inherent in the act, it is a slap in God's face, so to speak. Finally, the sin distances one from God.

In speaking of the moral, as opposed to the religious, aspects of *teshuva*, I use the term moral as that which relates to the wrong, to the evil, to its perpetration and its perpetrator; the presence of evil needs to be confronted and confounded. The religious aspect of *teshuva* relates more to the relationship to God, either at the level of affront or at the level of being divorced from God as a result of sin. When we engage in *teshuva* as a norm, we find ourselves focused on confronting the evil as such: correcting the sin and the sinner, more than upon the impact that sin has upon our relationship to God.

This is sharply delineated in the opening *halakha* (1:1) of the Rambam's *Hilkhot Teshuva*, which focuses on the obligation to address the particular sin that needs to be confronted and on the almost technical means of repairing it:

> If a person transgresses any of the *mitzvot* of the Torah, whether a positive commandment or a prohibition, whether willingly or inadvertently, when he repents, and returns from his sin, he must confess before God, blessed be He.

In the earlier chapters of *Hilkhot Teshuva*, the Rambam deals with *teshuva* as a mitzva, and as such, he focuses upon the element of evil and one's responsibility to confront it; only later, in the seventh chapter, does he discuss the relationship with God.

Furthermore, in the opening *halakha*, the Rambam speaks of *teshuva* that is occasional, in the sense that there are unanticipated moments when *teshuva* is required because a sin has arisen. Each sin requires its own *teshuva,* and each seems to be regarded in isolation, like an archipelago of islands, without looking at the totality. Yom Kippur, the mandated time of *teshuva,* demands of us, of course, an integrated and comprehensive purgation. And yet, possibly under the impact of the detailed "*Al Chet*" catalog, the lengthy confession recited on Yom Kippur, we often tend to focus on specific actions, on our many sinful acts, each of which requires its own particular *teshuva.*

The piecemeal character and limited range of *teshuva* have an impact upon its intensity as well. The intensity of normal *teshuva* is, I suspect, likely to be relatively mild. To be sure, if one's moral and religious sensibility is keen, and, if a particularly dastardly act has been committed, even a single failure may be devastating. For example, *mizmor* 51 relates to a particular transgression, which, however we understand its character and specific contents, affected King David deeply:

> When Natan the prophet approached, after he came unto Bat-Sheva [King David prayed:] Show me favor, O God, according to Your kindness; according to Your vast compassion erase my transgressions. Cleanse me abundantly from my iniquity, and purify me from my sin. For I acknowledge my transgressions, and my sins are ever before me. Against You alone have I sinned, and done what is evil in Your sight; therefore You are justified when You speak, and faultless when You judge. Indeed, I was fashioned in iniquity; with sin my mother conceived me. (*Tehillim* 51:2–7)

Where spiritual perception is sharp, even a single sin can be overwhelming. And, surely, apart from the specific content and context of a sinful act, each one entails the cardinal preference of personal will to that of God. This is rebellion, pure and simple, and therefore every sin should shake us to our roots. Nevertheless, this is not often the case. Even as we seek to repent for the particular sinful act and to make amends for it, and even as we harness our energies to realize all the components of the *teshuva* process (the abandonment of sin, regret for past action, acceptance of improvement for future action, and confession), we rarely sense cataclysmic upheaval or radical upsurge. Normal or moral *teshuva,* while sincere, is often restrained, if not muted.

CRISIS AS A CATALYST OF *TESHUVA*

By contrast, upheaval and upsurge lie at the epicenter of our second mode of *teshuva*, that of crisis. The relation of crisis and *teshuva* is itself multifaceted. One aspect is that *teshuva* is induced by crisis, to which it may constitute a response. The crisis in question can assume various forms. It may bespeak the awareness of failure: "Return, Israel, to the Lord your God, for you have stumbled in your iniquity" (*Hoshea* 14:2). It may also arise out of the throes of suffering, whether personal or collective.[2]

While it may be true as a psychological or sociological fact that the experience of crisis tends to induce *teshuva*, crisis may very well mandate *teshuva* halakhically as well. This would be parallel to the Ramban's approach to *tefilla*, prayer. Whereas the Rambam believed that once-daily *tefilla* is a biblically ordained positive commandment (*Hilkhot Tefilla* 1:1), the Ramban disputes this opinion, offering two alternatives. One is that the *obligation* of prayer is rabbinic in origin, though as a religious *fulfillment*

2. On the personal plane, the *Gemara* in *Berakhot* (5a) places almost the same charge on us as the *Gemara* in *Eruvin* above, but makes it conditional upon a certain individual situation: "Rava, and some say Rav Chisda, said: If a person sees that painful sufferings visit him, let him examine his conduct." Should a person examine himself only if he is suffering? The answer, of course, is that everybody must reflect on his deeds; but when one is suffering, it is a different kind of *teshuva*, a different kind of search, groping and grappling with one's spiritual state.

   Likewise, several passages in the Torah speak of *teshuva* within the context of collective tribulation and suffering, e.g.:

   > When you father sons and grandsons and have been established in the land.... The Lord shall scatter you among the nations, and you shall remain few in number among the nations where the Lord shall lead you. And there you shall serve gods, the work of men's hands, wood and stone, which neither see, nor hear, nor eat, nor smell. You shall seek from there the Lord your God, and you shall find Him, if only you seek Him with all your heart and with all your soul. When you are in distress, and all these things have befallen you, in the latter days, you shall turn to the Lord your God and obey His voice. (*Devarim* 4:25–30)

   and:

   > And it shall be, that when all these things happen to you, the blessing and the curse, which I have set before you, you shall return in your heart, among all the nations where the Lord your God has banished you. And you shall return to the Lord your God and listen to His voice, in accordance with all that I am commanding you today, you and your children, with all your heart and all your soul. (*Devarim* 30:1–2)

it is biblical in origin. The other possibility is that at the moment of crisis *tefilla* is biblically ordained, but at other times it is mandated only rabbinically.[3] The latter opinion means that in a time of crisis, a person should feel a sense of dependence on and need for God. In times of need, it is impossible to think in terms of self-sufficiency – that being the epitome of arrogance – and therefore a person needs to turn to the Source, who alone is able to satisfy his needs and to bring solace to his suffering.

So, too, with regard to *teshuva*. The verse, "When you are in distress...you shall turn to the Lord your God and obey His voice" (*Devarim* 4:30), may be intended to be understood in a double sense. First, it is predictive and promissory, an expression of the Rambam's remarkable assertion:

> Israel will be redeemed only through *teshuva*, and the Torah has already promised that, ultimately, [the people of] Israel will repent toward the end of their exile, and, immediately, they will be redeemed, as the verse states (*Devarim* 30:1–3): "And it shall be, that when all these things happen to you.... You shall return to the Lord your God.... The Lord your God will return your captivity and have mercy upon you." (*Hilkhot Teshuva* 7:5)

At another level, this can be viewed as normative, a blend of plea, assurance, and command.

THE CHARACTER OF CRISIS-INSPIRED *TESHUVA*

Teshuva prompted by a crisis focuses less upon the sin that needs to be confronted and corrected, and more upon the ramifications of sin upon one's relationship to God. In the terms I used earlier, it is more religious than moral. Consequently, it is described in teleological rather than corrective terms. There are verses which speak of *teshuva* as movement "from," such as, "Turn, turn from your evil ways" (*Yechezkel* 33:11), and other verses which speak of it as movement "to," such as, "Return to Me and I will return to you" (*Malakhi* 3:7), "Return, Israel, to the Lord your God" (*Hoshea* 14:2), or "Return to the Lord your God and listen to

3. See his commentary on Rambam's *Sefer Ha-mitzvot*, positive commandment 5, s.v. *katav*.

His voice" (*Devarim* 30:2). The former verses refer to normal, or moral, *teshuva*, while the latter verses refer to crisis-inspired, or religious, *teshuva*. The Rambam, unlike in his earlier treatment of *teshuva*, focuses in the seventh chapter on the rehabilitation of one's relationship with God:

> How exalted is the level of *teshuva*! Only yesterday this sinner was divided from God, the Lord of Israel.... He would call out [to God] without being answered.... He would perform *mitzvot*, only to have them thrown back in his face...
>
> Today, [after having repented,] he clings to the Divine Presence.... He calls out [to God] and is answered immediately.... He performs *mitzvot*, and these are accepted with grace and joy. (*Hilkhot Teshuva* 7:7)

In circumstances of genuine crisis, a person does not feel the need, or lacks the wherewithal, to try to tinker with the details of corrective *teshuva*. He is desperately in need of an anchor. He feels himself catapulted into outer space, free floating, and in his desperation and longing he looks to God and for God. Perhaps later there will be occasion to worry about the sins and the confession, but in his hour of most acute crisis, he is less engaged by the moral, and more with the spiritual. When compared with normal *teshuva*, crisis-inspired *teshuva* is likely to be both more comprehensive and more intense.

These qualities are reflected in the options for the halakhic source for *teshuva*. Although *Chazal* clearly regard *teshuva* as a wonderful opportunity and a weighty obligation, they provide no clear source for *teshuva* as a mitzva. The Rambam and the Ramban each chose different verses as sources – and how different these sources are!

For the Rambam, the root of the mitzva of *teshuva* is *viddui*, confession. He links these in his prefatory subtitle to *Hilkhot Teshuva*: "There is one positive commandment herein, namely, that a sinner should repent from his sin before God and confess." He cites the relevant verse in his opening paragraph:

> When he repents, and returns from his sin, he must confess before God, blessed be He, as the verse states, "Any man or woman who

> commits any wrong.... They shall confess their wrongdoing" (*Bemidbar* 5:6–7). This refers to verbal confession. (1:1)

This verse appears in *parashat Naso*, within the narrow context of a person who has stolen something and, when confronted, swears falsely that he is innocent. When he eventually confesses his guilt, the Torah mandates that he bring an offering and that he compensate the victim by repaying the value of the stolen item, plus a fine.[4]

The Rambam spoke of a person whose total lifestyle, personality, and scale of values are not in question. Rather, his source for *teshuva* addressed a person who has committed a grievous error, but a single error. The sin is a blot on his life and his person, but it does not bring into question his spiritual identity, his religious commitment, his fundamental relationship to God, his beliefs and practices, and his fulfillment of *mitzvot* generally. Of course, even in this case, *teshuva* is an effort; no one likes to confess, for it runs counter to one's sense of pride; no one enjoys paying the principal plus a fine. But presumably *teshuva* and its attendant obligations are manageable. *Teshuva* in this context is neither comprehensive nor intense, and it entails one's confrontation with a particular failure.

The Ramban, on the other hand, finds the source of the mitzva of *teshuva* in *parashat Nitzavim*, in a passage that he understands as both command and promise:

---

4. This law had already appeared in *parashat Vayikra*, and is repeated here to add several details. The relevant section in *Naso* reads:

> Speak to the children of Israel: Any man or woman who commits any wrong toward a fellow man by acting treacherously against the Lord, and that person realizes his guilt. They shall confess their wrongdoing; and he shall make restitution of the principal amount and add one-fifth to it, and he shall give it to him who was wronged. If the man has no relative to whom the restitution can be made for the guilt, the restitution to be made for the guilt shall be the Lord's, for the priest, besides the atonement-ram, with which he atones for himself. (*Bemidbar* 5:6–8)

While the *parasha* seems to open with an overarching mandate – "Any man or woman who commits any wrong" – the constriction to a specific case is almost immediate, both because the term "*ma'al*" (acted treacherously) here has a technical meaning, as in the end of *parashat Vayikra* (5:21), and because the phrase "he shall make restitution of the principal amount" is clearly a repetition of the basic pattern found in *Vayikra* (5:20–26).

> You shall repent and heed the voice of the Lord, and fulfill all His commandments which I command you today.... The Lord will return to rejoice over you for the good, as He rejoiced over your forefathers. If you shall listen to the voice of the Lord your God to observe His commandments and statutes that are written in this book of the Torah, for you shall return to the Lord your God with all your heart and all your soul. (*Devarim* 30:8–10)

The passage then continues:

> For this mitzva that I enjoin upon you today, it is not too hard for you, nor is it beyond reach. It is not in the heavens, that you should say, "Who among us can ascend to the heavens and take it for us and impart it to us, that we may do it?" Neither is it beyond the sea, that you should say, "Who among us can cross to the other side of the sea and take it for us and impart it to us, that we may do it?" For the matter is very close to you, in your mouth and in your heart, to do it. (*Devarim* 30:11–14)

What is "this mitzva that I enjoin upon you today"? The Ramban (*Devarim* 30:11, s.v. *ki karov elekha*) notes that "this mitzva" can refer either to the entire Torah or to a single mitzva. He then comments, with a nice grammatical distinction, that when the Torah denominates its entirety as a "mitzva," it uses the phrase *kol ha-mitzva*, "all the mitzva" (as in *Devarim* 8:1). However, the expression used here, *ha-mitzva ha-zot*, "this mitzva," refers to a specific mitzva, namely,

> to the aforementioned mitzva of *teshuva*, for the verses, "And you shall return in your heart" (30:1) and "You shall return to the Lord your God" (30:2), constitute the mitzva wherein He commands us to do so. And it is stated in the indicative mood [rather than the imperative] to suggest that it is a promise; this is something that will happen in the future.

The Ramban's conception, that "this mitzva" refers to *teshuva*, is to be understood against the background of the rest of the passage in *Nitzavim*:

> And it shall be, that when all these things happen to you, the blessing and the curse, which I have set before you.... You shall return to the Lord your God and listen to His voice.... If you shall listen to the voice of the Lord your God to observe His commandments and statutes that are written in this book of the Torah, for you shall return to the Lord your God with all your heart and all your soul. (*Devarim* 30:1–2, 10)

How drastically different this is from the Rambam! The *teshuva* here is comprehensive: "You shall listen to the voice of the Lord your God to observe His commandments and statutes," a general commitment; and it is intense: "with all your heart and all your soul," the totality of one's being. And while "this mitzva" is "not in the heavens" nor "beyond the sea," the *Gemara* (*Eruvin* 55a) points out that the verse implies that if it were in the heavens or across the sea, you would have to find a way of getting there.[5] In contrast, regarding the Rambam's source for *teshuva*, the *Mishna* (*Bava Kama* 9:5, 103a) tells us that if a person robs his fellow and swears falsely in denying it, he has to chase after the victim even as far as Madai in order to repay him; but presumably he would not have to ascend heavenward or transcend the ocean.

THE CRISIS OF *TESHUVA*

We have spoken of the relation of crisis to *teshuva* in two modes: first, *teshuva* as being induced by crisis; second, of *teshuva* as being mandated by crisis. Beyond what has been delineated, we need to recognize that *teshuva* is not just brought about by crisis; it is itself a crisis. To be sure, from a certain psychological standpoint, sin is manifest assertiveness, the implicit braggadocio of Milton's Satan and his motto, "Better to reign in hell than to serve in Heaven."[6] To a religious sensibility, however, sin, so vividly portrayed by Spenser as "close creeping 'twixt the marrow and the skin,"[7] is a corrosive cancer. Yearning for it and capitulating to it symbolizes and even constitutes the breakdown, if not the collapse, of the true spiritual personality.

5. The *Gemara* in *Eruvin* understands "this mitzva" to refer to Torah study and not repentance, but the implication of the verse is nevertheless the same.
6. *Paradise Lost*, Book 1, John Milton, 1667.
7. *The Faerie Queene* 1:10, Edmund Spenser, 1590.

Thus, within the process of *teshuva* itself, there can be a crisis. The acknowledgment of sin can be devastating, leaving the self in shambles. The *Mishna* (*Avot* 2:1) counsels: "Contemplate three things and you will not come within the power of transgression: know what is above you – an all-seeing eye, and an all-hearing ear, and all your deeds are recorded in the book." This implies that the recognition of sin will arouse a combination of fear, guilt, and shame. These feelings can shatter the self, even as the need to reconstitute, regroup, and rebuild is most urgent and most acute.

Within the context of sin and *teshuva*, one may find himself caught up in a threefold crisis: a crisis of identity, a crisis of capacity, and a crisis of standing before God. The process of *teshuva* then becomes daunting.

In these circumstances, when one's sense of self-worth and one's confidence in one's abilities are so thoroughly undermined, the cosmetic initiatives of normal *teshuva* alone will not do. One may correct a blemish here, a spot there. But what one needs is to be created anew. Will we attain that rebirth simply by zeroing in, as a result of the memory of previous lapses, on this improvement or that improvement? In order to attain regeneration, one needs to create energies and spiritual identities, even as one wishes to harness them. But while these tools are necessary in order to rebuild, they are precisely the tools that have been shattered.

We find ourselves up against the dilemma delineated by *Chazal*: "The prisoner cannot free himself from jail" (*Berakhot* 5b). Yet that is precisely what the *teshuva* of crisis entails: the need and the challenge for a prisoner to free himself from jail. Of course, he is not freeing himself all alone; there is divine assistance, both through redemptive reconciliation of "Return to Me and I will return to you" (*Malakhi* 3:7), and by the contribution of the divine assistance, *siyata di-shmaya*, that energizes the penitent, in the sense of "He who comes to be purified is assisted" (e.g., *Shabbat* 104a). That is a *mesaye'a*, an assistance – indeed, a *mesaye'a sheyesh bo mamash* (an "assistance of significance," as in *Shabbat* 93a) – but fundamentally the ball is in our court. "This matter is dependent," as R. Elazar ben Dordaya said, "only on me!" (*Avoda Zara* 17a). Thus, even when the crisis seems most calamitous, regeneration awaits.

WEEPING AND SUPPLICATION

We read in the *haftara* of the second day of Rosh Ha-shana, "With weeping (*bekhi*) they will come, and through supplications (*tachanunim*) I will bring them; I will guide them on streams of water, on a direct path in which they will not stumble, for I have been a father to Israel, and Efraim is My firstborn" (*Yirmiyahu* 31:8). The prophet spoke these words with regard to the return to the Land of Israel, but the Rambam spoke of the same elements with respect to the return to the God of Israel. In *Hilkhot Teshuva,* he outlines the normative components of *teshuva,* and describes the habitual activity of the penitent: "Among the paths of repentance is for the penitent to constantly call out before God, crying and entreating (*bekhi ve-tachanunim*)" (*Hilkhot Teshuva* 2:4). The same terms, *bekhi ve-tachanunim,* appear in the Rambam as in the verse in *Yirmiyahu.*

With respect to the weeping, there is a remarkable *midrash* in *parashat Tetzaveh* (*Shemot Rabba* 38:4). We read in the *haftara* of *Shabbat Shuva,* "Take words with you and return unto God" (*Hoshea* 14:3), and the *midrash* explains:

> This is what the verses in *Tehillim* (26:6–7) mean when they say, "I shall wash my hands in purity... to proclaim thanksgiving in a loud voice." Might I think that this means to offer bulls and rams? The verse teaches, "To proclaim thanksgiving." [Why do I need the verse to tell me this?]
>
> For Israel states, "Master of the World, when the princes sin, they may bring an offering and gain atonement (see *Vayikra* 4:22–26). If the anointed priest sins, he brings an offering and gains atonement (*Vayikra* 4:3–12). But we have no offering!"
>
> God said to them, "[Do not despair; you can bring an offering:] If the entire community of Israel inadvertently sins [then the congregation shall offer a young bullock] (*Vayikra* 4:13–21)."
>
> They said to Him, "We are poor, and we are unable to bring offerings."
>
> He said to them, "I seek your words, as the verse states, 'Take words with you and return unto God' (*Hoshea* 14:3), and I

will forgive all your sins. And 'words' refers to none other than the words of the Torah, as the verse states, 'These are the words that Moshe spoke' (*Devarim* 1:1)."

They said to Him, "We do not understand it." [In other words, just as they do not have money to buy offerings, they do not have the knowledge to learn Torah.]

He said to them, "Weep and pray before Me, and I shall accept it.

Your forefathers, when they were enslaved in Egypt, did I not redeem them through prayer, as it says, 'The Children of Israel groaned from their labor and cried' (*Shemot* 2:23)?

In the time of Yehoshua, did I not perform miracles through their prayer, as it says, 'Yehoshua tore his clothes, and fell on his face before the Ark of the Lord' (*Yehoshua* 7:6)? And what did I tell him? 'Extend the spear' (8:18), [leading to their salvation at Ai].

In the time of the Judges, I heard their tearful cry, as it says, 'And it was when the Children of Israel cried out to God' (*Shofetim* 6:7).

In the time of Shemuel, did I not hear their prayers, as it says, 'Shemuel cried out to the Lord on behalf of Israel, and the Lord answered him' (I *Shemuel* 7:9)?

And similarly regarding the people of Yerushalayim, even though they angered Me, I had compassion upon them because they cried before Me, as it says, 'For thus said the Lord: Sing with gladness, O Ya'akov' (*Yirmiyahu* 31:6).

Thus, I do not seek offerings from you but rather words, as it says, 'Take words with you and return to God,' and thus said David, 'I shall wash my hands in purity...to proclaim thanksgiving in a loud voice.'"

Torah is important and sacrifices are important, and for those with the facility to apply them, they can help in *teshuva*. But they don't have the existential force and significance of the *teshuva* of crisis. This is tied to the Rambam's statement, "Among the paths of repentance is for the penitent to constantly call out before God, crying and entreating"

(*Hilkhot Teshuva* 2:4). The weeping comes when one's defenses are down; and when the defenses are down, the offensive begins.

TESHUVA OF SUPPLICATION AND OF BURDEN

I spoke before of a possible parallel between *tefilla* and *teshuva* according to the Ramban: in times of crisis, the obligation of each is magnified and intensified. Likewise, with regard to supplication, there is a parallel between *teshuva* and *tefilla*. The *Mishna* draws a contrast between prayer as supplication (*tachanunim*) and prayer as a fixed task (*keva*).[8] The *Gemara* (*Berakhot* 29b) explains: "What is meant by *keva*? Rabbi Ya'akov bar Idi said in the name of Rabbi Oshaya: Anyone whose prayer is like a heavy burden upon him." Rashi (s.v. *ve-haynu*) elaborates: "The meaning of the word *keva* is [the attitude that] there is a set precept upon me to pray, and I must discharge my obligation." This means that one prays out of a sense of duty but doesn't necessarily identify with it or accept it as a value; it is not part of one's personality or essential being.

Just as there can be prayer that is *keva*, so too there can be *teshuva* that is *keva*. "It is like a heavy burden upon him." Yom Kippur rolls around and – what can you do? – it's time for *teshuva*. It says so in the books. You heard it as a child, you heard it when you were maturing as an adolescent, and you heard it when you became an adult; and you have to do *teshuva*. Clearly, that is not the *teshuva* of *tachanunim*. Just as prayer needs *tachanunim*, *teshuva* needs *tachanunim*; and the service of God in its totality needs to be *tachanunim*.

Of course, we act out a sense of duty and obligation, and that is a fundamental concept in Judaism: "Greater is the one who is commanded and fulfills, more so than the one who is not commanded and fulfills" (*Bava Kama* 38a, 87a; *Avoda Zara* 3a). But that does not mean, God forbid, that one who is commanded performs a mitzva while wishing he didn't have to. Rather, ideally he would do it even if he were not commanded, but being commanded, he does it more fully. The sense of identification, as opposed to the sense of "it is like a heavy burden," is

8. The *Mishna* in *Berakhot* (4:4) states descriptively that if one's prayer is *keva*, it is not *tachanunim*. This is clearly to be read in the spirit of the *Mishna* in *Avot* (2:13) that instructs one to ensure that his prayer be *tachanunim* and not *keva*.

essential to our conception of religious life in general, and to our conception of *teshuva* in particular.

There is another explanation of *keva* in the *Gemara* there: "The Rabbis say: It refers to whoever does not say it in the manner of *tachanunim*" (*Berakhot* 29b). There is a language of *tachanunim*. It is not necessarily something that can be described in linguistic terms; it is body language and a quality of experience. The *Chassidim* say that there are three levels of *niggunim*: tunes, or *niggunim* that have a libretto; *niggunim* that don't have a libretto; and third, a *niggun* without a *niggun*, something so internal that it doesn't even find verbalization in musical terms. That is a language of *tachanunim* – imploring, searching, and weeping.

INTEGRATING THE TWO TYPES OF *TESHUVA*

One critical point needs to be emphasized. Both strains of *teshuva* – crisis and norm – have their place. "Everything has its season, and there is a time for every desire" (*Kohelet* 3:1). There are circumstances when the focus needs to be upon the *teshuva* of norm, and others in which the call of the hour is to the *teshuva* of crisis. There are moments when the moral element of *teshuva*, the confrontation with sin, is central and overarching, and others where the religious element of return, the reconstruction and regeneration of one's self and one's relationship with God, is crucial.

We should not for a moment be drawn into deciding that one form of *teshuva* is valid and one is not. With an eye toward the totality of our religious experience, and with an eye to Yom Kippur in particular, we shall categorically refuse to choose between them. On the contrary, we shall strive not only to maintain each of them independently, but to attain integrated interaction.

Judaism has never been drawn into the debate between Protestants and Catholics regarding justification by faith or by works. We recognize the difference, but we don't recognize the conflict. What is central to halakhic life is the conjunction and interaction between their respective paths. The world of Halakha is one that is full of minute detail. Some people find it difficult to accept, preferring to speak in terms of spiritual generalities and axiological priorities. How does the Torah approach this? "Now, Israel, what does the Lord your God demand of you?" – the Torah offers a definition of the religious life – "Only that you revere the Lord your God, that you walk in His ways, that you love Him and that you serve the Lord your God with all your heart and with all your soul" (*Devarim* 10:12). The next verse details this generality: "To keep the commandments of the Lord and His statutes that I am commanding you today, for your benefit." The first verse speaks of ultimate religious values, twinned with universal values: fear of God, *imitatio Dei*, and love of God. Lest one think this is all one needs, that Halakha is somehow secondary, the next verse stresses the need to observe, safeguard, and develop the full range of Halakha, "the commandments of the Lord and His statutes."

The same conjunction appears in *parashat Ki Tavo*, which speaks of the crowning of God, so to speak, and the elevation of the Jewish people. It opens with a very clear normative charge: "This day, the Lord your God commands you to observe all these statutes and judgments; take care to fulfill them with all your heart and with all your soul" (*Devarim* 26:16). Here, "with all your heart and with all your soul" does not describe how one should fear and love God and follow Him, but rather how one should observe the "statutes and judgments." The next verse, "You have distinguished the Lord today to be your God, and to go in His ways," describes the acceptance of the majesty and yoke of Heaven, as well as *imitatio Dei*, and continues with the affirmation "to observe His statutes, His commandments, and His judgments, and hearken to His voice."

That conjunction, which runs like a thread through the Torah and throughout *Sefer Devarim* particularly, is the quintessential center of Torah existence and sensibility. This is true of the service of God generally, and of *teshuva* specifically.

In *parashat Nitzavim*, we encounter a similar conjunction: "If you shall listen to the voice of the Lord your God to observe His commandments and statutes… for you shall return to the Lord your God with all your heart and all your soul" (*Devarim* 30:10). I understand this to mean that part of the mitzva of *teshuva* itself is "to observe His commandments and statutes." We are charged to develop a religious sensibility that is attentive to minute detail – confrontation with and correction of sin – as well as to the building of the self and the repairing of one's relationship with God. We shall strive to invest our formal observance with experiential meaning and vitality; on the other hand, we shall strive to lend substantive body to our passionate mode of *teshuva*, to be guided and inspired by halakhic observance. The power of *teshuva* is that it integrates the dual strain: spiritual maintenance, focused upon correcting sin, and spiritual regeneration, stemming from religious crisis.

We have a concomitant desire to obtain something from our *teshuva*. Yom Kippur is a day of "compassionate judgment," as the Ramban says (*Vayikra* 23:24, s.v. *yihyeh*), the day of the Thirteen Attributes of Mercy. We turn to God in hope and anticipation that He, too, will relate to us on two fronts. Yom Kippur is, in one respect, the day of forgiveness of sins, as we say in the *Amida*: "The King who forgives our sins, and the sins of His people Israel, setting aside our wrongdoings every year." It is also a day of regeneration and reconciliation, even without reference to forgiveness of sins. If we became enmeshed in sin, with all the ramifications delineated earlier, then we hope and pray on "the great and awesome day of the Lord" (*Malakhi* 3:23) for forgiveness through supplication, for the erasure of our sins and punishment, and at the same time for the rehabilitation that is so essential.

King David, in the marvelous *mizmor* 51, addresses God with an eye to both elements of *teshuva*. On the one hand, he pleads for forgiveness of sin:

> Cleanse me abundantly from my iniquity, and purify me from my sin. For I acknowledge my transgressions, and my sin is ever before me. (*Tehillim* 51:4–5)

But he is not content with that; he also wants a relationship with God. He prays for a reborn and purified personality, attained through the interaction of divine grace and his own efforts:

> Create a pure heart for me, O God, and renew a steadfast spirit within me. Do not cast me away from Your presence, and do not take Your holy spirit from me. (*Tehillim* 51:12–13)

La-kol Zeman: *Teshuva* Within Four Time Frames of Our Lives

In classifying *mitzvot, Rishonim* invoked various organizing principles. The most familiar relate to the normative thrust of a mitzva, the way it is performed: the division between positive commandments and prohibitions, as in Rambam's *Sefer Ha-mitzvot* and in the *Semag*, or between those that devolve on the individual and those that are the responsibility of the community, as is done in the *Behag* and by Rav Sa'adya Gaon. Others, such as the *Sefer Yere'im*, focused upon the sphere to which *mitzvot* relate, differentiating between interpersonal *mitzvot* and those between man and God. The *Semak*[1] elucidated

Delivered as the Hausman/Stern *Kinnus Teshuva* lecture at the Gruss Institute in Jerusalem, Tishrei 5750 (1989).

1. *Semag*: *Sefer Mitzvot Gadol*, Rav Moshe of Coucy, thirteenth century France; *Behag*: *Ba'al Halakhot Gedolot*, Rav Shimon Kayyara, ninth century Babylonia; *Sefer Yere'im*: Rav Eliezer of Metz, a student of Rabbeinu Tam, twelfth century France; *Semak*: *Sefer Mitzvot Katan*, Rav Yitzchak of Corbeil, one of the late Tosafists, thirteenth century France.

a more recondite category: the temporal scope of a mitzva, whether it is limited to a specific period or is essentially timeless.[2]

Against this background, a simple question arises with respect to *teshuva*. Some *mitzvot* clearly have a very specific time frame; taking a *lulav* on Hanukka is patently foolish, and abstaining from work on Tuesdays is not only pointless, but, according to a *baraita* in *Avot De-Rabbi Natan* (11:1), proscribed. Contrariwise, just as obviously other *mitzvot* are supratemporal; the love and fear of God, the love for one's fellow, and the prohibition of *lashon ha-ra* all know nothing of time or place. But what of *teshuva*? To what extent is it for all seasons – *le-khol zeman* – and in what sense, if any, is it *la-kol zeman* (*Kohelet* 3:1), geared to a particular period?

Prima facie, *teshuva*, like other inner spiritual obligations, should be timeless. Is there a day or an hour unsuited for repentance? And yet when we are in the midst of the *Aseret Yemei Teshuva*, the Ten Days of Repentance, we are very much affected by our temporal setting. It is to this question of the relation of *teshuva* to time frames that I wish to address myself.

The answer, perhaps self-evident, is that *teshuva* bears a dual aspect. It is both for all seasons and rooted in a particular time – but with a difference. Basing himself on the *Gemara* in *Yevamot* (49b), the Rambam notes:

> Even though repentance and calling out to God are desirable at all times, during the ten days between Rosh Ha-shana and Yom Kippur they are even more desirable and will be accepted immediately, as the verse states, "Seek out the Lord when He may be found" (*Yeshayahu* 55:6). When does the above apply? To an individual. But with regard to a community, whenever they repent and cry out wholeheartedly, they are answered immediately. (*Hilkhot Teshuva* 2:6)

In contrast to the *Sefer Ha-chinnukh*, which suggests that *teshuva* during the *Aseret Yemei Teshuva* is simply preparation for Yom Kippur, the

---

2. Rabbeinu Bachya, in his introduction to *Chovot Ha-levavot*, similarly dwells upon the temporal scope of individual *mitzvot* as a significant characteristic, though not related to their enumeration.

Rambam grants this period independent status: *teshuva* and calling out to God, while always appropriate, are at this unique time "even more desirable." His focus, however, is on the efficacy of *teshuva*, saying it is "accepted immediately" or again, with regard to the community, "they are answered immediately."

I wish to focus instead upon differences regarding the reality of the *teshuva* experience proper: its character, process, scope, and emphasis. I submit that while, indeed, *teshuva* is both time-oriented and atemporal, these are not identical – neither with regard to obligation and fulfillment as halakhic categories, nor as general spiritual realities. My exposition will relate to four distinct temporal aspects of *teshuva*: occasional, annual, perennial, and perpetual.

"OCCASIONAL" *TESHUVA*

To begin with the first, it should be clear in this context that the term "occasional" is wholly divorced from the question of frequency. I use the word as in "occasional poetry," by which is meant that poetry which is elicited by an occasion, that whose creation was impelled by accident rather than design, by circumstance rather than initiative.

The primary halakhic sense of *teshuva* is, indeed, "occasional." From our earliest sources to our recent ones, we encounter it as, essentially, a response to a particular situation. The impulse may be a general spiritual collapse; Hoshea's plaintive yet insistent call, "Return, Israel, to the Lord your God, for you have stumbled in your iniquity" (14:2), is in response to libertine debauchery described earlier (*Hoshea* 13:6). In the Torah, it is foretold that the people's *teshuva* will follow their spiritual nadir of idolatry (*Devarim* 4:28–29). Similarly, the impulse may be a comprehensive spiritual and physical calamity, encompassing personal and national collapse (*Devarim* 30:1–2).

Alternatively, the stimulus may narrow to a single act. The Rambam famously opens *Hilkhot Teshuva* with just this scenario: "If a person transgresses any of the *mitzvot* of the Torah, whether a positive commandment or a prohibition, whether willingly or inadvertently," and he repeats the localized setting of a specific violation in describing the process of *teshuva* at the beginning of the second chapter.

The common denominator to both kinds of stimuli is that in both contexts we are dealing with *teshuva* mandated by an occurrence or a situation, and therefore oriented to responding to them and coping with them.

The great virtue of this *teshuva* lies in its immediacy, in both senses of the word. First, it brooks no delay:

> It was taught in the school of Rabbi Yishmael: If you saw a Torah scholar sinning during the course of the night, give it no thought the next day – he may have done *teshuva*. Do you think that only perhaps he did *teshuva*? Rather, he has certainly done *teshuva*. (*Berakhot* 19a)

Sin is not left as a festering sore, "close creeping 'twixt the marrow and the skin," in Spenser's marvelous phrase (*The Faerie Queene* 1:10). It is eviscerated at once, and the effort to control and ultimately reverse its damaging spiritual consequences is assigned priority. This, in turn, confers immediacy in a second sense, qualitative no less than quantitative. The freshness of the response lends both force and depth. One experiences not only remorse, but revulsion as well. Correspondingly, the resolve to desist from a relapse into the same sin is fueled by determination pervaded by urgency.

Occasional *teshuva*, particularly in its more specific manifestations, suffers from the defects of its virtues. Responding to the impact of a freshly experienced sin, a remorseful penitent may, perhaps almost must, perceive it myopically, and, in turn, relate to it symptomatically. Such *teshuva*, therefore, needs to be complemented by periodic *teshuva* – not only of a different date but of a different sort. What is the period? For those of the *Mussar* school this latter *teshuva* may be daily; for other pious Jews, possibly related to a monthly *Yom Kippur Katan*; and for most of us, ordinary Jews, it is bound up with Elul, the *Aseret Yemei Teshuva*, and Yom Kippur. The existence of this whole forty-day period is special, but of course it is not meant to deny the presence of *teshuva* at the occasional level when one has sinned.

ANNUAL *TESHUVA*

Rav Yisrael Salanter once said, "All year round ought to be like Elul, but Elul is still the main Elul." Clearly, the sense of the period is highly significant. Now, this annual stock taking bears a dual aspect. At one level, it is simply occasional *teshuva* writ large, but we arrive at the product through a given process.

According to some *Rishonim,* notably Rabbeinu Yona, there is a separate mitzva of *teshuva* on Yom Kippur, aside from the obligation that applies all year. The Rav related to this by drawing upon an analogy from Pesach, referring to the double prohibition of owning *chametz,* known as *bal yera'eh* and *bal yimmatzei* – that leavened products not be seen or found in a Jew's possession (based on *Shemot* 12:19, 13:7). According to some *Rishonim,* one violates these prohibitions only if one is aware of *chametz* that he owns. But the positive commandment of "*tashbitu,*" or "you shall eliminate [*chametz* from your possession]" (*Shemot* 12:15), does not call simply for dealing with the *chametz* which happens to have come to your attention; the mitzva is to search for the *chametz.* You must ferret it out and search for it with a vengeance, "in the holes and the chinks" (*Pesachim* 8a), "every place wherein *chametz* is taken" (*Pesachim* 2a).

Analogously, the Rav said, in the course of the year *teshuva* is mandated, essentially, at the same times one would bring sin offerings: when a person learns that he has sinned, he brings the sacrifice, which includes a mandated confession (*Vayikra* 4:28, 5:5; *Bemidbar* 5:7). The mitzva, as such, does not demand that a person get up every morning and begin examining whether he has committed a sin that requires such an offering.[3] But with regard to Yom Kippur and the whole period that precedes it, the obligation of "you shall be purified" (*Vayikra* 16:30) is to look, to search. To use a medical analogy, it is not so much treatment as a checkup. In some ways, once the sin is encountered, the kind of treatment that it then receives may be no different from that associated with occasional *teshuva* in the course of the year. But in other ways the annual *teshuva,* around Yom Kippur, may be qualitatively different.

In part, the scope *per se* adds a qualitative dimension to the *teshuva* of this season. If we may extend the medical analogy, there is a

3. The *Gemara* (*Keritut* 25a) says that Bava ben Buta thought that one was permitted to bring an *asham talui,* a provisional guilt offering, as a voluntary offering, which is not the generally accepted position on that issue. He would therefore bring such an offering every day in case he had committed some transgression. Generally speaking, of course, there is no such obligation.

qualitative difference between treating a particular symptom in isolation and treating it in relation to the whole patient. In the course of surveying one's general spiritual condition, and doing this by looking through both sides of a telescope, the macro- and the micro-survey, one sees not only the outlines of a particular sin but its context. And one sees not only his own individual failing on a certain occasion, but his whole gestalt as a sinner, what that means with regard to his spiritual personality generally, and its relationship to the Almighty particularly. In this, *totality* is essential to the procedure of annual *teshuva*.

On another occasion the Rav spoke of the last *mishna* in *Yoma* (85b), in which Rabbi Akiva extols the annual opportunity to be purified by God. The *mishna* there quotes the following verse among others: "The Lord is the ritual bath (*mikve*) of Israel" (*Yirmiyahu* 17:13). The Rav stressed that the reason the metaphor of a *mikve* is employed is that purity cannot be partial; one cannot immerse oneself by bits and pieces,[4] both in the sense that one cannot have a limited kind of purity, and that the immersion itself must be total on one given occasion.[5]

In this context the Rav also quoted a bold interpretation of the famous *mishna* (*Yoma* 85b) that Yom Kippur effects atonement for transgressions between man and God, but not for transgressions between a person and his fellow man, until the latter is pacified.[6] Most people understand this simply to mean that one's *teshuva* on Yom Kippur can take care of sins between himself and God, but one is still left with the burden of interpersonal sins. This opinion understands this *mishna* differently, insisting that if a person has not tended to the interpersonal sins, then Yom Kippur does not achieve atonement for one's sins against God either. As the Rav explained this position, we are dealing here with purification, and purification by definition cannot be partial. So the very scope of the *teshuva*, its totality, lends a qualitative dimension that occasional *teshuva*, even if it were done frequently, would not possess.

4. Rabbeinu Tam in the *Sefer Ha-Yashar* (Responsa 47–48) discussed the halakhic possibility of piecemeal immersion (*tevila le-chatza'in*), but his is a singular opinion in Halakha.
5. *Torat Kohanim, Emor* 4:7; Rambam, *Hilkhot Mikvaot* 1:7.
6. This opinion is found in the *Arukh La-ner, Nidda* 70b.

In part, the qualitative difference is due to distance no less than to scope. The perspective, clarity, and even the relative tranquility afforded by the passage of time provide insight as well as sweep. Some of the freshness and vibrancy of the *teshuva* may have been lost, but in compensation it is a *teshuva* that is more clearly focused and soundly understood. Religious romantics would cavil at the recourse to analysis within the context of searing, soul-searching *teshuva*. But the crucial term of *hakkarat ha-chet*, recognition of wrongdoing, entails something more than the mere knowledge of the existence and gravity of a given wrongdoing, or of sin in general. Doesn't that greater recognition, which, after all, is a major cognitive category, include the subtlety and profundity of this recognition? Hence, to the extent that annual examination enriches the recognition of wrongdoing, precisely because it is annual and not daily or occasioned by the hour of crisis, this annual examination enhances the quality of resultant *teshuva*. It becomes a repentance that can better encompass the root and branch of sin as well as its fruit, the contextual "path of the sinners" of which the Rav (as well as so many other moralists) so eloquently spoke, no less than the sinful act that resulted from it.

We have then a complementary relationship, quantitatively and qualitatively, between "occasional" and annual *teshuva*, where annual *teshuva* is regarded in one sense as the occasional kind multiplied, but, in another sense, something *sui generis*.

PERENNIAL *TESHUVA*

Our next time frame is perennial *teshuva*. This term, drawn from the botanical analogy, denominates *teshuva* that is repeated yearly for past sins, rather than recent or current ones. There is a dispute between *Tannaim* regarding this type of *teshuva*. It appears in various places, with the names somewhat shifted in different texts, but is most familiar to us from a *baraita* cited by the *Gemara* in *Yoma* (86b):

> Our Rabbis taught: As for the sins that one has confessed on one Yom Kippur, one should not confess them on another Yom Kippur; if one repeated the sin, then one should confess them on another Yom Kippur. And if he had not committed them again, yet confessed them again, the verse refers to him as "a dog who

> comes back to his vomit, so the fool who returns to his folly" (*Mishlei* 26:11). Rabbi Eliezer ben Ya'akov says: All the more so is such a person praiseworthy.

According to the first view, if you repeated during this past year the sin that you committed the year before, then now, on Yom Kippur, you would have to confess the first violation as well. But otherwise, if you did not repeat it, you shouldn't confess it again, and indeed, doing so is undesirable. By contrast, Rabbi Eliezer ben Ya'akov deems a person who repeats this confession to be praiseworthy, even though he already dealt with this sin in the past.

Rishonim disputed this point with respect to the Halakha, with the Rambam (*Hilkhot Teshuva* 2:8) ruling like Rabbi Eliezer ben Ya'akov, based on the verse in *Tehillim* (51:5), "I acknowledge my transgressions, and my sins are ever before me." By contrast, Rabbeinu Yona (*Sha'arei Teshuva* 4:21) accepts the first view of the *baraita*, and elaborates upon it, offering three reasons justifying the practice. First, if a person confesses and asks for atonement again, apparently he thinks that last year's *teshuva* was not efficacious, and he lays the blame not at his own doorstep, but at that of the Almighty. Secondly, focusing on the past can be a convenient way to neglect the present; turning one's attention to sins from five and ten years ago can easily divert attention from the more pressing and immediate pressures of sins which took place during the past year, whose fruits he may still be enjoying and which are part of one's immediate context. Finally, confessing only distant sins involves a kind of spiritual arrogance, as if he tells the world or himself that all he needs to do is settle old accounts, for there are no new ones.

So presumably *Tannaim* and *Rishonim* dispute whether an annual repetition of *teshuva* for the same occurrence of sin is in order. I say, "presumably," because quite frankly I find the position that a person ought not to review earlier transgressions to be totally inexplicable. Is it possible that sins, having once been expiated, can be consigned to one's spiritual dustbin? Can one's inner life, or the review of that life, be carved into so many temporal chunks, unrelated to each other, so that one remains oblivious to their cumulative impact? Categorically not. The whole of one's *pelerinage de la vie humaine*[7] needs to be retrospectively surveyed at every milestone. The lynchpin of classical ethics, exemplified by Socrates' dictum that "the unexamined life is not worth living" and no less part of the *Mussar* movement, clearly refers to the examination of life in its entirety.

What, then, of the dispute in the *Gemara* in *Yoma*? I believe it refers not to the question of whether one ought to review past sins generally, but to a much more narrowly focused issue. With reference to specific sins, the first view in the *Gemara* states that if one has already undergone the formal stages of *teshuva* – abandoning the sin, regret, acceptance of improvement, confession, and seeking atonement – it is not necessary to repeat the process annually with respect to the same incidence of sin. Expiation having been attained, it need not be sought again. But examination of earlier sins as part of a comprehensive remembrance of things past remains essential, because in fact it is in no way repetitive. The cumulative impact of a sin can be gauged only within a total context; and the kind of review related to a certain sin taken within a ten- or twenty-year period within one's life will differ from a review taken within a forty-year period. The implications and the subsequent developments are now seen in a broader and fresher light. To the extent that the contours of the total context have been limned anew in the course of this past year, the particular review this year, in relation to sins that were surveyed last year, the year before, or ten years before, has never been undertaken. Could Augustine or Proust have left the chapters on their childhood unaltered had they written them twenty years earlier or later?

Indeed, I was glad to find confirmation of my own intuition in Rabbeinu Yona, right after he defended the view of the first *Tanna* in the *Gemara*:

> And that which the verse states, "And my sins are ever before me" (*Tehillim* 51:5), has been interpreted by the *Midrash* as meaning that one's sins should be before his eyes and remembered in his heart, but he should not enunciate them.... It is not that you should regard these as if you have not done them, but rather, as if you have done them and they have been forgiven. (*Sha'arei Teshuva, op cit.*)

7. Lit., "pilgrimage of human life."

According to Rabbeinu Yona, past sins are part of one's experiential-existential reality, but the mitzva of confession does not apply to them. As a *midrash* from the *Yerushalmi* (*Yoma* 8:7) teaches, the process of current *teshuva* in relation to past sin is one which acknowledges both the sin and the previous *teshuva*.[8]

Perennial *teshuva* is not, then, the annual scenario, reproduced. It is an updated review of the past revisited. This perception brings us to our final time frame: perpetual *teshuva*.

PERPETUAL *TESHUVA*

Perpetual *teshuva* refers to constant *teshuva* – not the same thing repeated frequently, but that which is continual. It bears a dual aspect, abbreviating the period of reference in one sense, and extending it in another. We encounter, on the one hand, the notion that total *teshuva* can be compressed into a single experience, to be reenacted daily. I refer not just to penitence or expiation, with respect to individual sins, but to the totality of "Return, Israel, to the Lord your God, for you have stumbled in your iniquity" (*Hoshea* 14:2): renewed, salvific commitment and reconciliation. This is illustrated by a familiar *gemara* (*Shabbat* 153a) that relates to a *mishna* in *Avot* (2:10) and states:

> The *Mishna* elsewhere taught: Rabbi Eliezer said: Repent one day before your death. His disciples asked him: Does a person know the day of his death? He replied to them: Then all the more reason that he repent today, lest he die tomorrow; and thus his whole life is spent in repentance. And Solomon too said in his wisdom, "Let your garments be always white; and let your head not lack ointment."

Here we encounter the totality of *teshuva* every day, where "repent" refers not to a particular sin, nor to the introspection that we experience

8. To be sure, Rabbeinu Yona does conclude the passage by deviating somewhat from his initial position, insisting that "one must ask mercy all of his days for the forgiveness of his former and latter transgressions," for fear that one's *teshuva* was perhaps imperfect. Nevertheless, the thrust of the overall passage is clear.

daily, but to commitment to the Almighty that is to be confirmed and reinforced every day. This is one kind of perpetual *teshuva*, every day, all the time.

In another sense, however, perpetual *teshuva* is not a given procedure, incessantly repeated. It is rather an ongoing process – one moored in no particular time, because it is for all time. *Teshuva,* not in relation to a specific sin, but as striving for self-improvement, is an activity which ought to go on all the time. But, the question arises: if one is constantly examining, when is one living the life that is to be examined? Is the whole of life to be regarded as one constant process of examination? Presumably there is a wealth of experience to be attained; granted, evaluation of direction, purpose, and values will follow. But must examination be conducted at every moment of the experience?

One may recall a chapter in *Studies in Classic American Literature,*[9] in which D. H. Lawrence heaps scorn upon Benjamin Franklin, and particularly upon the account in the latter's autobiography where Franklin describes how he would keep a daily report card, a list of virtues and qualities with regard to which he felt that he had to work and develop, grading himself on how well he had done in the course of that day. From his romantic perspective, Lawrence sees this examination as being a deadening kind of experience, a substitute for life. "At all times," says the verse in *Kohelet* (9:8) cited by the *Gemara* in *Shabbat* (153a), "let your garments be white" – but are we, indeed, to conceive of the whole of life as one perpetual laundry?

This difficulty is itself dual: first, the devotion of time and effort to the process of examination diverts one from the realization of the values and experiences which are to be evaluated; and from a romantic perspective, the very process of this constant microscopic examination, floodlights penetrating into every nook and cranny of one's inner being, is felt to be deadening, involving a certain loss of vibrancy and spontaneity.

I must confess that I myself am somewhat torn between these respective positions. One may recall the passage in *Halakhic Man*[10] in which the *Mussar* movement is castigated for its incessant prodding, to

9. *Studies in Classic American Literature,* D. H. Lawrence, 1923.
10. *Halakhic Man,* Rabbi Joseph Soloveitchik, 1983, pp. 74ff.

which is contrasted the halakhic man, a person oriented more to the future than to the past, focused on the great challenges which confront him, without getting involved in all of this constant examination. I understand the passage, but I must say that I find it impossible to subscribe to either its tone or its substance. I can see it as being a kind of overreaction to some of the excesses of the *Mussar* movement, and yet, fundamentally, can one disagree with the position that the unexamined life is not worth living? The process of examination, and at a fairly high level of frequency, is essential for both the moral life and the religious life.

On the other hand, clearly, one presumes there must be limits; as one of Conrad's characters says, "One can't live with one's finger everlastingly on one's pulse."[11] It is difficult, though, to define, for myself and certainly for others, just how frequently, just how intensively and comprehensively these examinations ought to be taking place. With regard to this issue, much depends on what one assumes will happen if things develop spontaneously. The romantic objection is based, in part, upon a very optimistic conception of man: if only he would let his natural self flourish, the efflorescence would be all for the good. Judaism, while not in a totally Calvinistic vein, nevertheless subscribes to the position of the classical moral-religious humanism: that there is an evil inclination – "For the inclination of man's heart is evil from his youth" (*Bereishit* 8:21) – but that it can be overcome. But in order that it be overcome, one needs to invest much effort, thought, and emotion.

WHAT DOES PERPETUAL *TESHUVA* EXAMINE?

But, there is a second difficulty as well: what is being examined? Presumably it is no longer just particular sins, be they peccadilloes or major transgressions, or even the inventory of a given period's sins. Rather, the fabric, the thrust of one's total life is that which is laid bare for review. This includes that which has been done, and that which has not been done. It includes roads taken and roads not taken, which, as Frost knew very well, sometimes makes all the difference.

And if we are talking about examining at this level, can we omit anything? Ought we not examine not only how well we perform, but the

11. *Heart of Darkness*, Joseph Conrad, 1899, chap. 2.

tools themselves, the very standards of measurement? But then we must ask ourselves: Do we have an anchor? Are we not possibly cast adrift, because, as in Einstein's conception, the tools themselves are also going through the changes? And here, radical questions arise. When Socrates sat in that jail cell in Athens, would not proper examination have required him to ask himself: Perhaps Thrasymachus, with his opposing definition of justice, was right? Maybe Protagoras' theories of education and morals were better than mine? I doubt he asked those questions, but, surely, we need to ask ourselves where we draw the line: to what extent are we to simply measure with the tools that we have, and to what extent should we examine the tools as well? This can be an acute problem for us, within the context of Torah and tradition, the context of absolute truth and absolute standards.

Doubts with respect to the standards themselves, that is, skepticism regarding our cornerstone beliefs, can itself be something for which one must ask forgiveness. This is how Rav Y. Z. Mecklenburg, cited by the *Otzar Ha-tefillot,*[12] understands *tim'hon levav* in our *Al Chet* catalog recited on Yom Kippur:

> This has been explained well by Rav Y. Z. Mecklenburg *z"l,* who taught that this refers to the great and terrible sin of a person who has let himself be caught in the nets of philosophizers' empty harness, to be doubtful with regard to the veracity of major principles of Torah, the existence of the Almighty, providence, prophecy, the divinity of Torah, and so on. And it is that which is referred to in the foreign language as "skepticism," and in Hebrew is called *tim'hon levav,* because the empty heart (*lev*) is full of wonderings (*tim'hon*), questions, and doubts with regard to everything, inasmuch as faith and tradition have become weakened. And this is the terrible curse written in *Sefer Devarim* (28:28)...that a person is going to be affected by the babble and confusion of opinions and thoughts, until he attains a state of spiritual blindness, not knowing what to think and what to feel, and that, of course, is dreadfully unfortunate, because he has no peace and no spiritual calm unto himself.

12. See *Siddur Otzar Ha-tefillot Nusach Ashkenaz,* in the commentary "*Iyyun Tefilla*" on that phrase in the confession in *Tefillat Yom Kippur* (p. 1133).

Not only are we called to careful introspection with regard to how well we apply our standards, but we must try to probe the standards themselves. But it is here that this "terrible curse" of *tim'hon levav* lurks, confounding us further. The question then arises, where does one draw the line between laudable conviction and problematic certitude? While introspection is a cardinal element of *teshuva*, it can also be dangerous to faith, whether personal or communal.[13]

On the one hand, we would like to think of *teshuva* as being liberating and energizing, in part because of the process of purgation, and in part because of the great joy of the resolution of doubt.[14] On the other hand, if *teshuva* brings us to probe, to ask ourselves whether we are on the right road at all, whether we took a wrong turn somewhere or forgot to look back, then of course it can be paralyzing. One need not agree with the romantic interpretation of the character of Hamlet to recognize the syndrome of those who are "sicklied o'er with the pale cast of thought" (*Hamlet* 3:1) and as a result are psychologically immobilized, or, even if their energies are vital, still find themselves in a quandary because they don't quite know how, where, and when to apply this. In this manner, *teshuva* can raise very serious practical and psychological challenges.

BALANCING PASSION AND INTELLIGENCE: *TIM'HON LEVAV* IN THE TORAH WORLD

If I try to formulate an answer in theoretical terms, I too find myself in a quandary. But if I try to see these issues within our current context, surveying the present scene, I think that at least one evaluation can be clear: the need for balance, for a creative, even healthy, tension, between passionate commitment and intellectual humility in the Torah world.

13. The Rambam (*Hilkhot Avodat Kokhavim* 2:3) similarly speaks of the dangers of being led astray by incorrect thoughts. It is interesting to note that the heart appears both in the Torah's injunction to do *teshuva*: "Be restored through your heart" (*Devarim* 4:39), and in the warning not be led astray: "Do not stray after your hearts and eyes" (*Bemidbar* 15:39). Apparently, tensions inhere in the process of relying on one's inner resources for change, though they can be mitigated, and, to a certain extent, be resolved.
14. See the chapter "*Teshuva* and Joy."

Writing *Culture and Anarchy*[15] over a century ago, Matthew Arnold quotes two statements by Bishop Wilson, an English clergyman, at the very beginning of the chapter "Hebraism and Hellenism": "First, never go against the best light you have; second, take care that your light be not darkness." Arnold continues, addressing himself to the mid-Victorian English:

> We show, as a nation, laudable energy and persistence in walking according to the best light we have, but are not quite careful enough, perhaps, to see that our light be not darkness. This is only another version of the old story that energy is our strong point and favourable characteristic, rather than intelligence. But we may give to this idea a more general form still, in which it will have a yet larger range of application. We may regard this energy driving at practice, this paramount sense of the obligation and duty, self-control, and work, this earnestness in going manfully with the best light we have, as one force. And we may regard the intelligence driving at those ideas which are, after all, the basis of right practice, the ardent sense for all the new and changing combinations of them which man's development brings with it, the indomitable impulse to know and adjust them perfectly, as another force. And these two forces we may regard as in some sense rivals – rivals not by the necessity of their own nature, but as exhibited in man and his history – and rivals dividing the empire of the world between them.

Looking about us, at the Jewish world generally, and the Torah world specifically, with an eye to those two forces – the energy and passion to pursue one's goals, on the one hand, and the intelligence to adjust those passions on the other – where do we stand? Do we suffer from excess of one or the other? To what extent does the proper balance obtain? I believe that different parts of our Torah world are differently situated within this context. In the catalog of "*al chet*," we enumerate two different kinds of violations. There are "*al chet*" confessions where the

15. *Culture and Anarchy*, Matthew Arnold, 1869, p. 142.

phenomenon itself is a sin, such as "For the sin we have sinned before You of desecrating Your name," and there are also "*al chet*" confessions that speak of a given area, where the violation is not the listed activity *per se*, but a hint at actions in the context of that activity. Thus, in the enumeration of "For the sin we have sinned before You through food and drink," or "in business dealings," these are not only licit but very laudable areas of activity, in which sin lurks – eating forbidden foods, overcharging on a sale, etc.

In thinking of "the sin of... *tim'hon levav*," we may think along both tracks. There is a sense in which one might assume that *tim'hon levav* itself, the skepticism which we noted earlier, is a sin. But, I think that, at least for some, there is a sin of *tim'hon levav* which understands it as a very desirable and necessary part of introspection, with the sin being the failure to apply it intelligently and adequately.

Addressing the present scene, it seems to me that one sector of the Torah world – the *Charedi* community – is a world which has so much that is rich, admirable, and vibrant in terms of the depth of commitment and the intensity of Jewish life; but with respect to *tim'hon levav*, properly conceived as a value, it is sadly deficient. It is a world – and this is both its strength and its weakness – which is full of self-confidence and suffused with self-reliance. The weakness is that it often translates into self-aggrandizement and results in intolerance paired with aggressiveness and arrogance. Now these qualities grow out of the surfeit of certitude, of being certain not only that one is, generally speaking, on the right path, but down to the minutiae, that this is *the* way, and *the only way*. Rav Yisrael Salanter once said that the difference between *Chassidim* and *Mitnagdim* is one *rebbe* – the *mitnaged* thinks that all *Chassidishe rabbe'im* are hokum, and the *chassid* thinks that all the other *rabbe'im* are nothing, and only his *rebbe* is worthy.

The exuberance and certitude that are asserted and exuded are morally and halakhically problematic, as there is insufficient probing of two questions: How well do I conform to the standard which I have adopted; and to what extent is my light truly the maximal light, or might it be adumbrated in some kind of chiaroscuro situation, in some element of darkness? It is a question that, in the *Charedi* world, is not to be asked, though the answers are frequently clear.

Aside from this deficiency being both morally and religiously problematic for those involved (which is a question of one's own personal, communal failing), the impact upon the entire Jewish people can be very damaging. Because these certitudes can manifest in aggressiveness and the rejection of anything that is not precisely in accordance with one's particular stripe, these attitudes become highly divisive. Moreover, they can at times result in frightening *chillul Hashem,* desecration of God's Name, particularly in the Israeli public sphere where *Charedi* parties, whether in their campaigning before an election or in their jockeying for political position and advantage in its aftermath, can be fierce and unrelenting.[16] In this sort of instance, what is needed is not only personal *teshuva,* but a collective *teshuva* – because the failure, in a sense, is collective.

Here you have that laudable passion for righteousness, for right, which Arnold, in the paragraphs after citing Bishop Wilson,[17] correctly identified as being central to Judaism. But in this case, it is a passion for right that is insufficiently informed by introspection, by examining the tools, and by recognizing that maybe somebody else also knows something. The failure to engage in this kind of introspection is, in part, a defect of the virtue. To a great extent, it derives from a lack of historical perspective and from the supposition that the only model that the Jewish people have known is that of my particular *shtiebel.* This lack of perspective derives not only from sheer ignorance, but from the lack of the healthy kind of *tim'hon levav,* of wondering: Is this the correct model for this particular time, dealing with my particular era? Should I be taking this path or another path, personally or communally? There is no *tim'hon levav* at all – just passionate certitude, never to walk against your best light, yet never examining what is the nature of that light.

That is for one part of the Torah community. Another part of the religious community – the Religious-Zionist, Modern Orthodox, Centrist world, call it what you will – is, to a significant extent, in a very

16. I recall a couple of days before the 1988 Knesset election, hearing over the radio a reporter describing how the police and security forces were preparing for the elections, explaining that particular care was being taken to avoid violence and foul play in two major populations: the Arab sector and the *Charedi* sector!

17. *Culture and Anarchy,* p. 146f.

different situation. The kind of passion rooted in certitude (or maybe it is certitude rooted in passion) so typical of the *Charedi* world is, unfortunately, a great deficiency, but there is, nevertheless, a passion for righteousness in all areas and in all its forms. In the Centrist world, by contrast, there is a surfeit of *tim'hon levav*, and *tim'hon levav* appears in various manifestations – in some cases, unfortunately, pure and simple, in the form of the skepticism described in the text of the *Otzar Hatefillot* noted earlier. Those who are exposed to various cultural currents, and whose roots in Judaism and whose belief are insufficiently deep, are indeed shaken, at one level or another, by a measure of skepticism.

At another level, for many of those who, thank God, are not affected or afflicted by that kind of *tim'hon levav*, there is still another kind. While the *Charedi* world is so certain that it, and it alone, has absolute, comprehensive, detailed truth, the individual in the Religious-Zionist world often doubts its ideals and its ideology, its goals and its methods. Riven by conflicting loyalties, driven by a quest for integration, he finds himself in a state of tension. He likes to see that tension as creative – it has an appealing ring – but on the other hand, he's not quite certain. He has some difficulty in differentiating between inherent and accidental tensions. He hopes that his present difficulties in attaining the integration between the Jewish and the general worlds, between different orders of values and different values, are simply an aberration, not something that is inherently and intrinsically the result of some unending tension. Yet this remains, for many, an unrealized hope; the present difficulty is very much a real problem, leaving many unsure. They know that the evidence of history, in the course of which this kind of integration has certainly been a minority phenomenon, runs against this possibility.

So one notes a type of paradox. Ideologically, the Modern Orthodox conception is holistic. It thinks in terms of encompassing the whole of one's reality – social, political, economic, spiritual – as part of one integrated order of serving God. But this holistic worldview is, *experientially*, often accompanied by a sense of inner division and searching. On the other hand, in the *Charedi* current – which sees value as residing inherently *only* in the world of sanctity, narrowly conceived, and sees the rest as being of little moment – that philosophically divided world attains a degree of integration the Centrist community finds difficult to sustain.

Above all, there is the self-doubt that afflicts, and sometimes torments, much of the Modern Orthodox community, as it watches what seems to be transpiring around it. Contrary to the inner logic and the expectations of this Centrist community, contrary to all predictions of a generation ago not only within the Centrist world but within the *Charedi* world as well, the latter camp is perceived as growing stronger and stronger, while its own, Centrist, house is seen as struggling. While it may not be struggling in absolute terms – internally, the Modern Orthodox world is certainly much richer in Torah study and commitment to observance than it was several decades ago – it appears to be struggling, at least relative to its brethren to the right. Thus, an additional element of self-doubt creeps in.

So, we address ourselves in perpetual *teshuva*, and its demand for some sense of *tim'hon levav* properly conceived – questioning oneself and some of the details of one's interpretation and implementation. On the other hand, we may also need to repent for a certain excess of *tim'hon levav* – too much ambivalence and uncertainty, which make passionate commitment and implementation difficult.

TESHUVA FOR *TIM'HON LEVAV*

If we want to perform *teshuva* for this *tim'hon levav*, to what can we look? Obviously the *teshuva* depends upon the nature of the problem. For those who are suffused with a sense of passion and certitude, for those who bear their torch with total commitment, regarding everything else as darkness, then a measure of humility and self-examination is certainly in order. To that end one could counsel them to expand the base of their knowledge, to broaden their historical perspectives, and to have a greater awareness of the richness and diversity of Jewish experience, and by that I mean Jewish-Torah experience.

On the other hand, for those for whom the sense of *tim'hon levav*, of self-doubt, is all too deeply rooted, the prescription needs to be very different, perhaps in an opposite direction. First, it is necessary to develop and clarify, more fully and more incisively, the ideology of this particular mode of divine service. But second, inasmuch as the problem within our community is not so much one of ideology but more of implementation, of carrying out the execution of very grand and noble ideas, we must begin by asking, candidly, perhaps our reach has exceeded our grasp too much? Perhaps in trying to be so comprehensive, to address ourselves to so many issues and involve ourselves in so many areas of the contemporary scene, we are spreading ourselves so thin, personally and communally, that we are losing the center, perhaps even the epicenter.

Surely what we need is not only to express our commitments but to see to it that the ideology which guides us, as realized and as implemented, be worthy of the kind of passionate commitment we strive to inculcate. That means, of course, deepening faith, raising the level of mitzva observance, intensifying Torah institutions. It means establishing, above all, priorities which make it clear what is primary and what is secondary, and, to paraphrase *Yoma* 19b, to make the Torah a fixture and not a temporary element. And it means working harder, both personally and communally through our institutions, to ensure that proper priorities are indeed implemented.

Lest one think that I am inordinately pessimistic, let me say that when one surveys the Religious-Zionist Torah scene, in terms of its depth and intensity, certainly much has been done, a great deal attained, in the course of the last generation. But so much remains to be done; one is pained, genuinely hurt, by seeing the failure to address central issues with the kind of desperate urgency these require. For instance, the educational scene, given its cardinal importance, cries out for immediate attention. Education, when all is said and done, is not only, for us, *benei Torah*, a central value in its own right; it is the key to the quality of society and to the quality of its spiritual life. And to that let us proclaim and confess "*al chet*" openly – certainly the *Charedi* community, given its conception, its view of how life should be led spiritually, commits much more time, energy, and resources to religious education than does the Religious-Zionist camp. This is something that certainly needs to be reversed. As long as there is an educational gap, the Modern Orthodox will be afflicted by the subversive *tim'hon levav*, uncertain about their own views, and assuming that "real Torah" is to be found with those of a different camp.

CONCLUSION

Near the end of his life, Moshe *Rabbeinu* promises the people, "And the Lord your God will circumcise your heart, and the heart of your seed" (*Devarim* 30:6). The nature of that circumcision is the subject of a dispute between the Ramban and the Rambam. The Ramban (s.v. *u-mal*) assumes that the verse speaks of the messianic era. He says the evil inclination will be totally eradicated, and we will be returned, with divine assistance, to the pristine, pre-lapse period of purity of Adam, without sin and without desire for sin. The Rambam, in his view of the messianic era, is much more moderate, and does not envision such quasi-restructuring of human personality or society. To his lights, *teshuva* is always and intrinsically a human project, initiated from within the individual and the community; while the Almighty may respond with political tranquility and economic security to galvanize and fortify the effort (*Hilkhot Teshuva* 9:2), the endeavor remains exclusively in our own hands, ultimately ushering redemption (*Teshuva* 7:5). We must therefore work on our spiritual circumcision by recognizing our own problems and overcoming them, and not seek solace in either the problems or solutions of others.

If we are concerned with *teshuva* as a mitzva, be it a mitzva evoked by a particular occasion, a mitzva demanded by the arrival of a certain period, or *teshuva* as an ongoing process, repeated annually, or engaged in perpetually, then, of course, we are dealing with a degree of obligation incumbent upon us. It is upon us as individuals and upon us as a community, each in his own way. Addressing himself to the *yamim nora'im* of his own era, Moshe *Rabbeinu* states, "You shall circumcise, therefore, the foreskin of your heart" (*Devarim* 10:16). There is the Almighty's circumcision, and there is our circumcision. And hopefully, through our conjunction of these two, as we strive to purify our motives, to intensify our passions, and to harmonize and integrate our lives, out of the interaction of "He shall circumcise" and "You shall circumcise," we shall attain complete *teshuva* and complete forgiveness.

Teshuva: Ferment and Repose

Teshuva comprises, formally and psychologically, a cluster of diverse components: regret over past actions, abdicating wrongdoing, and acceptance of future correction. Yet a special place is reserved for *viddui*, confession to God. On one plane, *viddui* accompanies *teshuva*, as the Rambam formulates the heading to *Hilkhot Teshuva*: "There is one positive commandment described herein, namely, that the sinner should repent from his sin before God and confess."[1] On another plane, *viddui* is not an accompaniment but the acme, as suggested by the Rambam's description of the various stages of *teshuva* in the body of his text, where he concludes, "One must confess with his lips, stating the matters that he has decided in his heart" (*Hilkhot Teshuva* 2:2). Thus, in one respect, *viddui* is mandated as a parallel to *teshuva*, in another it serves as its apex. Hence, a brief survey of the primary texts and contexts of *viddui* may be illuminating and instructive of the contours of *teshuva*.

Delivered as the Hausman/Stern *Kinnus Teshuva* lecture at the Gruss Institute in Jerusalem, Tishrei 5765 (2004).

1. See also *Mishlei* 28:13: "*U-modeh ve-ozev yerucham* – He who confesses and forsakes [sins] shall be shown compassion."

TWO DIFFERING CONTEXTS OF *VIDDUI*

The reflexive form, "*ve-hitvaddu*," appears in the Torah in two *loci classici*. The first comes at the end of the *tokhacha*, the rebuke, in *parashat Bechukkotai*:

> Those remnants that are left of you shall pine away in their iniquity in their enemies' lands, and also in the iniquities of their fathers shall they pine away with them. And they shall confess (*Ve-hitvaddu*) their iniquity and the iniquity of their fathers, with their trespass which they trespassed against Me, and that they have also walked contrary to Me. (*Vayikra* 26:39–40)

The second appears in *parashat Naso* with reference to *gezel ha-ger*, theft from a convert who died leaving no heirs. This is the case of a person who stole or embezzled money or an object, took a false oath denying he had done so, and then confessed that, indeed, he had sworn falsely. In addition to restitution with an added premium, the Halakha requires he bring a guilt offering. Though the Halakha refers to a general sin, as *Chazal* explain (*Bava Kamma* 109a–110a), this passage elaborates upon a law already set down in *parashat Vayikra* to explain how restitution may be made to someone who died with no relatives, i.e., a convert. The verse says:

> They shall confess (*Ve-hitvaddu*) their wrongdoing, and he shall make restitution of the principal amount and add one-fifth to it, and he shall give it to him who was wronged. (*Bemidbar* 5:7)

While the term *ve-hitvaddu* appears in both contexts, the situations are certainly different, and hence the phenomena described by the term may be different. First, there is a question of scope. "*Ve-hitvaddu*" at the end of the *tokhacha* is not only in the plural form, but communal. Those who confess are a vestigial remnant, far off in some remote exile. "*Ve-hitvaddu*" in the passage of *gezel ha-ger* bespeaks a personal initiative, referring to a particular man or woman: "Any man or woman who commits any wrong toward a fellow man…" (*Bemidbar* 5:6). While here, too, the form "*ve-hitvaddu*" begins in the plural, the verse very quickly swings into the singular: "He shall make restitution" and "he shall give it." There is a difference in scope between these two contexts, in terms of who is doing the confessing.

Second, and perhaps more important, there is a significant difference regarding what a person is confessing. The "*ve-hitvaddu*" of the *tokhacha* relates to general – if not total – religious defection, with concomitant alienation from God. While the verse uses the singular "*avonam*" (their trespass), it bears a clear collective denotation, encompassing the comprehensive range of sin. In *Naso*, by contrast, the referent is a single sin, *gezel ha-ger*. Granted, *Chazal* (*Sifrei Zuta* 5) generalized from this paradigm to require *viddui* in the wake of any transgression, but the passage's focus remains defined and limited. So we have two distinctions – who is confessing, and with regard to what sin or sins he recites the *viddui*.

Related, but even more critical, is a difference in mood, and hence of mode. Positioned within the *tokhacha*, the *viddui* in *Bechukkotai* is envisioned within the context of exile and upheaval, against a background of a nation in shambles. *Viddui* is anticipated as a response to dissolution, as an acknowledgment of deviation, and as a halting first step on the road to rehabilitation and regeneration.

No such context is remotely in prospect in the passage of *gezel ha-ger*. Its matrix is a situation in which a person has violated a moral and halakhic precept, and seeks, as part of his *teshuva*, to recant and redress. The violation in question, swearing falsely, is certainly a serious transgression, considered one of the more severe violations (Rambam, *Hilkhot Teshuva* 1:4). Nonetheless, the prohibition is limited in scope, and the original misappropriation could have been a mere *peruta*.[2] Now, from a certain religious and halakhic perspective, every sinful act, no matter how minor, entails the defiance of God's will and a challenge to His authority. The injunction in *Pirkei Avot*, "Be as heedful in the fulfillment of a 'light' mitzva (*kalla*) as a grave one (*chamura*)" (*Avot* 2:1), applies, obversely, to sins as well.[3] Nevertheless, the Halakha has clearly

2. *Mishna, Bava Kamma* 103a.
3. The *Mishna*'s exhortation to be heedful is grounded, with reference to *mitzvot* as well as to sins, first in the hypothetical possibility that perhaps the true priority is reversed: "for you know not the reward granted for the *mitzvot*." But it is also predicated on the recognition that, quintessentially, every sin is severe, insofar as it entails the preference of one's own will to that of God as expressed in a divine norm.

recognized the demarcation of *kallot* and *chamurot*,[4] and were we to attempt to conjecture the state of mind of this confessing thief, there is little reason to assume he has been shaken to his psychological core. To the contrary, the *viddui*, halakhically and practically, is one phase in the checklist, and is on a par, in terms of one's psychological mindset, with the return of the principal and fine.

THE DIFFERING IMPULSES FOR *VIDDUI*

The difference in context between these confessions translates ordinarily into a difference in character and impulse. The impetus for the *viddui* in *Naso* is, presumably, a clear halakhic mandate, which therefore serves as the archetype for analogous initiatives with regard to other sins. That is how the Rambam opens *Hilkhot Teshuva*:

> If a person transgresses any of the *mitzvot* of the Torah, whether a positive commandment or a prohibition, whether willingly or inadvertently, when he repents, and returns from his sin, he must confess before God, blessed be He, as the verse states, "Any man or woman who commits any wrong toward a fellow man.... They shall confess their wrongdoing" (*Bemidbar* 5:6–7). This refers to verbal confession (*viddui*), and this confession is a positive commandment.[5]

As with regard to any mitzva, the Rambam tells you the technique, the content, and perhaps even the text:

> How does one confess? One states: "I implore You, God; I sinned, I transgressed, I committed iniquity before You by doing the following. Behold, I regret and am embarrassed for my deeds, and I promise never to repeat this act again." This is the essence of the confession. Whoever confesses profusely and elaborates on this matter is praiseworthy. (1:1)

---

4. Texts related to the theme of *kappara*, atonement, develop these lines most clearly. See, for example, the *arba'a chalukei kappara*, four different levels of atonement, noted in *Mekhilta Yitro, Massikhta de-ba-chodesh* 7, *Yoma* 86a, and *Yerushalmi, Yoma* 8:7.
5. The Rambam is basing himself on *Sifrei Zuta* 5:5.

The Rambam goes on to insist that this requirement applies to all sinners: those obligated to bring a sacrifice, those involved in torts, or those receiving capital or corporal punishment. We have here a halakhic procedure, and one's impetus to confess is presumably the mitzva, the fact that one is required to do so.

How does this compare with what we read in *Bechukkotai*? Those confessing in exile are shaken by remorse, driven by concern, and impelled by existential angst. Their *viddui* is not grounded in halakhic requirements, but is a desperate *cri de coeur*, an attempt to cope with a world in crisis and in tatters. Hence the inclusion of "the iniquity of their fathers" in their confession; at the level of formal confession, such an inclusion is highly problematic, and indeed, might violate *kibbud av va-em*, showing disrespect to parents and besmirching earlier generations.[6] But as soon as we recognize that the impulse here is an expression *mi-ma'amakim*, from the depths, responding to one's situation as part of an attempt to acknowledge, understand, and repent for the past, then one needs to deal with the total context, with the sources of the issue. Against such a background, the problem of confessing the sins of one's fathers along with his own sins is not so sharp.

By comparison – and I can only conjecture – the thief of *parashat Naso* presumably lives, acts, and confesses in relative stability. His *viddui*, rationally conceived, is rationally executed with a mindset fairly calm and reposed. His world is not in chaos; he performs his halakhically mandated act both punctiliously and spiritually, and is anchored within the safety and security of his country and community – so remote from "those remnants that are left of you shall pine away in their iniquity." We have the same term, but with very different content with respect to scope, context, and character.

FERMENT AND REPOSE: TWO TYPOLOGICAL PERSPECTIVES

The typological contrast between the two *vidduyim* is of far broader scope than just *teshuva*. We can see these two perspectives – one of torment and tempest, the other of calmness and serenity – in multiple

6. This is the reason that in many *siddurim*, in the phrase leading up to the *viddui*, "*Anachnu va-avoteinu chatanu*, We and our fathers have sinned," the word "*va-avoteinu*" is in parentheses.

dimensions of human perception and experience. For instance, with reference to one's view of the physical universe: some, such as the pre-Socratic Heraclitus, postulated nothing but ceaseless flux in the cosmic order, while Parmenides was enthralled by the pervasive unity in nature, perceiving all movement as that of ripples within a pool. In a more constricted vein, one detects a parallel diversity in the apprehension and experience of nature, particularly in poetry: consider the tempest in Lord Byron's *Childe Harold's Pilgrimage*,[7] set against the Romantic account of the Lake District in William Wordsworth's poetry.

The poles of ferment and repose are similarly evident in views of the human order, as regarding both the portrayal of what is, and, to an extent, of what ought to be. There are implications for social and political thought – what kind of society one wants and one admires – and there are also implications for moral and ethical theory, with possible religious implications as well. For instance, consider the celebrated question, going back to some pseudo-Aristotelian writings and familiar to many of us primarily through the Rambam's *Shemona Perakim* (especially chapter 6), as to whether the soul in conflict and torment who fights back negative impulses is to be preferred to the person with a kind of inborn natural virtue and metaphysical purity. To some extent, these are reflective of the ferment of one type of mindset, as opposed to the calm of the other type. If these two typologies obtain for one's view of the human order, they certainly apply to one's approach to religious life – coextensive with, and yet distinct in significant and crucial ways from, the mundane order.

FERMENT AND REPOSE AS TWO POLES OF RELIGIOUS LIFE

During the Ten Days of Repentance, we want to focus upon the ramifications of these respective categories for divine service generally, for *teshuva* particularly, and for our experience of Yom Kippur. In this context, we can relate to our twin categories not so much as responses, but rather as initiatives and desiderata – what kind of spiritual forces we want to mobilize, how we want to build and develop, from where we start and where we are headed.

7. Canto I, stanza 12.

With regard to religious existence, do we idealize *Sturm und Drang,* embodied within the dramatic and the heroic, revolving around conflict and confrontation, as is so admired in much of Western culture and literature? Or do we identify with cosmic, social, and personal placidity and strive to attain the equanimity so emphasized in much of Eastern mystical and religious thought? To anyone sensitive to the polyphonic voice of Judaism, the answer is self-evident: we strive to relate to both, and aim to attain both, in various contexts and in diverse expressions of our religious sensibility.

We see both within *Tehillim,* that most familiar terrain of religious experience. As one example, *mizmor* 63 gives vent to the element of inner drive, the ferment of the quest and the search:

> A psalm of David, when he was in the wilderness of Yehuda. Lord you are my God, earnestly I seek you, my soul thirsts for You, my flesh longs for You in a dry and thirsty land, where no water is, to see Your power and Your glory. (*Tehillim* 63:1–3)

The phrase "in a dry and thirsty land, where no water is" exemplifies the quest, the inner ferment, and even the inner torment of the search. But we place that side by side with another familiar psalm of David that we recite repeatedly:

> The Lord is my shepherd; I shall not want. He makes me lie down in green pastures; He leads me beside the still waters. (*Tehillim* 23:1–2)

Halakhic Observance

Similarly, we listen to both elements within ordinary halakhic existence. We emphasize – both in what we do and in how we relate to our activities – the interaction between the passional drive for the attainment of comprehensive goals and the commitment to minutiae in the fulfillment of halakhic norms. In this respect, the inner psychological and spiritual ferment that impels us with regard to the grander themes lives side by side with a calm dedication to detail at the level of fulfillment.

The interweaving of ferment and repose is exemplified by *chol* and Shabbat, dynamic activity and rest. *Rishonim* differed as to the exact relationship. Is the focus of our existence the creative activity of *chol*, the kind of ferment where we, in effect, do God's work, while Shabbat is meant for recharging our batteries?[8] Or is Shabbat the aim, and the "six days of work" are mere steps on the way? In any case, the interface of the ferment of the six days of work with the repose of Shabbat is crucial to our perception of both, and represents an archetype for the human situation.

In this context, the ferment of creative activity is valued, provided that it is purposive. We reject frenetic motion for its own sake; that is the inclination and the lot of the religiously disaffected and alienated, according to the *haftara* of Yom Kippur morning: "But the wicked are like the troubled sea, which cannot be still, and whose waters cast up mire and dirt; there will be no peace, says my God, for the wicked" (*Yeshayahu* 57:20–21). They are driven compulsively, but when the purpose is not clear, the activity is almost a curse. By contrast, when the activity is purposive, we certainly admire it and encourage it.

This World and the Next

Most often, we are inclined to think that the contrast between the dynamic and the static marks the difference between our world and the next. When the *Mishna* in *Avot* (4:17) states that "A single hour of *teshuva* and *mitzvot* in this world is more valuable than the whole of the World-to-Come," and on the other hand, "One hour of beatific joy in the World-to-Come is greater than all of this world," we are often inclined to assume that ours is the world of activity and ferment, and these are lacking in the World-to-Come. From a certain perspective, therein lies the superiority of this world: creating and acting, and the realization of human potential. But if we think of the wonders of repose, which is what the next world is all about, the experience has no parallel to this world; in the World-to-Come we enjoy and appreciate without creating, without change. Yet a striking *gemara* (*Berakhot* 64a; *Mo'ed Katan* 29a) qualifies even that: "Torah scholars have no rest either in this world or in the World-to-Come, as the verse states, 'They proceed

8. See *Kuzari* 3:5. *Avot De-Rabbi Natan* (version 2, chap. 21) understands "Six days you shall labor and do all your work" (*Shemot* 20:8) to mean that just as there is a mitzva to observe Shabbat, there is a mitzva to work the other six days of the week.

from strength to strength; every one of them appears before God in Zion' (*Tehillim* 84:8)." For our community's spiritual elite, even the next world is not a place of repose.

By the same token, the *gemara* in *Berakhot* is followed by another, more familiar statement: "Torah scholars increase peace (*shalom*) in the world"; and while *shalom* presumably refers to the social and civic order, something of an echo of *shalom* as repose is to be heard as well. Our world is built on the tensile interaction, perhaps the dialectic, between the elements of creative drive and reposed equanimity.

CRISIS AND RESTORATION

What is true of the world of divine service generally, is, I believe, equally true of the enclave of *teshuva*. *Teshuva* is often envisioned as engendered by crisis, as we see in two separate passages in the Torah. The first is read before Rosh Ha-shana in *parashat Nitzavim*, itself an extension of the prior *tokhacha*:

> And it shall be, that when all these things happen to you, the blessing and the curse, which I have set before you, and you shall return in your heart among all the nations where the Lord your God has banished you. And you shall return to (*ve-shavta ad*) the Lord your God, and listen to His voice, in accordance with all that I am commanding you today; you and your children, with all your heart and all your soul. (*Devarim* 30:1–2)

This passage is somewhat similar to what is described in *Bechukkotai*, but is very different in tone and mood. It does not suggest the same kind of despondency, it is less descriptive of the nature of the sin and relapse, and there is no mention of "they have also walked contrary to Me" (*keri*). Furthermore, the verse explicitly mentions *teshuva*; and this is not just any *teshuva*, but a comprehensive *teshuva*, both in terms of whom it encompasses – you and your family – and in qualitative terms, "with all your heart and all your soul." Overall, the passage is much more sanguine and hopeful. Nevertheless, it shares the common denominator with *Bechukkotai* that the *teshuva* comes as a response to crisis and suffering.

The same note is struck, in equally familiar verses, in the portion of *parashat Va'etchanan* that we read on Tisha Be-Av morning: "The Lord shall scatter you among the nations, and you shall remain few in number among the nations where the Lord shall lead you" (*Devarim* 4:27). Note, again, the reference to the exile described and prescribed in *Bechukkotai*. The verse continues:

> And there you shall serve gods, the work of men's hands, wood and stone.... You shall seek from there the Lord your God, and you shall find Him, if only you seek Him with all your heart and with all your soul. When you are in distress, and all these things have befallen you, in the latter days, you shall turn to (*ve-shavta ad*) the Lord your God and obey His voice. (*Devarim* 4:28–30)

Dispersion, exile, distress – these will be the sources of *teshuva*, so let us anticipate them. And again, while there is a common denominator with *Bechukkotai* in the origin of *teshuva*, in social and psychological ferment generated by crisis, a more hopeful note is struck here than there.

Nevertheless, the impetus of *teshuva* is hardly the total picture, for there is another facet to *teshuva*. The Bible speaks of *teshuva* in two grammatical formulations: *teshuva* "from (*mi-*)" something, such as "*Shuvu, shuvu mi-darkheikhem ha-ra'im... Beit Yisrael*, Turn, turn, from your evil ways... O House of Israel" (*Yechezkel* 33:11), and *teshuva* "to," expressed as "*el*" or "*ad*" – *teshuva* to something, or, more accurately, to Someone. The difference is clear. *Teshuva* "from" is a kind of moral *teshuva*, in that one is reacting against and distancing himself from something that is wrong (without reference to whether the wrong is ethical or spiritual, universal or particular). By contrast, the religious aspect of *teshuva* is one that focuses not upon the righting of wrongs but upon the restoration of one's relationship to God: "*Shuva Yisrael ad Hashem Elokekha*, Return, Israel, to the Lord your God" (*Hoshea* 14:2). The verses just cited, from *Nitzavim* and *Va'etchanan*, likewise refer to returning "to (*ad*)" God. These texts address the specifically religious element of *teshuva*.[9]

---

9. See also the section entitled "*Teshuva* 'From' and *Teshuva* 'To'" in the chapter "Mediocre *Teshuva* and the *Teshuva* of the Mediocre."

SELF-EXAMINATION: DUAL IMPULSES

The moral aspect of righting wrongs is reflected in twin statements in *Chazal*, which reflect two contexts and therefore characterize the two modes that I described previously.

The *Gemara* in *Eruvin* (13b) describes the long-standing dispute as to whether "It is better for man not to have been created." This dispute reflects whether one ordinarily perceives human existence in an optimistic vein, as most of us like to do, or pessimistically, as Hobbes described life: "nasty, brutish and short" (*Leviathan* xiii). Of course, the *Gemara* doesn't discuss whether it is good; God already declared that it was "very good" (*Bereishit* 1:30). But whether it is good is one thing, and whether it is pleasant is something else. In conclusion of that dispute the *Gemara* says, "It were better for man not to have been created," but "now that he has been created," he should engage in a measure of self-examination.

The theme of self-examination appears in another *gemara* as well:

> Rava, and some say Rav Chisda, said: If a person sees that painful sufferings visit him, let him examine his conduct, as the verse states (*Eikha* 3:40), "Let us search and examine our ways and return to the Lord." (*Berakhot* 5a)

The same recommendation appears here, but under different circumstances. The *Gemara* in *Eruvin* perceives self-examination as part of normal, daily living. It is a condition of existence. Under the calmest, most ordinary situations, one must examine his actions. The *Gemara* in *Berakhot*, on the other hand, speaks of this introspection as being required or suggested by one's encounter with suffering; it is a response, a way of grappling and coping with the suffering.

THE DUAL ASPECT OF *TESHUVA* ON YOM KIPPUR

How, finally, do we envision Yom Kippur and the *teshuva* attendant upon it? I believe that we again confront a dual phenomenon. This dual character is reflected, at least symbolically, in two distinct areas: the *vidduyim* of the day, and the very roots of Yom Kippur.

A) The *Vidduyim* of Yom Kippur

By *vidduyim* I refer to both the public confessions of the *Kohen Gadol* and the private confessions of the individual. The *Kohen Gadol* recited two confessions over his bull – the first for himself and his household, the second for the community of *Kohanim* – and recited one more confession, over the scapegoat, for the entire Jewish people. Without going into the details, let us note that the bull is related to sins in the Temple, to *tum'at Mikdash ve-kodashav,* the defilement of the Temple and holy matters. This is a narrow focus, similar to the *viddui* in the context of *gezel ha-ger*.

However, the associations with the *viddui* of the scapegoat are strikingly different, as is the scope:

> And Aharon shall lay both of his hands upon the head of the live goat, and confess over it all the iniquities of the Children of Israel, and all their transgressions in all their sins, putting them upon the head of the goat, and shall send it away by the hand of an appointed man into the wilderness. And the goat shall bear upon it all their iniquities to a barren land, and he shall let go the goat in the wilderness. (*Vayikra* 16:21–22)

Four times the word "all (*kol*)" appears. This rite pertains to the whole community of the Jewish people, and it relates to a primal and primeval association with the world of other spirits, as the Ramban discussed,[10] bordering on the world of mysticism. This is very different from the sins and atonement within the confines of the Temple itself.

There is something unnerving about this scene. After this broad and all-encompassing *viddui,* the appointed man crosses the fifty *mil* or so, solitary and alone,[11] confronting the vast wilderness, culminating in the scapegoat being pushed off the cliff, torn apart on the way down. This world of mystery, of unsettling uncertainty and anxiety, is in some ways similar to the world of *Bechukkotai,* but it is clearly very different from the much calmer and more circumscribed *vidduyim* over the bull.

---

10. *Vayikra* 16:8, s.v. *ve-goral.*
11. Described in the *Mishna* and *Gemara* in *Yoma* 66a–67a.

If we now turn from the public *vidduyim* to the private, personal ones, particularly those appended to the conclusion of the Yom Kippur *Amida,* two themes are struck there as well. On the one hand, we have the classical *viddui,* "*Ashamnu,*" dating back to the time of *Chazal,* and its extension and expansion to the "*Al Chet,*" by the *Ge'onim.* Qualitatively speaking, one is confessing sins. Some are more specific, e.g., "*Gazalnu,* We have stolen," whereas others are less so, e.g., "*Ashamnu,* We have incurred guilt." Fundamentally, however, it is like the confession of *gezel ha-ger,* as it is *viddui* that is engendered by a particular sin, just replicated many times over.[12]

But then, near the end of this confession, we come across a passage that relates to one's fundamental, existential identity: "My God, while yet I was unformed I was not worthy, and now that I have been formed, I am as though I had not been formed." One questions the validity, meaning, and value of one's own existence. This is reminiscent not of *gezel ha-ger* but of the passage in *Bechukkotai,* where one's basic existence is at stake. It is not a situation where the person is good but has committed a sin or two and has to make peace with God. No, the person confessing says, "*ke-ilu lo notzarti,* I am as though I had not been formed" – my life is meaningless, valueless!

To make that kind of statement, you have to be in a different mindset from ticking off a whole catalog of sins. This is a radical confrontation that calls into question the validity and the value of your existence and that places you in a world that is collapsing, in shambles. In this part of the *viddui* you say you are "like a vessel filled with shame and humiliation." Qualitatively, this is not the calculated, systematic *teshuva* where you list an alphabetical series of transgressions. This is a *teshuva* of crisis! Does anyone imagine, for a moment, that in the passage in *Bechukkotai,* when "they shall confess their iniquity and the iniquity of their fathers," they recite it according to the order of the *alef beit*? This is a very different kind of *viddui* and a different kind of *teshuva* if you really mean what you say. This is the *viddui* of a soul in ferment and torment, if the confession is honest and meaningful.

12. The chapter "The Integrity of *Teshuva*" elaborates upon this idea.

B) The Roots of Yom Kippur

I believe that a similar dual note is struck if we examine the roots of Yom Kippur. One root is historical: the day of receiving the second set of tablets and of the revelation of the Thirteen Attributes of Mercy, the path of repentance for the Jewish people, of appeasement of God and reconciliation with Him. Unquestionably, this context is one of *teshuva* and *viddui*. Moshe *Rabbeinu* states, in a declaration that is at once plea and acknowledgment, "O, this people has sinned a great sin, they have made them gods of gold" (*Shemot* 32:31). The account of the Golden Calf bears the hallmark of *Bechukkotai*. Its point of departure is frightening and alarming, what *Chazal* described as a kind of collective spiritual fornication, in the midst of a honeymoon,[13] resulting in total alienation from God with the concomitant threat of national extinction: "Let Me alone that I may destroy them" (*Devarim* 9:14)! It leaves the world riven asunder by sin and the people of Israel in shambles, devastated by abysmal failure. This is a scenario of "when you are in distress" (*Devarim* 4:30).

One does not need considerable literary skills or imaginative insight to picture how great and terrible must have been the ferment, collective and personal, during those eighty days of anxiety. To the extent that we appreciate that, and now strive to reconstruct and relive annually that primal Yom Kippur, we too undergo anguish; likewise, we strive, with creative dynamism, to be worthy of grace, pardon, and reconciliation. This is one root of Yom Kippur.

I would like to suggest that Yom Kippur has an additional root, one which is not historical but perennial. The verse states: "For on this day He shall atone for you to purify you of all your sins; you shall be purified before the Lord" (*Vayikra* 16:30). I ask myself, had there been no sin of the Golden Calf, had the people of Israel behaved properly, had everything proceeded from Egypt to Mount Sinai to the Land of Israel as planned, would the world have managed without a Yom Kippur?[14]

---

13. "A shameless bride who was unfaithful under the bridal canopy" (*Gittin* 36b).
14. Questions of this kind arise with regard to various *mitzvot*, which seem to be, as they are described in *Chumash*, a response to historical events. Similarly, we often speak of Torah's eternality, "having preceded the existence of the world" (*Shabbat*

Would there be no sins for which we require purification, no need for soul-searching and reconciliation? Would we all have been perfect?

I am conjecturing, but it seems to me that had there been no sin of the Golden Calf, nonetheless there would have been a need for purification; and this need would have been met by a periodic – presumably annual – day of taking stock, of quietly engaging in introspective examination of ourselves. This would have entailed examination of our deeds, not under the Damocles' sword of threatened extinction, but as a focus of constant spiritual existence.

Given that "there is no man who is wholly righteous on earth, who shall do only good and not sin" (*Kohelet* 7:20), such an occasion, on which we would be charged with coming to grips with our humanity and our failings, seems indispensable. To be sure, the Yom Kippur which I am hypothesizing probably would have been different. It would have been in the spirit of repose, there would have been *vidduyim* of *gezel ha-ger* replicated many times over, with no mention of *Bechukkotai* or of "now that I have been formed, I am as though I had not been formed." While it may be contended that the cumulative impact of many sins affects the qualitative nature of even *gezel ha-ger* and that transgressor's *viddui*, it does seem to me that the modality of the *teshuva* of repose, as well as the quest for the peace we seek in our response to God, would have remained an integral aspect of Yom Kippur.

PURIFICATION OF FERMENT AND PURIFICATION OF REPOSE

As we prepare for "the great and awesome day of the Lord" (based on *Yoel* 3:4, *Malakhi* 3:23), we approach it with an awareness of its multifaceted complexity. This complexity is characteristic of the religious life as Judaism has conceived it, within which there are the elements of ferment and repose as well as the interaction between them, and within which we neither deny, nor want to deny, the validity of either pole. It has been summed up in a marvelously Jewish formulation by a non-Jewish writer. Wordsworth once spoke tellingly of "central peace, subsisting at the heart of endless agitation."[15]

88b with Rashi *ad loc.* s.v. *tesha*, *Yalkut Shimoni*, I *Melakhim* 185, *Shir Ha-shirim* 988), yet somehow, whole *parashiyot* seem to be written in response to events. This is a more general question, which is not within the scope of this essay.

15. "The Sea Shell," in "The Excursion," Book IV.

This is the quest for the ferment interacting with repose, repose concurrent with the ferment. It is for this interaction of ferment and repose, of "central peace" with "agitation," that we prepare ourselves on the eve of Yom Kippur. We gird our spiritual loins for a grand effort, dynamic as well as calm, in a process of *teshuva*. And as we strive to rehabilitate and purify ourselves – dynamically, creatively, calmly – we turn to God with the hope and the prayer that He will purify us with an eye not only to the ferment, but to the repose.

Purification has various models. Purification of ferment is illustrated by the *halakha* that an earthenware vessel cannot be purified in a *mikve*, a ritual bath;[16] you have to break it and start afresh, *shevirat keli cheres*. This purification entails collapsing and rebuilding. Purification of repose is illustrated by *tevila*, immersion in a body of water; this mode is calm and restorative. We say to God we are "a vessel filled with shame and humiliation," perhaps worthy of being broken and reset. God should purify us as His wisdom perceives, but we hope and we plead of Him to give us the strength for the ferment, and to allow us the purification of repose. "May the Lord grant strength to His people; may the Lord bless His people with peace" (*Tehillim* 29:11). "Peace, peace, for the far and the near, says the Lord; and I shall heal them" (*Yeshayahu* 57:19).

16. Based on *Vayikra* 6:21, 11:33; *Shabbat* 84a; Rambam, *Hilkhot Tum'at Okhalin* 2:25, *Hilkhot Mikvaot* 1:3.

Renunciation, Divorce, and Rehabilitation

TESHUVA AS A UNIVERSAL AND A JEWISH CATEGORY

Teshuva constitutes a universal phenomenon. The gentile world acknowledges its significance as both duty and aspiration and has produced a valuable corpus extolling its character. *Chazal* indeed regarded *teshuva* as coterminous with human history, conjecturing in the *Midrash* that Adam and Chava, fresh from the exile from the Garden of Eden, discovered and initiated *teshuva* as dusk fell on a suddenly alien horizon, on the primal *erev* Shabbat.[1] When we recite *Selichot,* in the paragraph introducing the Thirteen Attributes of Mercy, we say that God "performs righteousness with all flesh and spirit," which includes the whole range of human existence and activity. And, of course, the fullest expression of the universal meaning of *teshuva* lies in the narrative of *Yona,* in which "Nineveh, the great city" (1:2) serves as the exemplar of repentance.[2]

Delivered as the Hausman/Stern *Kinnus Teshuva* lecture at the Gruss Institute in Jerusalem, Tishrei 5768 (2007).

1. *Avot De-Rabbi Natan,* chapter 1.
2. Similarly, Rabbeinu Yona opens his classic *Sha'arei Teshuva* with reference to *teshuva* as "among the Blessed One's kindnesses to His creations," which is all-inclusive.

Nevertheless, within the context of the special relationship of the Jewish people and God, *teshuva* acquires an additional dimension. Indeed, a *mishna* in *Avot* (3:18) speaks, on the one hand, of the special relationship between man and God, "Beloved is man for he was created in the image of God," and then a second level, "Beloved are Israel who are called children of God." The core of the assertion, "Beloved are Israel," is that the Jewish people in our totality have been accorded an elevated status, and that this has been conferred upon us uniquely. God's *tefillin*, says the *Gemara* in *Berakhot* (6a), bear the inscription, "And who is like Your people Israel, one nation on earth?" (II *Divrei Ha-yamim* 17:21).

On Rosh Ha-shana the Jewish people acknowledge the brotherhood of man under the fatherhood of God, and describe the idyll of the messianic era as a universal one: "And all shall form a single union to perform Your will with a complete heart."[3] But afterward we focus upon our particularistic election:

> You have chosen us from among all the other peoples. You have loved us and desired us, raised us up from all other tongues, sanctified us with Your *mitzvot*, and brought us closer to Your service.

Our unique place within the family of nations is an integral aspect of the Jewish eschatological vision, as articulated by both Mikha and Yeshayahu:

> But in the last days it shall come to pass, that the mountain of the house of the Lord shall be established on the top of the mountains, and it shall be exalted above the hills; and peoples shall stream toward it. And many nations shall come, and say, "Come, and let us go up to the mountain of the Lord, and to the house of the God of Ya'akov; and He will teach us of His ways, and we will walk

3. That element of unity is expressed also in the verse in *Zekharia* (14:9) that we recite daily in *Aleinu*, "And the Lord shall be king over all the earth; on that day the Lord shall be one and His name one."

> in His paths"; for Torah shall go forth from Zion, and the word of the Lord from Yerushalayim. (*Mikha* 4:1–2; *Yeshayahu* 2:2–3)

The ramifications of that election, so central to our sensibility and thought, are multifaceted and antithetical. The essence of that election is not solely the conferring of privilege and prerogative, but the setting of more rigorous standards, quantitatively and qualitatively, for the realization of divine service. When these standards are met, they accrue to our benefit and ennoble our spiritual being. *Chazal* say:

> God desired *le-zakkot* (to credit) the Jewish people; thus He increased the Torah and *mitzvot* on their behalf, as the verse states (*Yeshayahu* 42:21), "The Lord desires His righteousness, thus He magnifies and exalts the Torah." (*Makkot* 23b)

While in one sense the term "*le-zakkot*" means to credit, philologically it means to purify, to ennoble us.

Yet the possibility of failure to live up to those demands exists, and the history of that failure is writ large in the Bible and subsequent sources.[4] In the words of the prophet, "Only you have I known from all the families of the earth; therefore I shall call you to account for all of your sins" (*Amos* 3:2). So there is at the same time both a benefit and, potentially, a great price to be paid.

The critical fact is that this special relationship impinges upon the entirety of divine service, and specifically upon the realms of sin and *teshuva*. The concept of our election opens up vistas of sin and rebellion on our part, and, in consequence, it imposes demands of rehabilitation and regeneration. To the extent that we shun the outstretched hand and renounce our spiritual patrimony, shirking the responsibilities imposed upon us by our special status, we are then mandated to rejuvenate our spiritual selves and to mend our fences with God.

4. In a way, God's demands reflect the high regard in which He holds us. The *Midrash* says in a number of places (e.g., *Bereishit Rabba* 32:3, 34:2, 55:2; *Shir Ha-shirim Rabba* 2:2; *Tanchuma, Vayera* 20; *Midrash Tehillim*, Buber ed., 11:4) that God tests only those He thinks are capable of withstanding the pressure and responding appropriately to it.

RENUNCIATION OF NORMS AND VALUES

In the renunciation of that patrimony, we relate to three independent yet interwoven areas: norms and values; identity and status; and relationship and bonds. The *Mishna* in *Berakhot* (13a) explains the sequence of *Keriat Shema*: the first *parasha* demands acceptance of *ol malkhut Shamayim*, the yoke of Heaven, and the second speaks of *ol mitzvot*, the yoke of *mitzvot*. While we should glory in the responsibility imposed upon us, that response is not automatic. At times, we may feel that the burden of *ol mitzvot* is excessive – to some, problematic in theory, to others, problematic in practice. Then there are those who want, whether out of submission to base urges or out of rebelliousness, to renounce the entire corpus or parts of it. In addition, some rebel against the very thought that they will be told what to do. Others reject a certain specific norm as being out of sync with contemporary sensibility. In such cases, they may want to be identified with part of the system, and they may even observe part of the corpus out of a blend of conformity and commitment; but the concept of submission, of the yoke bearing down upon our necks, is more than they can stand.

The Torah designates a certain kind of servitude as a quintessential part of Jewish existence: "They are My servants whom I brought out of the land of Egypt" (*Vayikra* 25:42, 55). And we, as committed *benei Torah*, sing with joy, "I am a servant of the Holy One, blessed be He" (*Zohar, Vayak'hel* 206a, recited before removing the Torah). Indeed, this frees us from other kinds of servitude; halakhically one cannot indenture himself indefinitely to another master.[5]

But there are many who do not wish to be servants, even to God. They echo the memorable expression of Milton's Satan, "Better to reign in hell than to serve in Heaven."[6] There are others who are *benei basar*, the epicureans of this world, who seek out carnal pleasure and libidinous lust, and prefer these to a life of halakhic discipline. Another category consists of those who seek sheer passive existence, like that of

5. *Kiddushin* 22b, *Bava Kamma* 116b, *Bava Metzia* 10a.
6. *Paradise Lost* 1:1:263.

Tennyson's *Lotos-Eaters,* denizens of a land in which all breathe languid air, "a land in which it seemed always afternoon."[7]

RENUNCIATION OF IDENTITY AND STATUS

The flight from responsibility assumes a different character in a second mode of renunciation, that of status. God describes the Jewish people as occupying a special status: "*Beni bekhori Yisrael,* My son, my firstborn, Israel" (*Shemot* 4:22). Not only are the Jewish people part of God's family, they are His children; and not just children, but His firstborn. And the firstborn has a special status, which gives him privileges and responsibilities. It is only natural for the firstborn to enjoy the fact that he receives a double portion of the inheritance (*Devarim* 21:17). But there is less joy in assuming the burden of leadership and the mantle of responsibility that comes with the *bekhora.*[8] The special status of *bekhor,* the burden of responsibility that it places on one's shoulders, is of a different order from regular *mitzvot* such as meat and milk, prohibited marital relations, *tzitzit* and *tefillin;* consequently, the renunciation of that status differs from the first renunciation, that of *ol mitzvot.*

The firstborn bears a yoke that has to do with status, with *noblesse oblige.* When the selection of the Jewish people is described in the Torah, two terms are twinned: we are expected to be an "*am segulla,* chosen

---

7. *Chazal* identified the refusal to assume a burden of *ol mitzvot* with the world of *benei Noach.* On the verse from *Vezot Haberakha,* "God came from Sinai, shone forth from Se'ir, appeared from Mount Paran, and arrived from the holy multitudes" (*Devarim* 33:2), the *Gemara* (*Avoda Zara* 2b) asks, Why was God coming from Se'ir and Paran? *Chazal* say, in a daring statement, that God opened up the world of Torah and *mitzvot* to the highest bidder, offering it first to Yishmael and then to Esav, both of whom rejected His offer.
8. In the Torah there are a number of passages that speak of the *bekhora* and the mitzva of *pidyon ha-ben,* redeeming of the firstborn. Some describe the origin as the exodus from Egypt (*Shemot* 13:2, 12–15; *Bemidbar* 3:13, 8:17), whereas others designate the *bekhora* as something special simply because that which is first occupies a special place, not because of any connection to the exodus. The concept of *bekhora* includes firstborn animals (see *Bereishit* 4:4, *Shemot* 13:12–13); *bikkurim,* the first fruit (*Devarim* 26:2); *challa* (*Bemidbar* 15:20); *teruma* (*Bemidbar* 18:12); and *terumat ma'aser.* The Rambam in his *Commentary on the Mishna* (*Zevachim* 14:4) says that the delegation of the divine service to the firstborns started with Adam.

people," and a "*goy kadosh,* holy nation."[9] *Bekhora,* presumably, is the conjunction of these two elements. There are many who cherish the thought of being *am segulla,* God's treasure. But the Torah never speaks of *am segulla* as an independent category, divested of responsibility. If you want to be an *am segulla,* you must be a *goy kadosh.* But to be a *goy kadosh* is to aspire to be something that we are not as yet: "*Kedoshim tihyu,* You shall be holy" (*Vayikra* 19:2). This burden is much less pleasant and enjoyable, and therefore there are those who wish to renounce the *bekhora* and its attendant responsibility.

Some may minimize the status of *bekhor,* for it is a far cry from what it used to mean in agrarian communities. Today there are blessings aplenty to which one who is not a *bekhor* can aspire. But surely, we need to understand the lengths to which Rivka went in order to ensure that the blessing should be given to Ya'akov and not to Esav. What was at stake was not simply personal aggrandizement, the bounds of personal authority, and personal resources. What was at stake was the character of *bekhora,* and beyond that, the nature of human existence and moral responsibility. For Ya'akov, pervaded with a sense of personal, social, communal, and historical responsibility, *bekhora* meant *avoda,* the right and the duty to assume the mantle of service, the mantle of responsibility.

Esav had a different set of priorities. He was aware of the practical benefits of *bekhora,* and he was willing to adopt *bekhora* only to the extent that those benefits could be received. When it became apparent that he might never reap the fruits of the *bekhora,* he decided to sell it. "Behold I am going to die; for what do I need the *bekhora*?" (*Bereishit* 25:32). Today, the Esavs of the world, some within our own community, have internalized this philosophy and rejected the special status of God's firstborn.

RENUNCIATION OF RELATIONSHIP AND BONDS

There is a third level of renunciation, which relates to matrimony. Many metaphors in *Tanakh* express the relationship of God with the Jewish people, and one of the most common and most powerful is the amatory. At times it is expressed in thoroughly sexual terms, perhaps even

9. See *Shemot* 19:5–6; *Devarim* 7:6, 14:2.

sharply so. This is illustrated by the following verses from the *haftara* of *Nitzavim*, the last of the seven consolatory *haftarot* recited during the period from Tisha Be-Av until Rosh Ha-shana:

> You shall no more be termed: Forsaken; neither shall your land any more be termed: Desolate. But you shall be called: My delight is in Her (*Cheftzi-vah*), and your land: Espoused (*Be'ula*); for the Lord delights in you, and your land shall be espoused. For as a young man takes to himself a maiden, so shall your sons take you to themselves; and as the bridegroom rejoices over the bride, so shall your God rejoice over you. (*Yeshayahu* 62:4–5)

Elsewhere this is even more sharply defined: "For your Maker espouses (*bo'alayikh*) you; the Lord of Hosts is His name" (*Yeshayahu* 54:5). The message of that description, which speaks of reciprocal commitment and passion, is quite significant in its own right. But we need to look at the infrastructure it creates for infidelity and adultery. There can be no betrayal without prior fealty, no renunciation devoid of prior commitment.

The Rambam in *Moreh Nevukhim* (1:36) tries somewhat to limit the ascription of passion to God; it was, for him, part of the larger problem of anthropomorphism. He explains that the Torah and the prophets speak of God having "wrath (*charon af*)," "anger (*ka'as*)," and "jealousy (*kin'a*)" only with regard to idolatry.

The Ramban (*Shemot* 20:3 s.v. *ve-ta'am al panai*) calls the Rambam to task for this, citing many verses that speak of anger and wrath in contexts far from idolatry, such as, "And the anger of the Lord was enflamed against them and He departed" (*Bemidbar* 12:9), with regard to Aharon and Miriam. But, says the Ramban, in one respect the Rambam is right: "With regard to the term *kin'a*, it is true"; God is described as jealous exclusively with regard to idolatry. For example, when idolatry is mentioned in the Ten Commandments, the term "jealous (*kanna*)" is applied to God (*Shemot* 20:5). Gentile worship of idols does not please God, but His jealousy is not aroused. Why is there *kin'a* only with regard to the Jewish people? The Ramban explains:

> The reason for the *kin'a* is that Israel is the chosen nation of the Almighty God, who separated them as His, as I have explained above. And if His nation, His servants, turn to other gods, God shall set forth *kin'a* against them, as a man displays *kin'a* toward his wife when she turns to others.

The message concerning the Jewish people and its matrimonial station is very explicit. The term "*kanna*," as we know from the passage about the *sota* (*Bemidbar* 5:14), describes the kind of jealousy that enrages a man when he sees his wife consorting or having an affair with someone else. Idolatry, when practiced by gentiles, is objectionable, but gentiles are not married to God. By contrast, says the Ramban, "God, who separated [the Jewish people] as His ... shall set forth *kin'a* against them, as a man displays *kin'a* toward his wife when she turns to others."

For the Rambam, this jealousy has halakhic ramifications. Two modes of idolatry are discussed in Halakha: *ke-darkah*, which refers to worshipping a certain idol in accordance with its customary ritual, and *she-lo ke-darkah*, where one adopts one of the services done in the Temple, to be performed for God alone, and diverts it to idol worship (see *Shemot* 22:19). The Rambam in *Hilkhot Melakhim* (9:2) says that gentiles are charged only for serving an idol *ke-darkah*; they are not responsible for *she-lo ke-darkah*. Why? The answer, I think, is self-evident in light of the Ramban's explanation. Idolatry *ke-darkah* is an abomination *per se*, because it is a full expression of idol worship. But if a person worships an idol in a way that it is not ordinarily worshipped, *she-lo ke-darkah*, this does not constitute idol worship. Nevertheless, you have taken that which is unique to God and dedicated it to a false deity.

For the Jewish people that is a problem. "He that sacrifices to any god, save to the Lord only, he shall be utterly destroyed" (*Shemot* 22:19). The Jewish people can have a relationship only with God. Any expression of another relationship, even when it is not defined as worship from a strict legal perspective, is the transfer of fealty and loyalty from God, as expressed through a ritual done exclusively for Him in the Temple, to a figure of wood and silver. Such an act is prohibited to us, because we are chosen by God as an "*am segulla*" and a "*goy kadosh*."

DISSOLUTION OF THE MATRIMONIAL RELATIONSHIP

We discussed heretofore three kinds of renunciation – renunciation of the codex of Torah and *mitzvot*, renunciation of the special status of *bekhora*, and renunciation of the spousal relationship between ourselves and God. But there is a further step. The following passage appears in *parashat Vayelekh*:

> And the Lord appeared in the Tent in a pillar of cloud.... The Lord said to Moshe: Behold you shall sleep with your fathers; and this people will rise up and go astray after the gods of the strangers of the land into which they go to be among them, and they will forsake Me and break My covenant which I have made with them. Then My anger will burn against them on that day, and I will forsake them, and I will hide My face from them, and they shall be devoured, and many evils and troubles shall befall them; so that they will say on that day, "Are not these evils come upon us, because our God is not among us?" And I will surely hide My face on that day, for all the evils which they shall have perpetrated, in that they have turned to other gods. (*Devarim* 31:15–17)

The sections of the *tokhacha* in *Bechukkotai* and *Ki Tavo* are frightful. Yet they convey a sense that there is a limit, both to the Jewish people's sins and to God's response. This sense is more prominent in *Bechukkotai*, which concludes with the comforting thought, "Even still, with their being in the land of their enemies, I will not despise them nor abhor them to destroy them, to annul My covenant with them, for I am the Lord their God. And I shall remember the covenant with the early ones when I took them out of Egypt to be their God; I am the Lord" (*Vayikra* 26:44–45). The *tokhacha* in *Ki Tavo* does not end with this comforting note, I presume, for an obvious reason: that assurance can be given only by God. *Chazal* say that Moshe said the blessings and curses in *Ki Tavo* on his own (*Megilla* 31b). But still, when reading the whole *parasha*, one has the sense that both the transgressions and the response arise within the family relationship. The sins of the Jewish people are depicted as adultery, as the actions of a woman who has found a paramour, but who remains married and does not dream of departing the marriage. And while God, for His part, will punish the Jewish people for its infidelity, there is no threat that He will dissolve the marriage.

In contrast, that is precisely what is conceived and threatened in the passage in *Vayelekh*. It starts with an initial act of infidelity, the Jewish people "go[ing] astray after the gods of the strangers of the land." But then the next phase is "And they will forsake Me and break (*hefer*) My covenant." The term "*hefer*" in *Tanakh* and Halakha often means to violate, to breach a provision of a contract that you signed. But it is also used to indicate abrogation, dissolution: "If the husband annulled (*hafer yafer*) them on the day he heard them" (*Bemidbar* 30:13).[10]

I think the meaning here of "*hefer*," in light of the previous term, "they will forsake Me," should be taken in the sense of abrogated. Ordinarily, we would say that one cannot abandon God. "Where can I hide from Your face?" (*Tehillim* 139:7). But God threatens to disappear, as it were. "I will hide My face from them and they shall be devoured." God reiterates this message: "And I will surely hide My face on that day, for all the evils which they shall have perpetrated" (*Devarim* 31:17–18).

How is it possible for the Jewish people to dissolve the marriage? As we know, for Jews, the *get* has to be given by the husband. But there is another way. Gentiles do not need to give a formal *get*; one of the parties to the marriage can just decide to leave, and the marriage then dissolves automatically.[11] If the Jewish people renounce *malkhut Shamayim*, they become gentiles and, in so doing, they abrogate their relationship with God.

If that weren't enough, *Chazal* envision the Jewish people making the claim that they did not forsake God, but that God initiated the break. The *Gemara* in *Shabbat* (88a) mentions that, since there was some element of coercion, as it were, at the time of the giving of the Torah, the Jewish people could claim they accepted it under duress. The Ramban (*Shabbat* 88a, s.v. *ve-ha*) says that initially they accepted the Torah willingly, saying, "*Na'aseh ve-nishma*, We shall do and we shall hear

10. The *Mishna* in *Nedarim* distinguishes between *hafara*, cancellation of a woman's vow by her husband or father, and *hetter chakham*, abrogation of a vow by a scholar; the latter dissolves the vow altogether, while the former only suspends the vow.
11. *Yerushalmi, Kiddushin* 2:1; Rambam, *Hilkhot Melakhim* 9:8.

[the Torah]" (*Shemot* 24:7). But they understood there to be a condition: God gave us the Torah so that we would observe it in the Land of Israel. The pagan conception of the world conceives of geographical limitations on every deity: Athens, Sparta, Carthage, and every other land or city has its own deity that enjoys authority in its local domain, but it has no jurisdiction in the adjacent community. When the Jewish people were sent into exile, the *Gemara* in *Sanhedrin* (105a) conjectures that they asked: "A slave whose Master has sold him, does the servant have any responsibility to the former master?" The Jewish people reasoned: Now that we are in Babylonia, we owe fealty to the local gods. The argument is specious, but that was part of the justification of their renunciation. They claimed, "It is God's fault; He is responsible."

The prophets, by way of responding to this charge, gave two different responses. Yeshayahu says:

> Thus says the Lord, Where is the bill of your mother's divorce, with which I have sent her away, or which of my creditors is it to which I have sold you? Behold, for your iniquities you have sold yourselves and for your transgressions your mother was sent away. Why when I came was there no man? When I called, there was none to answer? Is My hand shortened at all that it cannot redeem? Or have I no power to deliver? Behold at My rebuke I dry up the sea; I make the rivers a wilderness. Their fish rot because there is no water, and die of thirst. I clothe the heavens with blackness, and I make sackcloth their covering. (*Yeshayahu* 50:1–3)

But in *Yirmiyahu* we read:

> The Lord also said to me in the days of Yoshiyahu the king, "Have you seen that which faithless Israel has done? She has gone up upon every high mountain and under every green tree and there has played the harlot. And I said, After she has done all these things, she will return to Me. But she did not return. And her treacherous sister Yehuda saw it. And I saw when, forasmuch as faithless Yisrael committed adultery, I had put her away and given

> her a bill of divorce, that her treacherous sister Yehuda was not afraid and went and played the harlot also." (3:5–8)

Whereas Yeshayahu denies the claim that God had written a *get*, here God is described as giving a *get*, albeit only a partial one, and only for a limited period of time. Yirmiyahu also describes a renunciation on the part of the Jewish people and a desire to abandon their special status, one expressed also in a verse from *Yechezkel* (20:32): "That which crosses your mind, that shall not be, that which you say, 'We shall be like the nations, like the families of the lands, to serve wood and stone.'" The people want to renounce the relationship, to be "like the families of the lands." In practical terms, it is a renunciation not only of the codex, but of the personal, intimate relationship with God.

TESHUVA FROM RENUNCIATION

The path of recovery from this entails *teshuva*, of course. Other passages in the Torah predict that *teshuva* will come forth as a response to suffering: "When you are in distress, and all these things have befallen you, in the latter days, you shall turn to the Lord your God" (*Devarim* 4:30), and "You shall find Him, if only you seek Him with all your heart and with all your soul" (*Devarim* 4:29). But here *teshuva* rises out of the depths of sin and renunciation, in a cycle described in *parashat Vayelekh* – not as a one-time historical event, but coming anew in every generation.

In light of this, how are we to conceive of *teshuva* for the renunciation of our special relationship with God? Will the *teshuva* of Nineveh suffice? Universal *teshuva* requires that one turn away from the sin, express remorse for the misdeeds of the past, accept upon oneself a corrective future path, and so on.[12] That normal *teshuva* undoubtedly is required, but for us it is not enough. That kind of *teshuva* suffices for the gentile world, which shares with us the idealization of *teshuva* and responds to sin through the context of *teshuva*. They have read *Sefer Yona* too.[13]

---

12. See Rambam, *Hilkhot Teshuva* 2:2; Rabbeinu Yona, *Sha'arei Teshuva*, 1:10 *et seq*.
13. Melville has a wonderful chapter (9) in *Moby Dick* about repentance.

But for us it is different. First, because more is expected of us. The bar was raised for us when we received the Torah. Our prayer should be more heartfelt, and our fear of Heaven should be more intense. Our *chesed* should be more generous, and our integrity should be more irreproachable. Our sense of justice and our concern for divine majesty should be at a higher level.

Not only is greater intensity expected of us, but we also have a more expansive complex of *mitzvot* to which we are committed. Furthermore, for us there is much more at stake. The ramifications of sin for us are not only right and wrong, but our status as firstborn, our living up to our elected status, and our intimate relationship with God.

The Rambam (*Hilkhot Teshuva* 7:7) speaks of the marvel of *teshuva* at a personal level. But the renunciation to which I address myself, and the kind of *teshuva* which it requires, extend beyond that. In the world of sin and *teshuva*, there is a dual difference between the *tzibbur* and the *yachid*, the community and the individual. On the one hand, the community is in a much better position: *Chazal* say that an individual generally has difficulty in gaining access to God, while regarding the *tzibbur*, we are told, "He is a mighty God and will not despise" (*Iyyov* 36:5), "Whenever we call out to him" (*Devarim* 4:7).[14] On the other hand, for the same reasons, the sin of the community is more grievous than the sin of the individual.

That means that we have much more work to do. We have to restructure our communities and restructure our nation. But we have to begin by restoring the relationship. We read in the book of *Hoshea* (2:9–10), regarding his unfaithful wife: "And she shall follow after her lovers, but she shall not catch them, and she shall seek them but shall not find them. And she shall say, I will go and return to my first husband, for then it was better for me than now." *Teshuva* begins with "I will go and return to my first husband." Hoshea describes a reconciliation that eclipses the original bond:

> And it shall be on that day, says the Lord, that you shall say, "My husband," and shall say no more to me, "My master." For I will take away the names of the *be'alim* out of her mouth, and they

14. *Rosh Ha-shana* 18a; *Yevamot* 105a; *Berakhot* 8a.

> shall be no more mentioned by their name. And on that day I will make a covenant for them with the wild beast, and with the birds of the sky, and with the creeping things of the ground, and I will break the bow and the sword and the battle out of the earth and will make them lie down in safety. And I will betroth you to Me forever; and I will betroth you to Me in righteousness and in judgment, and in loyal love, and in mercies. And I will betroth you to Me in faithfulness, and you shall know the Lord. (*Hoshea* 2:18–22)

We might ask, what does this have to do with us? We don't renounce Torah and *mitzvot*. We don't desire to abandon our firstborn status. And we don't suggest, God forbid, that we no longer owe fealty to the God who took us out of Egypt. We are anxious, *desperately* anxious, to hear the voice of God: "May He let us hear, 'I have forgiven you'" (from the *Selichot* for the Fourth Day of Repentance).

The answer, I think, lies in understanding the character of these kinds of sins in particular. Much of what I have discussed here will come under the general heading of secularism, as an ideology and a lifestyle. Secularism as an entity stands opposed to the world to which we are committed. But even if we are not, God forbid, secularists, we have to ask ourselves how seriously, how purposefully, do we want to advance *malkhut Shamayim* in the world? To what extent do we find ourselves fully engaged and fully committed to a life of Torah? Here, it seems to me, for ourselves and for our community, there is room for concern.

A strange phenomenon exists today within the Orthodox community. Some, animated by what can only be described as a jingoistic chauvinism, do not acknowledge the value and the validity of the gentile world altogether. If they could have their way, they would probably expunge *Sefer Yona* from the biblical canon; it doesn't quite meet their conception of what gentiles are like. On the other hand, there are many who absorb with relish much of what the gentile world has to offer, and who are not perturbed by the insidious influence of certain elements of that culture upon themselves, their children, their institutions, and their communities. So there is room for asking ourselves whether a taint of secularism has affected our lifestyle, because that is something which needs to be confronted by the power and force of *teshuva*.

When we approach Yom Kippur, it is a good time to be reminded, with all the power, depth and intensity at our command, of what the first *isru chag* of Yom Kippur entailed. This returns us to the Ramban, who brings to bear his wonderful conjectural capacity on the first verse of *Vayak'hel* (*Shemot* 35:1, s.v. *vayak'hel*):

> "And Moshe gathered the entire community of Israel" – This command includes "the entire community of Israel," the men and the women, for all contributed to the construction of the Tabernacle. And Moshe, after commanding Aharon, and the princes, and all the men of Israel all that God had spoken to him on Mount Sinai after he broke the tablets (*Shemot* 34:32), and placing a veil over his face (34:33), he returned and commanded that the entire community gather: men, women, and children. It may well be that this was on the day following his descent, the morning following Yom Kippur.
>
> He told the entire community about the Tabernacle (regarding which he had been commanded before breaking the tablets), and that since they had been forgiven by God, and He had given the second tablets, and established a new covenant to walk in their midst, they had returned to their original level and to their nuptial love. And they came to know that His presence would be among them as He had commanded originally, as it says, "And they shall make a *Mikdash* for Me, and I shall dwell in their midst" (*Shemot* 25:8). Thus Moshe commanded them now everything that he had been commanded to teach them originally.

Humility and Pride in *Teshuva*

THE DANGERS OF PRIDE

From time immemorial, moralists and pietists have railed against the failings of pride and have warned against its imminent dangers. First, at the plane of personal ethics, pride generally involves a deplorably distorted appraisal of status and worth on the one hand, and presents an egocentric posture on the other; both are morally reprehensible. Second, pride, particularly its exaggerated form, poisons not only one's personal moral state, but one's interpersonal relations as well, introducing an aura of supercilious condescension in the mere act of tolerating a person one clearly regards as being inferior. Finally, pride represents spiritual corrosion with respect to the individual and the community both, in that it enables us to ascribe to our own talents and efforts a confidence better credited to God.

From a religious dimension, pride even more daringly and dangerously subverts some of the most fundamental components of religious life: submissive awe, radical subjugation, and comprehensive servitude. At its most extreme, pride stimulates the rebellious impulse, issuing a

Delivered as the Hausman/Stern *Kinnus Teshuva* lecture at the Gruss Institute in Jerusalem, Tishrei 5769 (2008).

challenge to divine authority, as we find with Aeschylus' Prometheus, Milton's Satan, and their confreres throughout history. The quest for fame, "that last infirmity of noble mind,"[1] obscures the cardinal truth as to where we stand objectively, and where we should stand religiously.

Pride certainly comes in for condemnation in our own tradition as well. From the very inception of humanity, pride – particularly intellectual pride – is represented as the root of Adam and Chava's primal sin. Even before Chava "saw that the tree was good for food, that it was desirous for the eyes" (*Bereishit* 3:6), the serpent stroked the human ego: "For God knows that on the day you eat of it, then your eyes shall be opened and you shall be as gods, knowing good and evil" (3:5). A handful of generations later, we encounter the generation of the Tower of Babel, whose sin – "And let us make ourselves a name" (*Bereishit* 11:4), admittedly couched in ambiguity – was evidently bound up in the context of their reputation, which the *Gemara* (*Sanhedrin* 109a) envisions with the following scenario:

> Rabbi Yirmiya ben Elazar stated: They were split into three groups. One group said: We will ascend heavenward; we will settle there. A second group said spitefully: We will engage in idol worship. A third group said: We shall ascend heavenward and wage war.

Pride is thus singled out for condemnation as a quality that is evil, morally and religiously, from the earliest generations of humanity.

Our traditional condemnation of pride is not confined to the implications of biblical narratives, however expounded. To be sure, the quest for glory, and the fame and pride attendant upon it, are not clearly prohibited, either in the *Gemara* or the *Rishonim*;[2] nevertheless, there is no dearth of authoritative condemnation in other texts and other contexts. *Avot* is replete with exhortations against pride. To offer a small

1. From John Milton's "Lycidas."
2. Some authorities did seek a clear prohibition; nonetheless, the Rambam includes the pursuit of fame and pride not as a specific prohibition but on the list of things that are reprehensible and require *teshuva* (*Hilkhot De'ot* 2:2–3).

sampling: "One should be very, very humble of spirit" (4:4), and: "Jealousy, desire, and glory remove a person from this world" (4:21). Another *mishna* challenges the tendency of self-congratulatory credit: "If you have studied much Torah, do not ascribe credit to yourself, because for this you were created" (2:8) – you are merely fulfilling that which is your fundamental duty and destiny.[3]

THE *GEMARA* ON PRIDE

But if you want to look for a more central text, the richest lode to mine is certainly the *Gemara* in *Sota* (4b–5a), where we find a number of teachings in parallel, yet certainly different, veins. "Rabbi Yochanan states, any man who is haughty," and out of haughtiness assumes that everything is in his control, "in the end he will stumble with another's wife" and cross the clearest and sharpest of lines. The *Gemara* continues to make striking comparisons:

> Rabbi Yochanan states in the name of Rabbi Shimon ben Yochai: Any man who is haughty, it is as if he serves idols, for the verse states here: "A haughty person is an abomination to God" (*Mishlei* 16:5), and the verse states there: "You shall not bring an abomination [i.e., anything related to idolatry] into your home" (*Devarim* 7:26).... Rabbi Yochanan, for his part, said: It is as if a person has denied the most basic of dogmatic truths.

These phrases might be taken as a bit hyperbolic, and elsewhere other qualities and actions are compared to idolatry,[4] but here I think the suggestion is that both idolatry and pride compete with God for loyalty within a person's heart and soul. Like idolatry, haughtiness impinges, so

---

3. While the *mishna* speaks specifically of Torah study, Rabbeinu Yona and other commentators add that the same concern about taking pride in one's accomplishment applies also to the areas of fear of Heaven and fulfillment of *mitzvot*. See also *Shir Ha-shirim Rabba* 1:9.
4. A classic example is the *Gemara* in *Shabbat* (105b), which states that if a person gets angry and loses control of himself, it is as if he worships idols. Other contexts in which that comparison is made are found in *Pesachim* 118a, *Ketubbot* 68a and 110b, *Bava Batra* 10a, *Sanhedrin* 92a, *Makkot* 23a, and *Nidda* 13a.

to speak, on God; thinking so highly of oneself, one becomes a competitor and an opponent to the Almighty. But from another perspective, qualities are defined as an abomination to God in various verses not because they directly compete, so to speak, with divine authority, but because these are phenomena that God abhors.

The *Gemara* continues to seek other ways to understand the abominable nature of the haughty individual. Rabbi Chama bar Chanina equates the haughty person with one who engages in forbidden sexual relations.[5] By this assessment, the haughty person is not truly countermanding divine authority *per se*, but rather is conflicted between pursuing his own inclinations and obeying God; in the end he gives priority to his own needs – but that is the limit of his offense. The *Gemara* then returns to the realm of idolatry, likening the haughty person to one who "built a *bama*," an altar at an alternate location to the Temple, a phenomenon described recurrently in *Sefer Melakhim* as the bane of all those kings who sought to inculcate the fear of Heaven in the people, yet failed;[6] this may hint that pride, too, is difficult to uproot because it is so deeply ingrained in the human personality.

The *Gemara* (5a) continues by speaking of what lies in store for such a person: "He will be reduced"; this is followed by additional sharp statements, typified by Rabbi Elazar's remonstrance that "Anyone who is haughty, it is fit to chop him down like a tree worshipped by pagans." The overall thrust is, of course, severe condemnation of haughtiness.

The passage concludes with a dispute as to whether pride may nevertheless be, in a very small proportion, a favorable element. One opinion is that one may have "an eighth of an eighth" of pride, or less than 2% of one's total personality, while another view is that a person should be totally cleansed of pride or self-aggrandizement. Even with regard to the view that one should have a little bit of pride, the reason for allowing that pride is unclear. By contrast, I imagine we often consider even much more than 2% entirely legitimate, encouraging a "positive self-image," such that the 2% are not only allowed but recommended! Rashi explains that the talmudic allowance is limited to a person in

---

5. The Torah refers to illicit sexual relations as "abominations" (*Vayikra* 18:27), suggesting a comparison to the haughty person.
6. I *Melakhim* 15:14, 22:44; II *Melakhim* 12:4, 14:6, 15:4, 15:35.

charge of civil affairs, a local politician who, in order to assert authority, needs to cultivate an authoritative image.[7] But whatever popular opinion holds today, the range and depth of opposition to pride as being sinful, immoral, and pernicious is quite clear in the *Gemara*.

Small wonder, then, that after the Rambam sets forth his general theory of morality in the first chapter of *Hilkhot De'ot*, advocating a *via media* (middle path) for the majority of people, in the second chapter he retracts a bit and states there are some qualities with regard to which, indeed, extremism is no vice. Certain qualities call not for a moderate *via media*, but for a radical extirpation and the adoption of the alternate extreme. Not surprisingly, pride tops the list:

> The proper way is not to be modest alone. Rather, one should be low of spirit, and his spirit should be very low, this is why the verse states regarding Moshe that he was "very humble" (*Bemidbar* 12:3) rather than simply "humble." (*Hilkhot De'ot* 2:3)

In light of all that is implied in *Tanakh* and explicit in *Chazal*, we might concur with C. S. Lewis' rendering of Augustine: Pride does not just go before a fall; pride is, itself, a fall.[8]

DOES HUMILITY HAVE A ROLE IN *TESHUVA*?

It is precisely at this juncture that we stumble upon an obstacle. What does the centrality of *teshuva* suggest about humility? Does the rejection of any element of pride enhance *teshuva*, or does it possibly impede it? Does the conviction of Avraham *Avinu*, "I am but dust and ashes" (*Bereishit* 18:27), taken by *Chazal* as being a fairly extreme formulation,[9] provide the optimal milieu for *teshuva*, as well as positing for us a destination?

Prima facie, I think the answer should be resoundingly negative. I say that first with respect to those denominated today as *ba'alei teshuva* – individuals who have crossed a Rubicon and adopted a lifestyle of Torah

7. S.v. *echad mi-shemona*.
8. *Words to Live By: A Guide for the Merely Christian* (Harper Collins, 2007), p. 33, re-stating Augustine's *City of God* XII:1.
9. *Chullin* 89a.

and *mitzvot* – and also in the much more limited sense used by *Chazal* of those who repent from a particular sin.[10] In either case, but especially the first instance, transmutation requires a significant reservoir of ideological, psychological, and spiritual powers, which inspire the change, energize it, and direct it to a successful resolution.

Let us analyze the process more specifically. It entails two related, yet distinct, elements: the *ba'al teshuva* must wring out the old and ring in the new. He or she first needs to dismantle the barricades that had, both objectively and subjectively, constituted a divider between the self and God.[11] He also needs to grapple with the challenge of developing a new persona creatively and constructively: is he going be a renovated version of what he had been previously or will he be something totally different? And whether he intends a more moderate or radical form of *teshuva*, he needs both to plan how to implement the change, and actually to implement it. Destroying one's previous identity and lifestyle and adopting and adapting to a new one are prodigious tasks. How does one do so, and who is to engage in these awesome tasks?

In this connection, I am reminded of the remark made by Rabban Yochanan ben Zakkai to the Roman general Vespasian during the siege of Jerusalem (*Gittin* 56b). The *Tanna* referred to the general as royalty, and was immediately charged by the general with treason. Rabban Yochanan ben Zakkai defended himself by citing a verse from *Yeshayahu* (10:34): "And the *Levanon* shall fall by a mighty one," meaning that a mighty one would be required to destroy the *Levanon*. Inasmuch as this general was on the verge of overrunning the *Beit Ha-mikdash*, understood as "*Levanon*" (based on *Devarim* 3:25), apparently he had to be "a mighty one," a ruler. I believe we are not taking too much poetic license if we suggest that there is an "inner *Levanon*" as well, the inner sanctum of the human personality, with its various components. And *Yeshayahu*'s phrase suggests that when that human temple is defiled and desecrated, it requires "a mighty one" to dismantle it on the road to restoration and regeneration.

10. Rambam (*Hilkhot Teshuva* 2:1) clearly has this narrower ambience in mind, as does, presumably, the *Gemara* (*Yoma* 86b).
11. As the Rambam (*Hilkhot Teshuva* 7:7), contrasting the pre-*teshuva* stage to the post-*teshuva* phase, notes, "Only yesterday this sinner was divided from God."

So if a person is to engage in *teshuva,* and to lower the boom on his personal *Levanon,* on his own inner sanctum, the question is, from where is the internal strength coming? Where, if not the wellsprings of personality, shall the might necessary to destroy the *Levanon* be generated and summoned? A desperate cry must come as a *cri de coeur,* issued *de profundis,* from the depths of the heart. One needs a cry like the *shofarot* at Jericho, which were able to destroy the walls by sound alone. How else shall the ramparts of the soul come tumbling down? And afterward, in the curative, restorative, and, above all, creative second phase, from where shall come the drive and momentum requisite for molding a renascent, regenerate soul?

As we know, the world of Halakha and *avodat Hashem* is built, to a very great extent, on the concept of *bechira,* of choice. Indeed, so central is the concept of choice to the Rambam's total outlook, to *teshuva* particularly and divine service generally, that he offers a paean to free will at the epicenter of *Hilkhot Teshuva.*[12] Take, in sharp contrast, Protestantism. As he developed the main dogmas of Protestantism, Luther spoke of the aspiring regenerate, lying in utter passivity, awaiting the injection of divine grace, like a woman who lies waiting for impregnation of manly seed. To counter Luther, in 1524 the Dutch humanist Erasmus wrote a small treatise, *De Libero Arbitrio* ("On Free Will"), espousing the centrality of free will to the Christian conception of religious life even after the Fall. In the emerging war of words, the next year Luther published *De Servo Arbitrio* ("The Bondage of the Will"), contending that Erasmus had held a "knife to his throat"[13] by getting to the heart of the matter in forcing him to clarify and defend his views. If Erasmus was seen as holding a knife to Luther's throat, might not the Rambam be conceived as holding a machete?

But what does choice entail? Choice is power, authority, inner strength. And when we think of *teshuva,* we indeed think of constructive action, of building and molding.[14] *Teshuva,* in a certain sense, is a

12. The fifth through seventh chapters out of ten chapters of *Hilkhot Teshuva.*
13. Conclusion, VIII, p. 319 in the Packer-Johnston translation (1957).
14. See the famous Rashi, citing *Bereishit Rabba* 39:14, on the verse, "The souls they fashioned in Charan" (*Bereishit* 12:5), which highlights Avraham and Sarah's acts of human construction.

sort of auto-conversion, and just as a convert is considered halakhically like a newborn baby,[15] so too the *ba'al teshuva* is like a new person. As the Rambam, in a celebrated passage, states:

> Among the paths of repentance is for the penitent to constantly call out before God, crying and entreating; to perform charity to the best of his ability; to distance himself far from the object of his sin; to change his name, as if to say, "I am a different person and not the same one who sinned"; to change his behavior in its entirety to the good and the path of righteousness; and to travel in exile from his home. Exile atones for sin because it causes a person to be submissive, humble, and meek of spirit. (*Hilkhot Teshuva* 2:4)

All of that is part of *teshuva*. Interestingly, when the Rambam speaks of molding a new identity, it is the identity of a humble and low-spirited person. But here I come back to the question: Is it so self-evident that the two – humility and *teshuva* – go together? If one is humble and low-spirited, does he have the force of personality, the depth, the imagination, and the cognitive capacity for creating a new personality? When we try to relate free will to *teshuva*, we must ask: What does the centrality of free will suggest about humility? Do they naturally go hand in hand and does the exercise of free will make one more humble, or is there some gap, even some antagonism, between them?

HUMAN DISTINCTIVENESS AS THE ENGINE OF *TESHUVA*

An almost self-evident reply to this question may be found in one of the most famous Renaissance humanistic texts, Giovanni Pico della Mirandola's *Oration on the Dignity of Man*. In that work, the author, a Florentine scholar familiar with our tradition and quite friendly with some of the leading Torah scholars of northern Italy at the time, dwells upon the distinctive human ability to choose freely, and to choose not only a particular action, but a certain identity. Pico was reared on the notion, which goes back to Plato, of a kind of great chain of being,

15. *Yevamot* 22a, 48b, 62a, 97b; *Bekhorot* 47a; *Shulchan Arukh, Yoreh De'a* 269:10, *Choshen Mishpat* 33:11.

running from God, down through the angels, through a whole scale of different levels of existence. For every other species on earth, there is a fixed position on the ladder, assigned divinely and naturally. Only man, given his freedom and manifested through his action, determines his post, where he stands and where he is stationed, potentially superior to the angels or inferior to the insects.

That uniqueness, we would probably suggest to ourselves, is crucial to the process of *teshuva*. If *Levanon* will fall only at the hands of the mighty, it is precisely being a mighty one, with power and authority, with the ability to assert these capacities and exert them, that enables *teshuva* to take a person out of the state of inertia and into the field of motion and change. If one is defined and conceived as "dust and ashes" as Avraham declared, or as "nothing," based on the self-assessment of Moshe *Rabbeinu* (*Shemot* 16:8), that nothingness will be unequal to the task of dismantling an old personality and creating a new one. As admirable as humility may be in many respects, it simply will not suffice for *teshuva*. Minimally, an element of self-esteem is crucial to the process.

That element, a sense of one's worth, is itself multifaceted. It includes, first, an explicit confirmation of human worth by the *ba'al teshuva*. Were he animated by the spirit of the nihilistic portions of *Kohelet*, exemplified by "Man has no preeminence over the beast, for all is vain" (3:19), then just as an animal knows nothing of *teshuva*, man would similarly know nothing of *teshuva*. If ours is a life that, in the words of one of Tennyson's early poems (*The Two Voices*), is "a life of nothings, nothing-worth, from that first nothing ere his birth, to that last nothing under earth," we should find neither the impulse nor the capacity for *teshuva*.

But the Jewish tradition, like the humanistic one, emphatically asserts the singular character of the human species, warranting (as the Rambam and other *Rishonim* asserted) a level of *hashgacha peratit*, personal providence, denied any other species.[16] Repentance is rooted in

---

16. To be sure, the Rambam and others allow that the animal order may be guided, at most, by a "generic *hashgacha*," a providence applied to the whole genus or species. That, of course, is a far cry from the level of providence exerted on human beings, both as a species and as individuals. See *Moreh Nevukhim* III:17–18.

the assumption that we are sufficiently worthy to be cared about by God – and if He cares, we too, *a fortiori,* should care.

This point, so crucial to the experience of *teshuva* in general, and to Yom Kippur in particular, is brought home most powerfully in *tefillat Ne'ila.*[17] At twilight, as the day draws to a close, we speak at first in a voice reminiscent of the nihilistic parts of *Kohelet*:

> What are we, what is our life... what is our righteousness... what is our strength, what is our might? What can we say before You, Lord.... Are not all the mighty like nothing before You... the wise as if devoid of wisdom, and the perceptive as if devoid of understanding? For their deeds are mostly desolate, and the days of their lives null before You, and man has no preeminence over the beast, for all is vain.

As long as that is the perception, that man is regarded as implanted within the naturalistic universe, indeed there is no *teshuva*. But then we do an about face, emphasizing human differentiation and distinction, with which the possibility of *teshuva* begins: "You set man apart from the beginning, and You considered him worthy to stand before You." *Teshuva* is thus grounded in the assumption that human personality has worth, that human existence has meaning, and that human life has purpose. It is energized by a humanistic impulse – religiously humanistic, to be sure, but still humanistic.

The contrast of man's worthlessness on the one hand, and his power, position, and uniqueness on the other hand, is memorably echoed in *Tehillim*:

> When I behold Your heavens, the work of Your fingers, the moon and the stars which You ordained, what is man that You are mindful of him, and the son of man that You take account of him? Yet You have made him a little lower than the angels, and You do crown him with honor and majesty. You give him dominion over Your handiwork; You have put all things under his feet. (8:4–7)

17. The Rav *z"l* noted this very point in *Ish Ha-Halakha*, pt. 1, chap. 11 (*Halakhic Man*, p. 69).

The majesty spoken of here vis-à-vis the natural world is also that majesty and power that a person can bring to bear upon himself or herself in the quest for *teshuva* in every generation. Beyond the assumption that *teshuva* is desirable, there is a conviction that it is feasible, bespeaking a confidence that goes together with the conviction.

All this implies human power, assertiveness, and authority. While our citations speak primarily in a collective vein – "what is man?" – that sense of worth and significance exists at the individual plane as well. It is not only collective humanity but each person who is endowed with everything that *mizmor* 8 asserts. Each of us is important enough for God to address Himself to us, guide us, and challenge us. And we are each sufficiently empowered to be able to respond and to energize ourselves to act. In the first person voice of *mizmor* 139:

> Lord, You have searched me and known me. You know my sitting down and my rising up, You understand my thought far off.... I will praise You for I am fearfully and wonderfully made; marvelous are Your works, and my soul knows that very well. (*Tehillim* 139:1–2, 14)

THE DANGER OF CONDESCENSION

Yet this trumpeting of collective and personal worth only serves to reinforce our quandary: what role does humility play in the *teshuva* process, if any? The Rambam asserts, "*Ba'alei teshuva* are generally quite humble and low of spirit" (*Hilkhot Teshuva* 7:8). Now, is the Rambam making a normative statement, prescribing what ought to be, or is he merely being descriptive, stating what happens to be the case?

While this is a fair question, we must also ask if the Rambam's idealization even comports with our experience and withstands the test of factual scrutiny. Have we not all met some *ba'alei teshuva* whose retrospective wallowing in past sin, compared with the glory of subsequent enlightenment, is almost insufferable? Are not we, ourselves, often tinged with the infection? Unfortunately, one of the regrettable opportunities of *teshuva* is the opportunity it affords to contrast my own virtue with the failures of my peers. To the inspiring, positive aspects of conviction and confidence may be pinned the less favorable aspect of condescension, misusing the quality of pride in my own divine service generally, and in my *teshuva* particularly.

We must admit, with appropriate and necessary spiritual candor, that some assertions of *Chazal* that rightly laud the *ba'al teshuva* – for example, "In the place where *ba'alei teshuva* stand, the fully righteous do not merit to stand,"[18] or the fact that *teshuva* performed out of love of God is able to transmute even willfully committed sins into merits[19] – can be internalized to the point that some of those who perform *teshuva* become infected, regrettably, with a sense of superiority.

But does the risk of adopting an attitude of superiority enable us, in any way, to dismiss the centrality of *teshuva* as the quintessence of religious life? It is unthinkable that we might fail to reconcile our deep commitment to humility with our simultaneous commitment to the value, challenge, and responsibility of *teshuva*. This is true not only during *Aseret Yemei Teshuva*, but throughout our lives. Can we suggest a resolution that can break down the apparent antinomy and give us a handle on what kind of *teshuva* and what kind of pride are concordant, that the "two may walk together" (based on *Amos* 3:3)?

THE MODEL OF MOSHE *RABBEINU*

As we search for a solution, let us take our cue from Moshe *Rabbeinu*, not in the role of an individual *ba'al teshuva*, but in his capacity as leader of a nation shaken to its roots and striving to attain rehabilitation after the sin of the Golden Calf.

The Torah itself attests to the centrality of humility in the character of Moshe *Rabbeinu*: "The man Moshe was very humble, more so than any man on the face of the earth" (*Bemidbar* 12:3). Moreover, his humility is not confined to his confrontation with God. It is clearly present in the human context, as evidenced by his ability to absorb criticism rather than respond to it, and also when he posits about himself and Aharon, "Who are we that you murmur against us?" (*Shemot* 16:7–8). So Moshe *Rabbeinu* is the humble one, par excellence.

18. *Berakhot* 34b; see also *Hilkhot Teshuva* 7:4.
19. *Yoma* 86b.

And yet, this very humble human being poses to God the most audacious of requests, even demands. First, in the meetings prior to the Thirteen Attributes of Mercy, he seeks informative and ingratiating enlightenment: "Now, therefore, I beseech, if I have found favor in Your eyes, show me Your ways, that I may know You, that I may find favor in Your eyes, seeing that this nation is Your people" (*Shemot* 33:13). Subsequently, he pleads not for knowledge, but for pure, epiphanous revelation: "I beseech You, show me Your glory" (33:18).

How can the man who is "very humble, more so than any man on the face of the earth," make such audacious requests? Surely, more than any other mortal, he understands the limits of investigation, the bounds embodied by the injunction, "Inquire not in that which is beyond you" (*Ben Sira*, cited in *Chagiga* 13a). I presume Moshe *Rabbeinu* relied in part on the fact that the desired knowledge was not sought solely, or even primarily, in order to satisfy personal curiosity or to advance any other form of self-aggrandizement. It was sought, as the context indicates ("Seeing that this nation is Your people"), in order to facilitate Moshe's mission to request forgiveness and atonement for the Jewish people. His unalloyed goal was to help realize the conjunction of "You are one" and "Who is like Your nation Israel, one nation upon the land?" (*Mincha* for Shabbat).

But this is not the whole story. The answer, particularly with regard to "Show me Your ways," inheres in a fundamental distinction between human probing and divine revelation. Exploration, undertaken as human initiative, is indeed confined and limited; not all boundaries can be breached and secrets revealed. But revelation freely willed and initiated by God, to which a man may be exposed and from which he might derive benefit, might open a crack in the "the thick cloud" (*Shemot* 19:9) enveloping the Divine Presence. If I am correct in perceiving the distinction between the human pursuit of knowledge and divinely initiated revelation, then perhaps uncovering Moshe's own thought process in this request is relevant to our issue of how humility and pride might work together in *teshuva*.

DEFINING HUMILITY: WHENCE DO ONE'S POWERS DERIVE?

In trying to understand these verses, we intuit that humility is not defined solely by the content of one's self-image, the quality of one's character, or the level of talent, knowledge, and accomplishment one requires of oneself. It is determined, no less, by one's conception of the source to which these accomplishments and talents are ultimately attributable. There is a marked difference between ascribing one's character and achievements exclusively to one's personal ability, as opposed to crediting them to *siyata di-shmaya,* divine assistance. Indeed, these are two entirely different perceptions of the self, the former characterized by pride, and the latter by humility.

Likewise with regard to *teshuva.* Consider, for example, the famous formulation by *Chazal,* "A person who initiates a process of purification is granted divine assistance."[20] Or, in a sharper mode, *Chazal* encouragingly assert that God tells the Jewish people, "My children! Open for Me an opening of *teshuva* as slight as the point of a needle, and I will open for you an entry wide enough for carriages and wagons to pass through."[21] *Teshuva* suffused with a sense of God's involvement, with the sense that my powers are attributable to Him, is fundamentally and qualitatively different from that perceived as purely the result of my own effort and achievement.

Moshe begged for knowledge of God in order to be able to perform his task even better. Whence did this ambition derive? It was deeply rooted in a sense that anything he accomplishes is entirely empowered and enabled by God. It is audacious in one sense, and yet very humbly presented in another.

This distinction, in a very different context, appears in *Ekev.* Moshe was concerned that upon entry into *Eretz Yisrael,* where plenitude awaits,

> Your herds and flock shall multiply, and your silver and gold shall multiply, and all that you have shall multiply. Then your heart shall be lifted up, and you shall forget the Lord your God, who brought you out of the land of Egypt, from the house of bondage. Who led you through that great and awesome wilderness.... Who brought forth water for you from the rock of flint. Who fed

20. *Yoma* 38b, *Avoda Zara* 55a, *Menachot* 29b.
21. *Shir Ha-shirim Rabba* 5:2.

> you manna in the wilderness.... And you shall say in your heart, "My power and the might of my hand have gotten me this wealth (*ha-chayil ha-zeh*)." But you shall remember the Lord your God, for it is He who gives you the power to gain wealth, that He may establish His covenant, which He swore to your fathers, as it is this day. (*Devarim* 8:13–18)

You indeed have "*ha-chayil ha-zeh,* this wealth," ability and accomplishments, and you are not asked to abandon it or eviscerate them. Rather, you are asked to assess them properly and to ascribe them spiritually. In one sense, it is *my* power and *my* might; in another sense, it is that which you have been granted by God, "for it is He who gives you the power to gain wealth."[22]

For Moshe *Rabbeinu*, there was not, God forbid, a single iota of "your heart shall be lifted up and you shall forget"; confronted with the Divine Presence, which he thirsted to know and experience better, he was suffused with the sense that "it is He who gives you the power to gain wealth." Moshe *Rabbeinu* understood this fully. Likewise, we must ask ourselves with reference to our own *teshuva*: Do we see our effort to return, to improve, to be regenerated and re-created as originating exclusively in our own will, undertaken and executed under our own power, a supreme instance of "picking oneself up by one's bootstraps"? Or do we see God centrally involved in the process, helping motivate the initial stirrings, supporting the ongoing progress, and indispensable to its ultimate success?

This understanding of humility conjoined with pride can be found in what we – ordinary Jews far below Moshe's level – say at the end of the *viddui*, the confession prayer on Yom Kippur: "My Lord... I stand before

22. In the introduction to the prohibitions his *Sefer Mitzvot Ha-gadol* (s.v. *ve-hinnei*), Rav Moshe of Coucy recounts how he set out to write a work about all the *mitzvot,* and he was pleased that he would be able to spread God's word far and near. And then a dream came to him – presumably in light of his good feeling – informing him that he had forgotten to include the most important prohibition, "Beware lest you forget God" (*Devarim* 8:11). When you get so engrossed in your learning or in other aspects of serving God, and you begin to credit the accomplishment and aspiration to yourself, then you have forgotten God.

You like a vessel filled with shame and humiliation." The focus is, appropriately, on a blend of shame and guilt that serves as a reflection of the preceding *viddui* and our severely wanting behavior; filled with shame, we cannot be fully proud. On the other hand, we are only "*like* a vessel" – the comparative *kaf* – but not actually mere pottery. We can and should be gratified in what we are doing; unique among all creatures, we can plan and monitor our actions, and we can marshal our powers and abilities to advance the agenda of *teshuva*, both personally and communally. The sense of accomplishment and of worth is the engine that drives *teshuva* and provides momentum and inspiration for it; it is part of the Jew's worldview and personality, and there is no desire to eradicate it. But never let us forget how the engine is fueled, and Who put it there in the first place.

JEWISH ELECTION AND *TESHUVA*

In dealing heretofore with the question of *teshuva* and humility, I have touched upon one facet of the tension between humility and *teshuva* and its possible resolution. That facet has a universal ring, and it could have concerned the inhabitants of Nineveh as much as the Jewish people. But we may single out another factor, more endemic to our unique, indigenous relationship to God, namely, our election, which can become a significant factor in the relationship between humility and *teshuva*.

We may therefore ask: Does the sense of Jewish election produce more humility or less? This issue confronts us all year, but all the more so on the unique days of the High Holidays, especially Yom Kippur. To be sure, Rosh Ha-shana is, broadly speaking, conceived and experienced in universal terms, though not uniformly so. If we consider the *Musaf* blessings of *Malkhuyot, Zikhronot,* and *Shofarot,* we can see the breakdown: *Malkhuyot* is, by and large, universal; the *Chafetz Chayim* said that if the gentiles knew how much we pray for them on Rosh Ha-shana, they would print *machzorim*! *Shofarot,* on the other hand, is entirely focused on the Jewish people. The middle blessing, *Zikhronot,* is the critical transition from one to the other, beginning with "All creations are accounted" and moving on to "He who remembers the covenant."

Yom Kippur is different. It focuses on the Jewish people, as its historical origin is within the context of the recovery from the sin of the Golden Calf; and it is centered on the unique service performed in the

Temple, which is, of course, particularistic. Gentiles can bring offerings in the Temple, but not as part of the unique service of Yom Kippur. So on Yom Kippur, consciousness – even subliminal awareness – of our status and stature vis-à-vis God is markedly sharper and deeper than on Rosh Ha-shana, and that can have an impact on the nature of our *teshuva*.

But the awareness and reality of our election is a two-edged sword. It can promote not just heightened devotion and closeness; it can also feed arrogance, chauvinism, and condescension. This sharpens the possible conflict between humility and *teshuva* on Yom Kippur, because humility is more difficult to come by when you are told you're the salt of the earth.

On the other hand, if one has been properly educated and nurtured, and has properly prepared for "the great and awesome day of God" (*Malakhi* 3:23), then the very experience of the sanctity of the day can intensify one's awareness that it is the Lord your God "Who gives you the power to gain wealth." The deeper exposure to and experience of God that we aim to have on Yom Kippur intensifies our sense of where our power and might are coming from. The might for running an army, the might for running a business, the might for running a society, and, above all, the might for running a life of Torah and *mitzvot*, personally and collectively: it all comes from the Lord your God.

Exposure to *malkhut Shamayim*, divine majesty, has the effect of intensifying the sense of human weakness, and yet it is capable of so much more. The Rambam speaks to two central *mitzvot*, the love and the fear of God:

> What is the proper way to love and fear Him? When one ponders His actions and wondrous creations, recognizing His boundless, incomprehensible wisdom, he will immediately love, praise, glorify, and gain a strong desire to know His great Name, as David said, "My soul thirsts for God, for the living God" (*Tehillim* 42:3). And on pondering these very matters, he immediately recoils, fears, realizes that he is a small, lowly, dark creature, limited in knowledge, standing before Him whose knowledge is perfect, as David said (*Tehillim* 8:4–5), "When I behold Your heavens... what is man that You are mindful of him?" (*Hilkhot Yesodei Ha-Torah* 2:1–2)

The exposure to the divine at once enhances the sense of human frailty, even as it stimulates the passion for love and fear. If the Rambam says this with regard to the experience of scanning the heavens, then likewise on Yom Kippur; the majesty of God, the confrontation with the divine, is more intensely felt on Yom Kippur than on other days, and therefore it elicits more of a response.

One of the most striking descriptions of revelation in the Bible is when the Thirteen Attributes of Mercy were revealed to Moshe. Every time we recite the Thirteen Attributes of Mercy, we should reflect not only on the qualities that were enumerated but on the scenario during which they were revealed; thereby we are enthralled, engaged, more deeply involved with God. Even though there is a danger that humility will be eroded precisely on Yom Kippur, this can be mitigated if we fully understand our exposure to the Divine Presence on Yom Kippur, if we feel the stirrings of the love and fear of God not just when we look at the heavens, but all the more so when we express the Thirteen Attributes of Mercy (as we do repeatedly on Yom Kippur).

So, indeed, humility can and should co-exist with *teshuva* on Yom Kippur – not only the humility of attributing our own accomplishments to God, that He is the One who gave us "the power to gain wealth (*chayil*)," but also specifically the humility that is stimulated by, and emerges from, our experience of "the great and awesome day of God." While we seek to experience the sanctity of the day, and while we seek to recognize the source of our *chayil*, we should strive to experience *chayil* in another sense as well: looking to achieve, however incrementally, our longer range eschatological vision embodied in the verse, "They proceed from strength to strength (*me-chayil el chayil*); every one of them appears before God in Zion" (*Tehillim* 84:8).

Teshuva and Joy

Prima facie, the emotion of joy is entirely absent from the process of *teshuva*.[1] As we scour our tradition's sources that deal with *teshuva*, their substance and tone present quite the opposite portrayal of the penitent's psychological state. We begin, of course, with the Rambam and his classic formulation in *Hilkhot Teshuva*:

> Among the paths of repentance is for the penitent to constantly call out before God, crying and entreating, to perform charity to the best of his ability, to distance himself far from the object of his sin... to change his behavior in its entirety to the good and

---

Delivered as the Hausman/Stern *Kinnus Teshuva* lecture at the Gruss Institute in Jerusalem, Tishrei 5767 (2006).

1. When I speak of joy, I refer neither to festive celebration as such, nor to hedonistic experience, but rather to emotional and spiritual gratification, pleasurable and satisfying in its own way, but still very different from some of the elements that we associate with joyous celebration. For those who have read C. S. Lewis' autobiography *Surprised by Joy*, the term joy would have far richer associations, but these too I leave to the back burner. (Lewis' title is derived from the title and opening line of one of Wordsworth's sonnets, "Surprised by joy – impatient as the wind," written in the aftermath of the death of his three-year-old daughter, Catherine.)

> the path of righteousness, and to travel in exile from his home... because it causes a person to be submissive, humble, and meek of spirit. (2:4)

Similarly, the *Roke'ach*, Rabbi Elazar ben Yehuda of Worms, the last major member of *Chassidei Ashkenaz*, composed a prayer for a person who wants to accomplish *teshuva* properly. He stands before God and says:

> And I cry with the tears of my heart, streams of water flow forth from my eyes, for the fact that I did not observe Your Torah; the pain and crises of my heart have widened, and I have changed my attire to sack... and I admit my sins before You with the sharp travails of my heart (*tzarat libbi*)... and I bemoan my sins.... May my bitter tears extinguish Your wrath, extinguish with the blood of my melted heart the fire I have enraged in You... and may the pouring out of my soul wash away my transgressions like water. (*Ha-Roke'ach Ha-gadol, Hilkhot Teshuva,* p. 30, s.v. "*tefillat ha-shav be-kol kocho*")

In this excerpt, part of a much longer, heart-rending prayer, the *Roke'ach* speaks of wellsprings of tears flowing from his eyes, of utter anxiety and sadness. The whole spirit of the piece is the sense of deep mourning and tragedy.

Rabbeinu Yona, in *Sha'arei Teshuva,* lists some of the primary principles of *teshuva.*[2] The third one is *yagon,* the sense of mourning and tragedy: "He should think with deep anxiety and mourning how terrible it is that a person has countermanded the orders of his Creator, and see to it that there is much sadness (*yagon*) in his heart... and gasp in bitterness." He continues in this vein about the significance of *yagon,* and starts the next paragraph, "The different levels of *teshuva* and its gradations are a function of the extent of bitterness and the intensity of the sadness."

These citations – drawn from a wide variety of sources and traditions, differing both geographically and by religious temperament – all speak in the same voice: joy is not a concomitant characteristic of *teshuva.*

---

2. *Sha'arei Teshuva* 1:3, paragraphs 12–13.

THE EXPERIENCE OF SIN AND *TESHUVA*

If we consider the experience of confronting sin and the urge and effort to redress it, we will confirm our intuition concerning the place of joy in *teshuva*. This is powerfully expressed in the personal plane by King David, after the prophet Natan forced him to face his transgression. *Mizmor* 51 conveys the devastating sense of experiencing and confronting sin:

> Have mercy upon me, O God... erase my transgressions. Cleanse me abundantly from my iniquity, and purify me from my sin. For I acknowledge my transgressions, and my sins are ever before me. Against You alone have I sinned, and done what is evil in Your sight.... Indeed, I was fashioned in iniquity; with sin my mother conceived me.... Hide Your face from my sins; erase all my iniquities. (*Tehillim* 51:2–11)

Just as there is no room for joy in this description, joy is likewise absent from the metaphors used to describe sin and *teshuva*. First, sin is often referred to as a spiritual disease – a disease not the less dangerous and debilitating for being, if not self-induced, at least self-enabled.

Second, sin is often described as *tum'a*, defilement. In the Bible this term has a dual sense; at times it refers narrowly and technically to a particular halakhic status, and at other times it refers to a general kind of spiritual defilement from sin.[3] *Yechezkel* (36:25), for example, speaks of how God promises that He will cast pure water upon us and purify us from all the defilements, and the Torah states that on Yom Kippur "You shall be purified before the Lord" (*Vayikra* 16:30). In addition, we pray on every Shabbat and Festival, "Purify our hearts to serve You with truth."

Third, beyond the medical and halakhic metaphors, sin is regarded in religious and psychological terms as a failure, both to oneself and to God, which engenders deep shame. The sinner feels ashamed

3. One can easily extend the halakhic distinction between two kinds of *tum'a*, that which emanates from within a person, and that which is externally generated or stimulated, to sin as well: some violations are primarily internally motivated, while in the case of other transgressions, though the individual is personally culpable, the role of external pressures or temptations is particularly salient.

of himself that he was unable to withstand temptation and maintain his standards, and he is ashamed to confront God. *Chazal* speak of this shame in a positive sense.[4]

Fourth, we often speak of the response to sin in terms of grief and mourning. *Megillat Eikha* (3:39) states, "Over what shall a living man grieve (*yit'onen*)? Each one over his own sins." *Yit'onen* derives from *onen*, one who experiences the initial shock immediately after a death, prior to burial, and refers to the sense of grief that is felt at that time.[5] Over what does the sinner feel grief-stricken? His is a threefold concern, relating to past, present, and future. A person asks himself how could he have done such a thing, and he feels defiled. He experiences an almost visceral sense of revulsion, like one who hasn't showered for a month, or like a person who suddenly feels insects crawling all over him.[6] This is with respect to the past.

In the present, there is a loss of the most valuable and cherished relationship a person can have. The Rambam describes the sinner's alienation from God as a kind of natural consequence: "Only yesterday [before he repented] this sinner was divided from God, as the verse states (*Yeshayahu* 59:2), 'Your iniquities have been a barrier between you and your God'" (*Hilkhot Teshuva* 7:7). What can be worse for a person than to be cast off from the face of God, to have no access, no relationship?

With regard to the future, the sinner is terribly anxious. He fears that perhaps the alienation is not a temporary phase and that there has been a permanent rupture in the relationship; this greatly aggravates his concern about the alienation. Moreover, he is concerned about possible punishment for the sin. So the mourning touches various bases:

---

4. Based on the verse, "That His fear (*yirato*) may be upon your faces (*peneikhem*) so that you not sin" (*Shemot* 20:17), the *Gemara* (*Nedarim* 20a) identifies *boshet panim* (shame) as the root element of a pervasive *yirat Elokim* (awe of God) that prevents sin. See "*Teshuva*: Impetus and Motive," note 6.
5. I am applying here the two stages with respect to mourning that the Rav *z"l* so eloquently articulated: the initial shock (*aninut*) and the gradual return to normalcy over a long period of time after the finality of burial (*aveilut*). Likewise, I believe, with regard to sin, there are two stages of response to it.
6. It is not for naught that, in *Sefer Chassidim*, the scenarios suggested for *teshuvat ha-mishkal*, penitential actions commensurate with a sin, include sitting in a tub of freezing cold water and having ants crawl all over you. The sinner is revolted by his actions and by himself.

revulsion with regard to the past, alienation with respect to the present, and anxiety with regard to the future.

A fifth aspect of the experience of sin is the transgressor's sense of feeling trapped. As *Tehillim* graphically expresses:

> From where shall I flee from Your spirit and where, from Your face, can I escape? If I go heavenward, You are there; if I want to descend to the netherworld, there You are. If I take wing with the dawn to come to rest on the western horizon, even there Your hand will be guiding me, Your right hand will be holding me fast. (*Tehillim* 139:7–10)

There is no fleeing, no escape.[7] And while this sense of entrapment appears in a different context in the verse, it would nevertheless greatly exacerbate the experience of sin.

Finally, the experience of sin is one that is conceived in terms of disintegration. One who sins has "a contrite and crushed heart" (*Tehillim* 51:19), a personality which is no longer a single unit, but broken.[8]

In sum, as we survey the experience of sin and therefore *teshuva*, there are many strands running through it: a sense of being ill, defiled, and a failure. There is grief and anxiety about the past, present, and future, and a feeling of being trapped and broken. We certainly do not encounter joy, and probably do not expect to.

THE POSSIBILITY OF JOY IN *TESHUVA*

And yet, can it be that the world of *teshuva* – one of the major axes of divine service – is wholly morose and depressing, with nothing to provide encouragement or to ennoble? Does the sun never pierce the clouds of guilt-induced crisis?

Speaking for myself, my intuitive response is: *Chas ve-shalom*, impossible! Within the context of Yom Kippur, there is evidence to suggest

7. The refrain "*Yachbi'enu,*" recited in *Selichot* for the third day of the Ten Days of Repentance, similarly captures this sense of entrapment.
8. This sentiment is echoed in the *Selicha* of *Adon Befokdekha*, recited on *erev* Rosh Ha-shana: "Turn, Master, to the sadness of spirit, see the brokenness of heart."

that, at some point, the sun breaks through and there is light again. In the *Shulchan Arukh*, the ruling is that on the night after Yom Kippur one should eat a semi-festive meal, for it is a bit of a Festival (*Rema, Orach Chayim* 624:5).[9] And to speak from my own interactions with the Rav *z"l*, if anybody needed something from him, the best time to speak to him was the night after Yom Kippur, when he was in the best mood of the year. But these instances are both after Yom Kippur, after sin has been dismissed and abolished and we have enjoyed the grace of God. That is not the primary time of the mitzva of *teshuva* and not the occasion of sin, so it does not quite count as relief within the gloom of sin and repentance.

If we look for some expression of joy in the midst of Yom Kippur itself, we find it in the *Musaf* service. Near the end of *Ammitz Ko'ach* (*nusach Ashkenaz*), after the descriptive account of the Temple service itself has been fully presented, there is a passage that describes the response of *Klal Yisrael* to the completion of the service:

> With purity and cleanliness they will be cleansed and purified; they will be renewed like the new angels of morning.... They will utter from their throat the exaltations of God, glad song with their tongue, new song with their mouth. They will rejoice with trembling, serve with awe the Holy One of Israel, who sanctifies the holy people, to express, to sing, to drum, to sound the cymbal, to conduct the instruments.... [They will be] drawn to approach His gates with glad song, and attaining joy and gladness forever. Joyous and celebrating with His Name all day long, happy with the gladness of His Presence.

The description of joy – not just an inner joy, but festive, almost raucous, celebration: song, dance, use of instruments – takes place in the midst of Yom Kippur, before the day has atoned for our plethora of sins.[10]

9. Later *posekim* quote a *midrash* on the verse "Go, eat your bread in gladness...for God has already accepted your works" (*Kohelet* 9:7) to support this position. *Tosafot* (*Shabbat* 115b, s.v. *ve-amai*) say in the same vein that after Yom Kippur those who serve God are in a celebratory spirit, having found grace.

10. The *Yerushalmi* (*Yoma* 8:7) and the *Tosefta* (*Yoma* 4:17) say that the atonement that is not effected by offerings but rather by the essence of the day, *itzumo shel yom*, takes place at the moment of sunset.

But if we are looking for a sense of joy within the process of *teshuva,* this too is small consolation. Our concern is not so much with the result: of course, if forgiveness is attained, who wouldn't be happy? The question, however, is not how we respond to the conclusion, but to the process. Is our awareness of sin wholly charged with what Calvinists would describe as "religious melancholia," a type of spiritual depression? Is *teshuva* the kind of semi-clinical, phased phenomenon described in James' *Varieties of Religious Experience,* joy appearing only at the culmination of the process? Or is there some saving grace, some element of joy inherent in the process that is licit and perhaps even demanded, despite the pervasive anxiety and the sense of tension? My personal, intuitive answer is an emphatic yes, but I need to elucidate my sources and reasoning.

The notion that some element of *simcha,* joy, can be conceived within the context of sin and *teshuva* has halakhic ramifications. The *halakha* is that if *yom tov* comes in the midst of *shiva,* the *yom tov* abrogates the *shiva.* This is unlike Shabbat, where private mourning, *devarim she-betzin'a,* is still in effect. What about Rosh Ha-shana and Yom Kippur? The *Tannaim* debate this (*Mo'ed Katan* 19a), and we rule that these days also abrogate *shiva.* The Rav *z"l* assumed that this could only be if joy were part of the character of the day, and therefore, in experiential terms, a day could not be both one of mourning and one of joy. Apparently, then, the *Tannaim* thought that joy applies on Rosh Ha-shana and Yom Kippur.[11]

Similarly, the Rosh (*Rosh Ha-shana* 4:14) quotes a version of prayer that we, today, have abandoned. In the holiday *Amida,* after "*Atta vechartanu,* You have chosen us," the second part begins "*Va-titten lanu Hashem Elokeinu be-ahava,* You have given us, Lord our God, with love." On the *regalim,* we continue with the phrase "*mo'adim le-simcha chaggim u-zemanim le-sasson,* Festivals for celebration, holidays and times

11. The *Sha'agat Aryeh* dealt with this issue as well in a responsum (102), but approached it from a different perspective. In his view, the sanction of *melekhet okhel nefesh be-yom tov,* cooking on holidays, is based on the mitzva of *simcha;* since *melekhet okhel nefesh* is permitted on Rosh Ha-shana, obviously the mitzva of *simcha* applies on Rosh Ha-shana. This approach, of course, does not help with Yom Kippur, which is arguably more critical to our subject.

for joy," but we omit these words on Rosh Ha-shana and Yom Kippur. The Rosh quotes *Ge'onim* who did have this version, reflecting the fact that the High Holidays were part of a complex of joyful holidays. Apparently, for these *Ge'onim* some form of joy is not only a desideratum but a conscious aim of these days, a part of their reality.[12] Of course, *Chazal* stressed the awesome moment and sense of anxiety of these days sufficiently to exclude the recitation of *Hallel*.[13] This fact notwithstanding, these *Ge'onim* saw that the element of *simcha* could be part of the definition of a day that is pervaded by and devoted to *teshuva*.

JOY AS PART OF *AVODAT HASHEM*

To put it differently, the possibility that an element of *simcha* should relate to *teshuva* cannot be foreclosed, and I say this with respect to three distinct elements, each progressively more focused. First, the Rambam, after his account of *Simchat Beit Ha-sho'eva* (*Hilkhot Lulav* 8:15) and the great festivity that characterized it, concludes with a more general statement about joy with regard to divine service:

> The happiness with which a person should rejoice in the fulfillment of the *mitzvot* and the love of God who commanded them is a great service. Whoever holds himself back from this is worthy of retribution, as the verse states (*Devarim* 28:47): "Because you

12. A question naturally arises: according to the Rav's position that *simcha* applies to Rosh Ha-shana and Yom Kippur, why do we omit this phrase on those days? While I don't recall whether the Rav ever related to this question, I don't think we need to be too concerned about it. There are two issues: one is the character and purpose, as it were, of the day; the other has to do with whether a particular mitzva applies. The question of *aveilut* addresses whether there is *simcha* altogether on Rosh Ha-shana and Yom Kippur. Once the day is defined as a *yom tov*, then the mitzva of *simcha* applies, and so *aveilut* is suspended. On the other hand, the formulation we have in *tefilla* rests on the day's purpose, whether it was given for the realization of *sasson ve-simcha* or for other goals. As such, the *Amida* on Rosh Ha-shana and Yom Kippur need not include the phrase relating to *simcha*.
13. The *Gemara* (*Rosh Ha-shana* 32b; *Arakhin* 10b) justifies the lack of *Hallel* on Rosh Ha-shana and Yom Kippur by asking: How could one recite *Hallel* when the books of life and death are open, and each person is being judged? Nonetheless, an element of *simcha* can and does exist there.

> did not serve the Lord, your God, in joy and good-heartedness".... There is no greatness or honor other than celebrating before God, as the verse states (II *Shemuel* 6:16): "King David was dancing wildly before the Lord."

The joy and love of God that a person experiences during the performance of a mitzva is, itself, a great *avoda*, a great expression in the service of God. The proof text that the Rambam cites is from the *tokhacha*, the rebuke passage of *Devarim*, and comes after a long list of frightful things that are going to occur should the people sin: "Because you did not serve the Lord, your God, in joy and good-heartedness and plentitude" (*Devarim* 28:47). This is normally taken to mean that when things were going well, you did not worry about God, turning to Him instead only in times of crisis. The *tokhacha* is therefore saying, inasmuch as you didn't worship God, and you revolted when you were in a state of prosperity and joy, now you will suffer and be forced to turn to Him under conditions of desolation and desperation. Rabbeinu Bachya,[14] however, explains the verse differently. It is not that you didn't worship God when you were prosperous; on the contrary, you worshipped Him – but it was lackluster and mechanical worship, lacking all *simcha*. Presumably, Rabbeinu Bachya is basing himself on this statement of the Rambam,[15] who apparently sees in this verse a source for the concept that the *simcha* that is to accompany a mitzva is an *avoda* in itself. Now let us ask ourselves: if, indeed, our *avoda* must be done with joy, would this not apply to *mitzvot* such as *teshuva* as well?

Thus, the first link between *teshuva* and joy relates to *avoda* generally. We can now go a step further, relating to *avoda* more narrowly. *Chazal* understood the term "*avoda*" as it appears in the Torah in a variety of ways: at times, it refers to the whole world of our relationship with

14. Commentary on the Torah, *Devarim* 28:47, s.v. *tachat*.
15. Rabbeinu Bachya has a small encyclopedia, *Kad Ha-kemach*, that is a collection of *midrashim* organized by topic. In his discussion of *simcha* (letter *samekh, simcha*, s.v. *ha-simcha ha-zot*), he says that the *simcha* which accompanies a mitzva is more significant than the mitzva itself! That refers to a particular kind of *simcha* of course, not the kind of *simcha* engendered by non-mitzva considerations. But it is a radical statement nonetheless.

God,[16] while in other contexts, such as the verse in *Keriat Shema*, "and to serve Him with all your heart and soul" (*Devarim* 11:13),[17] *Chazal* took pains to establish a separate category of *mitzvot* that are defined as *avoda* in a more specific sense. After rejecting the possibility that the sacrificial order is meant, since that was addressed elsewhere, two answers are offered: one is "*le-ovdo zo tefilla*," the other is "*le-ovdo zeh talmud*," service of God as manifest in prayer and in Torah study. There are thus three *mitzvot* that have been singled out to be *avoda*: sacrifices, Torah study, and prayer.

Pondering this *midrash halakha*, we can ask ourselves: how exclusive is this club of *mitzvot*? If we seek the entry card into this distinctive group, we would say these are *mitzvot* that involve not just a particular performance, but rather entail the totality of one's relationship to God, particularly the meeting with the *Shekhina* and one's submission and servitude. This is what prayer is all about, and *Chazal* deemed Torah study a vivifying and pervasive experience as well.[18] If these are the general criteria, then *teshuva*, which involves not only the depth and intensity of one's relationship with God, but the very existence of the relationship itself, must qualify as *avoda* as well. And if joy is essential for *avoda* in general, how much more so should it be part of *mitzvot* that are more intensively *avoda*! Just as joy needs to accompany prayer and Torah study, as we recite in the *birkhot ha-Torah*, "Please make the words of the Torah sweet in our mouths," joy must likewise accompany *teshuva*.

The first two respects related to *teshuva* as part of larger categories. But what is the nature of joy in relation to *teshuva* specifically? Here we come to a third dimension: I think it is endemic and inherent within the experience of *teshuva* – not only of its *denouement*, but of the process

16. There are verses which speak in that vein, for instance, "You will serve God and He will bless your food and your drink, and I will remove illness from you" (*Shemot* 23:25). Presumably, that refers not to any particular *avoda* or mitzva, but to the whole range of our relationship with God.
17. *Sifrei* 41, s.v. *u-le-ovdo.*
18. For example, "Even when one person sits and studies Torah, the Divine Presence is with him" (*Berakhot* 6a).

itself, isolated from its benefits. A *midrash*[19] addresses a stark contradiction between two verses in *Tehillim*:

> One verse states, "Serve the Lord with joy" (*Tehillim* 100:2), but another verse states, "Serve the Lord with fear" (*Tehillim* 2:11)! Rabbi Aivo taught, when you stand in prayer, your heart should be glad ("*yehei libbekha same'ach*"), for you are serving the most-high God."[20]

Rabbi Aivo distinguishes here between two components of the experience of prayer. The first has to do with the content of the mitzva: in prayer, you position yourself before God, addressing Him, praising and thanking, petitioning and imploring Him. Together, these elements exemplify *yira*, the sense of awe, of which the Rav on many occasions spoke so fully and richly, based on Rashi and the Ramban. It is the sense of "*omed lifnei Ha-Melekh*"; you stand before the Royal Emperor, *Melekh Malkhei Ha-Melakhim*. But there is also the context: that of *your* standing before God; *you* – little you, a *shokhen batei chomer*, one housed in earthly matter[21] – are addressing Him, engaging in a dialogue with the King of Kings! Reflecting on the fact that you are, as it were, ushered into the presence of God, is a source of infinite joy.

You can also rejoice over the fact that you have been created as a spiritual being with talents and abilities which the rest of the created world does not have. Your life can be given over not simply to animalistic experience and mundane matters; you have the capacity for *avodat Hashem*.

If it is true of prayer that "your heart should be glad," I submit it is doubly true of *teshuva*. Of course, I am not suggesting for a moment that a person should be happy that he was a sinner and now is able to come to God to repent. But after a person has lapsed, and has the experience that "just yesterday he was hated before God, distanced, cast out, abominable," if he has the opportunity to do *teshuva* and once again be "beloved" (*Hilkhot Teshuva* 7:6), will he

19. *Midrash Tehillim Shocher Tov* on *mizmor* 100, *piska* 2.
20. The *midrash* does offer a second answer based on a chronological distinction between this world and the next, but that is not to our present purpose.
21. Based on *Iyyov* 4:19.

not be enthralled, just as you rejoice in prayer, to be in the presence of God? Can there be any greater source of joy than your opportunity to be *chozer bi-teshuva*, a penitent, as well as actually being one? The sinner has access, an appointment with God. With all the sense of despondency, defilement, and failure, you are nevertheless "a prisoner freeing himself from prison."[22] Shall we not rejoice at the privilege accorded us?

NE'ILA: EXPRESSING APPRECIATION FOR *TESHUVA*

Recognition and appreciation of this opportunity, let alone reveling in it, is not a daily experience. In the blessing in the *Amida*, we take *teshuva* for granted and only ask God to accept us and encourage us to do *teshuva*. Expressions of appreciation for the fact that there is such a thing as *teshuva* appear primarily in the *Ne'ila* service, and there it appears at two levels.

Shortly before the concluding passage of the silent *Amida*, we highlight the uniqueness of our spiritual existence, at the human plane as opposed to the animal. In terms reminiscent of the nihilistic chapters of *Kohelet*, we first express that man is worthless, devoid of significance, equated with the animal,[23] and then we do an about-face:

> [Nevertheless,] You set man apart from the beginning (*atta hivdalta enosh me-rosh*), and You considered him worthy to stand before You, for who can tell You what to do, and if he is righteous what can he give You?[24]

Here we distinguish humans in universal terms from the animals, because *teshuva* is a universal category, not a uniquely Jewish one, as we know from Yona and Nineveh and from the way *Chazal* speak of the *teshuva* of Adam. We say, "You set man apart from the beginning" by granting him power "to stand before You"; even before *teshuva* is mentioned in this prayer (though it is, of course, its context), we highlight the fact that

22. Based on, and in contrast to, *Berakhot* 5b.
23. "Man has no preeminence over the beast, for all is vain" (*Kohelet* 3:19).
24. The Rav wrote about this extensively in *Halakhic Man*, Part I, chap. 10.

God gave man a permanent appointment to enter into His presence.[25] We simply express appreciation for the fact that God has singled us out, as part of the human race, from the world of the animal.

But then our words in *Ne'ila* turn to Yom Kippur, which, unlike the predominantly universal Rosh Ha-shana, is much more national in character: "And You have given us, Lord our God, with love, this Yom HaKippurim... for You are the forgiver of Israel."[26] And then we speak of the particular *chesed* with regard to *teshuva,* and the opportunity that we, as members of *Knesset Yisrael* have been given, to be *chozrim bi-teshuva.* "Happy is your portion Israel! Before whom are you purified, and who purifies you? Your Father in Heaven" (*Mishna Yoma* 85b).

In both cases, "to stand before You," even in excruciating spiritual pain, in anguish and anxiety, is the source of *simcha.* Even if at some point you wish you could get away, even if you wish you were not a Jew, this is only a delusion; this is what the *yetzer ha-ra* wishes. The *oved Hashem* in you does not wish that at all. Though the spiritual and psychological pain can be terrifying, we are nonetheless joyous, as we are profoundly appreciative of the ability to stand before God and engage in *teshuva.*

RELATING THE TERROR AND THE JOY OF *TESHUVA*

There are various models to define what the interactive relationship may be between what we have described as the terrifying content and the joyous context in the process of *teshuva.*

Rav Schneur Zalman of Liadi, the first *rebbe* of Chabad, relates to this issue in at least two different places. In *Likkutei Amarim,*[27] the central text of the *Tanya,* he writes:

---

25. Though we are discussing *Ne'ila,* the universal element is present in other penitential prayers as well. Thus, even the introductory paragraph to the *Yud-gimmel middot ha-rachamim,* the Thirteen Attributes of Mercy, which focuses on the covenant between God and the Jewish people, nonetheless makes the point, "*oseh tzedakot im kol basar va-ruach,* You perform righteousness with all flesh and spirit," highlighting the universal dimension of repentance and forgiveness.
26. See the chapter "*Teshuva*: Ferment and Repose," in the section "The Dual Roots of Yom Kippur."
27. End of chapter 34.

> All the abovementioned particulars regarding the diverse joys of the soul do not preclude the person from considering himself shameful and loathsome, or from having a contrite heart and humble spirit, at the very time of the joy. For the sense of shame... is occasioned by the aspect of the body and the animal soul, while his joy comes from the aspect of the divine soul and the spark of Godliness that is clothed therein and animates it, as has been discussed above (chapter 31). After this manner it is stated in the *Zohar* (II:255a; III:75a), "Weeping is lodged in one side of my heart, and joy is lodged in the other."

The kind of humility and self-effacement that the Ba'al Ha-Tanya had been advocating previously in that chapter is not inconsistent with a sense of joy, because each relates to a different element of the human personality. Humans are conjoined of matter and spirit, the animal and the human. The self-effacement relates to the animal part of him, whereas the joy, the celebratory element, relates to the spiritual, to the divine spark that is in him. He quotes the *Zohar* that two elements coexist within the heart, weeping and joy.

To be sure, in the *Iggeret Ha-teshuva*,[28] the Ba'al Ha-Tanya expands upon this theme and refers to this passage from the *Zohar* as well, but he takes the cutting edge off its message by creating a temporal division:

> Joined to this is the faith and confidence, the heart being firm and certain in God that He desires goodness, and is gracious, and merciful, and generously forgiving the instant one pleads for forgiveness and atonement of Him.... Not the faintest vestige of doubt dilutes this absolute conviction.

Here the joy derives from the faith and conviction that God "is gracious, and merciful, and generously forgiving." The penitent can, at the same time, cry and be joyous: today we cry, but our tears are mixed with joy, because we know that tomorrow we are going to dance.

28. Chapter 11, near the beginning.

Reb Tzadok Ha-kohen of Lublin conveys something of this same notion, though not quite in the sequential vein. Reb Tzadok relates to a sinner who, filled with despair, doubts whether he is deserving of the promise by *Chazal* that if a person wants to initiate self-purgation, he will receive divine assistance (*Yoma* 38b):

> The advice against this kind of inner doubt is the *simcha* and inner confidence that certainly God, in His great compassion and kindness, will accept him as having performed complete *teshuva* before Him, [while at the same time] he is filled with great bitterness over his sin. This [combination] is perfectly modeled after the *tekia-shevarim-terua-tekia* that is blown on Rosh Ha-shana, for it is known that the *tekiot* represent *simcha,* and the *shevarim-terua* represents the groan and the wail.... This is why it is stated, "A song of David, when Natan the prophet came to him" (*Tehillim* 51:1), for this [the joyful song even though Natan was accusing David of a terrible sin] is the flat (*peshuta*) *tekia* sound that is sounded before the *terua*, representing the *simcha* and song, confident that God will answer him.... And it is also truly a complete *teshuva,* for at that very moment, simultaneously, [he is surrounded by] the light and the revelation, and this is the joy that follows [the *tekia*].[29]

Reb Tzadok is saying that the way to relate to this inner doubt is to conjoin two elements: on the one hand, the experience of *teshuva* and the anguish that accompanies it, and on the other hand, the conviction that one will be answered and that God will be understanding and forgiving. He does not describe these elements as being two successive stages as the Ba'al Ha-Tanya does, but as two simultaneous facets of the *teshuva* experience. The inner core of the experience, its specific focus, is indeed the bitter pill of sin; yet it is embedded in the external framework of the positive relationship to God. So there is something here of the message I have been trying to convey: according to Reb Tzadok, one who comes to engage in *teshuva* feels despondency and a sense of tragedy regarding

29. *Tzidkat Ha-tzaddik,* Part III – *Tikkun Ha-berit,* no. 129.

the terrible thing he did, but this is counterbalanced by the certainty and the joy that God will accept his *teshuva*.

Reb Tzadok presents an interesting analogy to *tekiat shofar*. The *halakha* is that the simple, flat sounds (*peshuta*), what we call *tekiot*, both precede and follow the inner part, the *terua*, a sound that suggests anxiety and tragedy.[30] Like the structure of the *teshuva* experience, the *shofar* blasts have a surrounding framework, and an essence within that framework. Although *tekiot* are ineluctably sequential, conceptually it's a sandwich: the *peshuta* is the flat sound of joy and celebration, as it is written: "God (*Elokim*) ascends with a *terua*, and the Lord (*shem Havaya*) with the [*tekia*] sound of the *shofar*" (*Tehillim* 47:6). While the inner core is the *terua* – the sense of sin as indicated by the divine name of justice, the outer *tekia* reflects the intimate, compassionate name of *Hashem*. A person partakes of and experiences that "sandwich," which is the nature of *teshuva* and its interaction with joy.

Reb Tzadok adds one element, partly by way of referring to *mizmor* 51, which we cited above. The psalm is historically situated when Natan the prophet comes to King David to rebuke him over his sin with Bat-Sheva. Yet it counterintuitively begins, "*Mizmor le-David,*" a term that usually suggests some of kind of joy or singing. But what did Natan tell him? That his behavior was utterly immoral and reprehensible! So why the *simcha*? Reb Tzadok says King David's confidence that God would answer him is the prior *tekia*, and the rebuke is the middle part, the *terua*. The *tekia* after the rebuke, according to Reb Tzadok, is "the light and the revelation" piercing through the clouds, which is coterminous with the *teshuva*. The grief and the joy are simultaneous, unlike in the Ba'al Ha-Tanya, which, as I read him, sees the relationship of the two as more mechanical and segmented.

BETTER ONE HOUR OF *TESHUVA*

After our excursus into the various types of joy relevant to *teshuva*, what is the message with which we are left? Of course, the deep sense of disintegration, of "*shivron levav*" underscored in *mizmor* 51, is unavoidable in *teshuva*; indeed, we speak often of God being close to and healing

30. *Rosh Ha-shana* 33b–34a; *Shulchan Arukh, Orach Chayim* 590:1.

the brokenhearted.[31] While few of us can avoid thinking of and hoping for *teshuva*'s future benefits,[32] we can also find the *simcha* in today's *teshuva*, irrespective of the benefits that will be conferred as a result of it. As the *Midrash* states, the very fact that you can stand before the Holy One, blessed be He, is of inestimable benefit.

C. S. Lewis once wrote that the message he had learned from the British Idealists, a nineteenth-century philosophic school, was that "It is more important that Heaven should exist than that any of us should reach it."[33] The same is true of *teshuva*. While we all hope and pray to reap the fruits, it is – from an ultimate, spiritual point of view – more important that the world of *teshuva* exists, along with the *simcha* from acknowledging that fact, than that we should ever get there to reap the benefits.

But we don't need to look only at C. S. Lewis and the British Idealists; this idea is stated in a *mishna* in *Avot*. Rabbi Ya'akov states:

> Better one hour of *teshuva* and good deeds in this world than the entire life of the World-to-Come; and better one hour of the spiritual bliss in the World-to-Come than the entire life of this world. (4:17)

Two modes of existence and experience are contrasted. In metaphysical terms, even momentary experience of the spiritual bliss of basking in the Divine Presence is superior to the totality of all kinds of joys and pleasures a person can have in this world. But in moral terms, this world, where you will be challenged and where you will respond, is preferred

---

31. *Tehillim* is replete with references to God's relationship to such crushed spirits:
    "True sacrifice to God is a contrite spirit; God, You will not despise a contrite and crushed heart." (51:19)
    "He heals their broken hearts and binds up their wounds." (147:3)
    "God is close to those who are brokenhearted, and those who are crushed of spirit, He will redeem." (34:19)
32. Even within *mizmor* 51, so focused on the oppression of sin, King David notes the joy rooted in hope and faith in the fruits of *teshuva*: "You will make me hear gladness and joy; bones which You had crushed will rejoice" (verse 10), and "Return to me the gladness of Your salvation, and Your generous Spirit will support me" (verse 14).
33. *Surprised by Joy* (London, 1955), chapter 13.

to the next world, where you are going to be metaphysically pampered; a single hour of *teshuva* and good deeds now is weighted over all of the World-to-Come. In other words, the hour of meeting Him and standing before Him is so much more meaningful than all the dividends and fruits that we are going to reap. "Your heart should be glad for you are serving the most-high God."

What sort of *teshuva* earns such adulation? *Chazal* refer to *teshuva me-ahava, teshuva* out of love, in contrast to *teshuva mi-yira,* out of fear. As the Rambam understands the distinction (*Hilkhot Teshuva,* chap. 10), performance of a mitzva out of love means doing it *li-shmah,* with no regard to the reward. *Teshuva me-ahava* is thus *teshuva* in which one engages for the encounter *per se,* for the mutual love that is the theme of *Shir Ha-shirim*. The depth and intensity of this relationship is for us an aspiration; and on the part of God, it is a pure gift than which there is none greater.

So do we have joy in *teshuva*? We do not have the type of joy that is oblivious to the tragedy, that disregards the pain, and that tries to paper over the failure. All of those agonizing elements are present. But transcending all is the fact that we are there, to confront, to be challenged, and to respond. And we are there to feel the full power and glory of the momentous encounter between ourselves and God in the experience of *teshuva,* and in particular *teshuva me-ahava,* which is the purest and noblest form. True, Judaism does not prohibit thinking about tomorrow's benefits, but we can still idealize the *li-shmah* aspect of *teshuva* and recognize it to the point where it informs the nature and experience of our *teshuva*.

Yom Kippur – the time of the renewal of the covenant of "The King has brought me into His inner chamber" (*Shir Ha-shirim* 1:4) – is precisely the moment of the encounter, the marvelous opportunity which is given to us. While we hope and strive to purify ourselves, first and foremost, we are eternally grateful for and animated by the very opportunity to stand *lifnei Hashem,* before God.

About the Author

RABBI AHARON LICHTENSTEIN *zt"l* (1933–2015) was an eminent rabbinic educator, scholar and thinker who served as *rosh yeshiva* of Yeshivat Har Etzion for over forty years.

Born in France, he escaped just before the German invasion and arrived in the United States in 1941. He was educated at Yeshivat Rabbi Chaim Berlin under the tutelage of Rabbi Yitzchak Hutner *zt"l* and Rabbi Ahron Soloveichik *zt"l*, and continued at Yeshivat Rabbenu Yitzchak Elchanan, where he was granted rabbinic ordination by his mentor, Rabbi Joseph B. Soloveitchik *zt"l*. After receiving his Ph.D. in English Literature from Harvard University, he briefly taught literature at Yeshiva University and afterwards taught Talmud there. As founder of YU's *kollel* and its head for a decade, he set the tone for its continued development.

Moving to Israel in 1971, he joined Rabbi Yehuda Amital *zt"l* in heading Yeshivat Har Etzion, an advanced Torah institution whose students, believing the defense of Israel to be a moral, national, and halakhic imperative, also serve in the Israeli military. Together they built the yeshiva into a world-renowned center of Torah learning and service to the Jewish people. In addition, Rabbi Lichtenstein was rector of Herzog College and *rosh yeshiva* of Yeshiva University's Gruss Kollel in Jerusalem.

Rabbi Lichtenstein's views on religious, social, and personal issues were widely sought both in Israel and the Diaspora, and his influence was extended by his many disciples who serve as rabbis, educators, and communal leaders worldwide. A tireless pedagogue, he lectured extensively and published several volumes of studies on Talmud, Jewish law, and Jewish thought. His publications in Talmud include *Minchat Aviv*, *Kedushat Aviv*, and the *Shiurei HaRav Aharon Lichtenstein* series, and his publications in Jewish thought include *Leaves of Faith* (two vols.), *Varieties of Jewish Experience*, *Musar Aviv*, *By His Light*, and *Seeking His Presence*. In recognition of his contributions, he was awarded the Rabbi Kook Prize for Original Torah Literature in 2013 and the Israel Prize for Torah Literature in 2014. Several collections dedicated to studying his thought and halakhic scholarship have appeared in recent years. Rabbi Lichtenstein continues to be regarded by many as an intellectual and spiritual beacon, and as a role model par excellence of Judaism's highest ideals.

RABBI DR. MICHAEL S. BERGER is Associate Professor of Jewish Law and Ethics at Emory University in Atlanta, Georgia. His courses and articles focus on medieval and modern Jewish thought, Jewish ethics, and contemporary religious identity formation. He authored *Rabbinic Authority*, and edited Rabbi Joseph B. Soloveitchik's *Emergence of Ethical Man*, part of the MeOtzar HoRav series. Since 2001, he has served as a program officer for the Avi Chai Foundation, and teaches regularly for the Wexner Heritage program.

RABBI REUVEN ZIEGLER is Chairman of the Editorial Board at Koren Publishers Jerusalem and Director of Research and Archives at the Toras HoRav Foundation. A founder of Yeshivat Har Etzion's renowned Israel Koschitzky Virtual Beit Midrash, he has served as its editor-in-chief for more than two decades. He is the author of *Majesty and Humility: The Thought of Rabbi Joseph B. Soloveitchik* and numerous essays, and editor of many volumes, among them works by Rabbi Joseph B. Soloveitchik, Rabbi Yehuda Amital, and Rabbi Aharon Lichtenstein.

The fonts used in this book are from the Arno family

Maggid Books
The best of contemporary Jewish thought from
Koren Publishers Jerusalem Ltd.